T0309256

The Economics of the Stock Market

PRAISE FOR *THE ECONOMICS OF THE STOCK MARKET*

'Awe-inspring, encompassing, convention-flouting analysis, hard stick-your-neck out empirical discoveries, and counter-intuitive hypotheses. Endlessly stimulating and intensely useful.'

Avner Offer, Chichele Professor Emeritus of Economic History, University of Oxford

'This is a bold book that questions virtually all the assumptions of prevailing neoclassical theory. By rejecting the concept of the "representative agent", proposing instead that households and corporate management have totally different motivations, Smithers shows how finance plays a crucial role in explaining developments in the real economy. Leverage, ultimately driven by demographics, raises growth but threatens it too. His attacks on theory, particularly the Modigliani-Miller theorem, are supported by careful empirical work that also reveals important and unexpected financial constants. Throughout, the book sparkles with insights based on decades of close observation of how financial markets really work. Theorists must confront this reality, not try to ignore it.'

William White, Senior Fellow at the CD Howe Institute and former economic adviser to the Bank for International Settlements

'Andrew Smithers addresses fundamental questions about the operation of financial markets and their interaction with corporate decisions. He does so in a way that leads him to question a great many of the predictions of corporate finance and of resource allocation that are taught to students of economics. Some will part company with him along the journey but few will be bored and all will benefit from having propositions central to their world view questioned.'

David Miles, Professor of Economics, University College London

'Most economists tend to think of financial markets as being efficient, notwithstanding an increasing body of evidence that there is a predictable component to movements in share prices. In this book Andrew Smithers sets out a view very different from the mainstream position of how share prices are determined. A key feature of his analysis is that periods of high returns are likely to be followed by periods of low returns—there is low frequency negative serial correlation. The book provides an account of the factors that can give rise to this, based around the argument that different market participants have very different objectives and views of what risk is. The book poses a substantial and important challenge to financial economics. It is therefore important that the book should be published and the author's views debated.'

Martin Weale, Professor of Economics, Kings College London

'This is a very formidable project and great accomplishment! The author has produced both a comprehensive critique of received doctrine and a constructive approach to a macroeconomics that integrates finance with the real economy.'

Bill Janeway, economist and venture capitalist (Warburg Pincus)

'Advances a major new paradigm for the relationship between securities markets and the economic system. Andrew Smithers' insights have been stimulated not least by the opening decades of the twenty-first century, with monetary authorities across the globe mired in more or less blind recourse to so-called quantitative easing (QE) on a vast scale—and with the economics profession conspicuously at a loss to judge the impact of this policy on the course of events.'

Peter Oppenheimer, Student, Christ Church Oxford

'Andrew Smithers is a free thinker, happy to confront conventional corporate finance theory in the several respects in which this latter has gone astray. He does so on the basis of careful study of the data combined with much practical experience and great analytical ability. In particular, his assessment of the woeful implications of the bonus culture on the incentives and decisions of corporate managers is of first-order importance.'

Charles Goodhart, Professor Emeritus LSE and
a former chief adviser to the Bank of England

'This is Andrew Smithers boldest sortie yet in his battle against the Efficient Market Hypothesis, the doctrine that financial markets always price shares correctly on average, so that finance can be excluded from analysis of the economic equilibrium. As Smithers convincingly shows the neoclassical macro model is poorly supported empirically. Drawing inspiration from Keynes, he calls on economists to provide a theory which accords better with reality—and human welfare.'

Professor Lord Robert Skidelsky

The Economics of the Stock Market

Andrew Smithers

OXFORD
UNIVERSITY PRESS

OXFORD

UNIVERSITY PRESS

Great Clarendon Street, Oxford, OX2 6DP,
United Kingdom

Oxford University Press is a department of the University of Oxford.
It furthers the University's objective of excellence in research, scholarship,
and education by publishing worldwide. Oxford is a registered trade mark of
Oxford University Press in the UK and in certain other countries

© Andrew Smithers 2022
Foreword © Andy Haldane 2022

The moral rights of the author have been asserted

First Edition published in 2022

Impression: 1

Published in the United States of America by Oxford University Press
198 Madison Avenue, New York, NY 10016, United States of America

British Library Cataloguing in Publication Data

Data available

Library of Congress Control Number: 2021947441

ISBN 978-0-19-284709-6

DOI: 10.1093/oso/9780192847096.001.0001

Printed by Sheridan Books, Inc., United States of America

To Kit and Pelham

Foreword

Andy Haldane
Chief Executive, the RSA

Larry Summers once famously observed, tongue-in-cheek, that much of modern-day finance theory concerned itself with pricing a second bottle of ketchup, once the price of the first bottle was already known. While an over-statement, this quip contained an element of truth. Much of modern finance, and in particular asset pricing, theory relies on arbitrage relationships between different asset types (the second bottle of ketchup), largely taking as given macroeconomic fundamentals (the first bottle). Finance and economics were, in this sense, fundamentally detached.

That theoretical detachment between asset pricing and fundamentals, or between the financial and real sides of the economy in these models, pre-vailed only under some strict behavioural assumptions. Prominent among these were that the limits to arbitrage between asset types (bonds and equi-ties, long- and short-duration assets) were small and short-lived and that the behaviour shaping these markets could be well approximated by that of a single representative investor and household. In other words, companies' behaviours typically played a somewhat secondary role, if at all. And so too did heterogeneity between investor and household types.

Although highly stylized, this approach to modelling found its way into many mainstream macroeconomic models from the 1980s onwards. Many of these models viewed both money and finance, and the corporate sector, as a 'veil' which could effectively be looked through when understanding the drivers of the economy. Financial factors—the financial sector and financial markets—had at best a secondary role in explaining business-cycle dynamics and likewise the financing and investment choices of companies. These omissions were a not insignificant contributor to the intellectual oversight that culminated in the Global Financial Crisis of 2008/09.

This stylized approach to asset pricing and financial choice also dominated academic discourse over much of the past half-century. Often, this focused on the co-determination of asset prices across different risk classes and dur-ations. In the 1970s and 1980s, this led to the identification, and indeed pro-liferation, of various asset pricing puzzles—the 'equity premium' puzzle, the 'risk-free rate' puzzle, the 'uncovered interest parity' puzzle. These were puzzles that were believed to be rooted in the limits to arbitrage. And attempts to explain them were typically found by tweaking the behavioural assumptions underpinning the representative investor.

The past decade has seen a serious questioning of these approaches. The Global Financial Crisis, and empirical failures of the workhorse asset pricing and macroeconomic models, have led to a re-evaluation and re-think of modelling practices. For example, when it comes to understanding the economy, newer strains of models have emerged in which finance in general—and banking in particular—play a much more central role in shaping its dynamics, not just during times of crisis, but over the normal course of the business cycle. That has left us much better placed to assess, for example, the dynamics of the economy after the Covid crisis than after the Global Financial Crisis.

When it comes to academic research on asset pricing and finance, several new and exciting strands of thinking have emerged over recent years to help resolve some of the puzzles in finance and to link financial factors to observable macroeconomic behaviours. That has included an increased focus on so-called behavioural finance—the application of psychology to understanding the behaviour of investors, individually and collectively, and its implications for asset price dynamics. And it includes models which explicitly take account of heterogeneity in the behaviour and balance sheets of different investor types. These have helped resolve various asset pricing puzzles and close the gap between theoretical models and empirical practice.

This provocative and stimulating book by Andrew Smithers provides a different take again on the determination of asset prices and their link to the macroeconomy, based on his own research and practical investment experience over a long and distinguished career. There are a number of ways in which Smithers' model deviates from the mainstream. Let me highlight two. First, it puts centre stage an aspect of finance often less focused on—namely, the economics of the *stock market*. Second, it puts centre stage the behaviour of the managers of *companies*, as distinct from their household owners, linking this to the fortunes of the stock market.

While these might sound like relatively modest modifications of the core model, Smithers draws out a set of implications that are often significantly at odds with conventional thinking, both when it comes to the determination of asset prices and the functioning of the economy. To give an example, in Smithers' framework the level of bond yields and equity returns are not co-determined. That leaves the gap between them—the equity risk premium—able to deviate significantly from 'normal' levels for protracted periods.

Smithers' brings empirical evidence to bear, largely drawn from the United States, to explain and justify these alternative hypotheses.

Putting the behaviour of managers of companies at the centre of a joint explanation of asset market and the macroeconomy is, I think, a significant step forward in enhancing our understanding of both. The way the risk appetite of company managers is shaped by stock market performance, in ways which affect investment and financing choices, are issues not yet fully, or adequately, incorporated into mainstream macroeconomic models. Certainly, that is true by comparison with the effort devoted to studying consumption choices by households.

One of the signature macroeconomic challenges of our time—a challenge made more acute by the Global Financial Crisis and by Covid—is the global productivity slowdown. This has many and various causes. In a growth accounting sense, a significant part of it reflects a slowing in the rate of capital accumulation of companies in a large number of advanced economies. Smithers' model provides a clear and compelling explanation for this behaviour, rooted in the short-term behaviour of managers of, and investors in, companies, with the performance of the stock market at its centre.

Many in the economics profession, the investment management profession, and beyond will probably take issue with some (or many) aspects of the model, the evidence, and the hypotheses Smithers sets out here. In fact, it would be disappointing if they did not. Because this book provides, for me, just the sort of revisionist thinking and intellectual challenge the economics, investment management—and indeed policymaking—communities need if our models are to match the data, in particular over the longer run, and if they are to offer a more useful guidepost for decision-making in the future than has been the case in the recent past.

Acknowledgements

This book is the result of over sixty years' concern with economics and stock markets, starting in 1956 when I went up to Clare College Cambridge to read economics. In addition to having the good fortune to being supervised by Brian Reddaway, I attended the classes of Nicky Kaldor, and, if I remember correctly, lectures by Robin Marris, both of whom I quote. I then worked in investment banking, mainly in investment management, at S.G. Warburg, where I learnt how companies and financial markets operate and how different this was from the way that economists have usually assumed. On retiring from banking I set up Smithers & Co., an economic consultancy, in which I was joined on a part-time basis, on Brian Reddaway's introduction, by Martin Weale. After a few years we were joined by Stephen Wright, another of Brian's pupils and later by James Mitchell, who worked with Martin in the National Institute of Economic and Social Research.

I wrote many papers with Martin, Stephen, and James and they have continued to be a great help with all the ideas which have gone into this book. Stephen co-authored *Valuing Wall Street* with me and we taught together a module for a course, sponsored by a charity and superbly managed by Russell Napier, on the stock market. Derry Pickford, who was a colleague at Smithers & Co., contributed much to our discussions and took over as Stephen's teaching partner on this course when I stepped down. Economics is a science, though even more often than most other sciences, it is often pursued unscientifically, and debate is thus essential for its development and I am grateful for the time many distinguished economists and financial journalists have been prepared to devote to discussions with me. In addition to those previously mentioned I would like to express my particular thanks to Charles Goodhart, Haruhiko Kuroda, David Miles, Masaaki Shirakawa, Bill White, Martin Wolf, Rob Armstrong, and Andy Haldane, whose offer to write the Foreword I accepted with speedy gratitude.

I owe, as with nearly all the books and papers that I have written, a great debt to Vanessa Brown. Not only does she proofread them for typographical errors but draws my attention to badly constructed sentences that are illogical, lack clarity, or are badly phrased. Those that survive are, however, my fault.

Contents

List of Figures   xvii
List of Tables   xxi

1. Introduction   1

2. Surprising Features of the Model   7

3. The Model in Summary   14

4. Management Behaviour, Investment, Debt, and Pay-out Ratios   21

5. Corporate Leverage and Household Portfolio Preference   31

6. The Growth of Corporate Equity   34

7. The Yield Curve   37

8. The Risk-free Short-term Rate of Interest   41

9. Equity, Bond, and Cash Relative Returns   45

10. Stock Market Returns Do Not Follow a Random Walk   51

11. The Risks of Equities at Different Time Horizons   55

12. The Time Horizon at Which Investors Will Prefer Equities to Bonds 59

13. Changes in Aggregate Risk Aversion   61

14. Monetary Policy, Leverage, and Portfolio Preferences   65

15. Valuing the US Stock Market   68

16. The Real Return on Equity Capital Worldwide   75

17. Money- and Time-weighted Returns   84

18. The Behaviour of the Firm   87

19. Corporate Investment and the Miller-Modigliani Theorem   95

20. Land, Inventories, and Trade Credit   105

21. How the Market Returns to Fair Value   109

22. Fluctuations in the Hurdle Rate   111

23. Tangibles and Intangibles   115

24. Other Problems from Labelling IP Expenditure as Investment   121

25. Inflation, Leverage, Growth, and Financial Stability   127

26. Tax   132

27. Portfolio Preference and Retirement Savings   137

28. Life Cycle Savings Hypothesis   140

29. Depreciation, Capital Consumption, and Maintenance   143

30. Comparison with Other Approaches   147

31. The Efficient Market Hypothesis   154

32. Summary   156

33. Comments in Conclusion   158

Appendices
1. The Duration of Bonds and Equities   161
2. The Valuation of Unquoted Companies in The Financial Accounts
   of the United States—Z1   163
3. Measurement of the Net Capital Stock and Depreciation in the
   United States   165
4. Data Sources, Use, and Methods of Calculation   167

Glossary   171
Bibliography   179
Index   183

List of Figures

1. United States: Non-financial interest cover, profits before tax, and profits before depreciation   24
2. United States: Non-financial companies' leverage   25
3. United States: Average life of fixed produced assets   26
4. United States: Real bond yields rolling averages over sixteen and thirty years   26
5. United States: Mean reversion of value of produced tangible capital stock/NDP   27
6. United States: Corporate pay-out ratios and GDP % p.a., change over previous thirty years   28
7. United States: Corporate profit retentions and GDP   29
8. United States: The yield spread ten years minus one year   38
9. United States: Real long bond yields, long period rolling averages   38
10. United States: Yield curve for risk-free interest rates   39
11. United States: Real short-term interest rates   42
12. United States: Real short-term interest rates since 1913   42
13. United States: Real long-term bond yields   43
14. United Kingdom: Real consols/long bond yields 1703 to 2016   44
15. United Kingdom and United States: Average real long bond yields since 1871   44
16. United States: Cash, bonds, and equities real returns over previous thirty years   46
17. United States: The equity risk premium   46
18. United States: Real bond yields and equity value   47
19. United States: Yields on TIPS and q 48
20. US equities: Annual volatility and returns 1801 to 2018   52
21. US equities: Negative serial correlation shown by non-overlapping periods of circa seventy years   53
22. United States: Equities' annual real returns   56
23. United States: Real return to equity investors 1801 to 2020   56
24. United States: The long-term stability of volatility of one-year real equity returns   57
25. United States: The long-term stability of volatility of thirty-year real equity returns   57
26. United States: Distribution of equity log returns 1871 to 2019   58

27. United States: Lower-bound real returns on equities with two probabilities
   with two average returns   60

28. Time horizon (T) at which US investors will prefer equities to bonds   60

29. United States: Household ownership of equity assets   66

30. United States: Monetary base as % of GDP and Treasury yield spread
   (twenty-year minus one-year)   67

31. United States: Stock market value—q and CAPE   69

32. United States: Hindsight value using one to ten and one to thirty years' data 71

33. United States: Hindsight value using one to thirty and one to fifty years' data 72

34. United States: Hindsight compared with q and CAPE   72

35. United States: Value of the stock market measured by hindsight 1801 to 1968   73

36. Belgium, France, Germany, Italy, and Japan: Average of real total return indices 80

37. World inflation   81

38. International growth and equity returns   82

39. Australia, Belgium, Canada, Denmark, and France: Serial correlation
   of equity returns in local currency   82

40. Germany, Italy, Japan, the Netherlands, and New Zealand: Serial
   correlation of equity returns in local currency   83

41. South Africa, Spain, Switzerland, and the United Kingdom: Serial
   correlation of equity returns in local currency   83

42. United States: Corporate profit margins   85

43. United States: Non-financial companies' net new issues as % of net worth   86

44. United States: Corporate sector's share of total output   88

45. United States: Business and non-financial corporate investment as % of total 88

46. United States: Non-financial companies' interest rate of net debt   96

47. United States: Business investment and the cost of capital, measured
   after depreciation and before interest and tax   100

48. United States: Business investment and the cost of equity   101

49. United States: Non-financial companies' land, inventories, and trade
   credit as % of tangible assets   106

50. United States: Non-financial corporate profits adjusted for changes
   in land prices   107

51. United Kingdom: Non-financial companies' land as % of total tangible assets   108

52. United States: Net additions to the capital stock and q 110

53. United States: The change in management incentives   112

54. United States: Corporate investment and tax rate   112

55. Foreign direct investment in United States   113

56. United States: Intangibles as % of total business investment   119

57. United States: Non-financial companies' net profit margins 123

58. United States: Non-financial gross profit margins 124

59. United States: Gross ICOR 125

60. United States: Net ICOR 125

61. United States: Non-financial corporate leverage 128

62. United States: Non-financial companies' debt as % of tangible assets 128

63. Monetary base as % of GDP and Treasury yield spread (twenty-year
    minus one-year) 129

64. United States: Effective rate of corporation tax and labour share of output 133

65. United Kingdom and United States: Tangible produced fixed capital/output
    ratios 134

66. United Kingdom and United States: Non-financial companies' profit margins 135

67. United States: Identifiable pensions assets as % of net financial assets
    and personal disposable income 139

68. United States: Volatility of S&P 500 EPS and NIPA profits after tax 152

List of Tables

1. US percentage of the population over 65   29

2. Direction of the impact on bond yields, corporate leverage, and output growth in response to changes in the fiscal deficit and investors' portfolio preferences   32

3. Long-term yield curve (average yields on risk-free return minus one year on bonds of different maturities)   39

4. Average risk-free return on bonds of different maturities   43

5. R^2 correlations between US real log % equity and bond returns   47

6. Comparison of data on negative serial correlation comparing non-overlapping and overlapping time periods for five and ten years   54

7. Comparison between implied and observed growth in US quoted company dividends   70

8. Comparisons between growth of GDP and equity returns for countries experiencing capital destruction 1899 to 2019   77

9. Comparisons between growth of GDP and equity returns for countries experiencing little or no capital destruction 1899 to 2019   77

10. Comparisons between periods 1899 to 1955 and 1955 to 2019 for equity returns for countries experiencing capital destruction   78

11. Comparisons between periods 1899 to 1955 and 1955 to 2019 for equity returns for countries not experiencing capital destruction   78

12. Comparisons between periods 1899 to 1955 and 1955 to 2019 for growth of GDP for countries experiencing capital destruction   79

13. Comparisons between periods 1899 to 1955 and 1955 to 2019 for growth of GDP for relatively fortunate countries   79

14. United States: Relative importance of quoted, unquoted, and unincorporated non-financial business in 2018, by net worth and fixed non-residential investment   89

15. Correlations between business fixed investment as % of GDP and the cost of capital   101

16. Impact on 2018 data of inclusion of intangible spending in investment   122

17. Required decline in tax rate for stable RoE if interest is disallowed as an expense for corporation tax on non-financial companies and interest rates unchanged 2019   130

18. Household direct and indirect ownership of US fixed produced assets 2018   138

1

Introduction

Economic theory has changed little over the past fifty years. The consensus, termed the neoclassical synthesis, has been subject to refinements and tinkering, but left fundamentally unchanged. Despite attacks, such as Nicholas Kaldor's comment on 'the intellectual sterility engendered by the methods of Neo-classical Economics'[1] it was, until recently, believed to provide a solid basis for policy—a view which was, however, treated with scorn by Hyman Minsky who wrote that 'Modern orthodox economics is not and cannot be a basis for a serious approach to economic policy.'[2] It was previously assumed that by following the precepts of the neoclassical consensus the economy could be kept in balance, with mild fluctuations in unemployment and inflation occurring around a trend of steadily rising output. But following the financial crisis and the great recession of 2008 the questioning of this view has become increasingly vociferous.

The major weakness of the previous consensus is seen by many to lie in the failure to incorporate finance into its economic models. Half the US economy's output is produced by companies whose behaviour is determined by the fact that their shares are quoted on the stock market. Once this is accepted, the economic model that follows is very different from the neoclassical consensus. Unlike the latter its assumptions are testable and prove robust when tested and it radically changes our understanding of how the economy operates and leads thereby to different policies, largely because it shows that corporations behave differently from households and quoted companies differently from unquoted ones. The failure of the current consensus is shown by its dependence on assumptions which either are untestable or, if not, fail when tested. The determination to stick to accepted assumptions and ignore the evidence that they are invalid shows that neoclassical economists have much in common with Hobbits who 'liked to have books filled with things that they already knew, set out fair and square with no contradictions.'[3]

---

[1] 'Marginal Productivity and the Macroeconomic Theories of Distribution: Comment on Samuelson and Modigliani' by Nicholas Kaldor (1966) *Review of Economic Studies* 33.
[2] *Stabilizing an Unstable Economy* by Hyman P. Minsky (2008) McGraw-Hill.
[3] *The Lord of the Rings—Part 1: The Fellowship of the Ring—Prologue Chapter* by J. R. R Tolkien (1954) George Allen & Unwin.

The Economics of the Stock Market. Andrew Smithers, Oxford University Press. © Andrew Smithers 2022.
Foreword © Andy Haldane 2022. DOI: 10.1093/oso/9780192847096.003.0001

The main faults in the consensus arise from two aspects of its construction. Firstly it largely ignores the strength of the 'corporate veil' and assumes that the private sector behaves as it if were the same as the household sector and secondly it holds that a satisfactory model can be constructed in which finance has little place. I avoid the first and seek to make a significant step towards rectifying the second. The stock market is not the only way that finance needs to be included in a valid model of the economy, but it is an important part of it.

The main concern of the owners of shares in quoted companies, and even to a greater degree those who manage their money, is the current value placed on them by the stock market, and this short-term assessment has naturally absorbed much of the vast resources of the financial services industry. It has also deflected the attention of economists from the market's longer-term behaviour, so that we need to shift our main concern from its unpredictable short-term fluctuations, which are simply noise in the statistical sense, to its longer-term more predictable ones. To understand how the stock market works we need to explain two of its key characteristics which include the stability and level of the long-term real return on equities and the stability and strength of the mean reversion of their cumulative return to trend.[4]

While mean reversion cannot be proved, it can only be shown to be probable, there appear to be two other important constants which are otherwise rare in economics and seldom known precisely. These are the produced fixed tangible capital output ratio and the labour share of output. The value of one of these three constants can be deduced from that of the others and as they are also derived independently of each other and are mutually consistent they provide strong evidence for mean reversion of each one considered separately. I put great emphasis on the stability of the real return on equities which has gained far less attention than it deserves. One reason for this lacuna is that much of the financial literature concentrates on excess returns (the return on equities over a supposedly 'risk-free' asset such as cash) which, contrary to the authors' usual expectations, are not mean reverting. The importance of the stationarity of the real return on equity comes not only from the conclusions that follow from it but also because of the support it gives to the stability of both the capital output ratio and the labour share of output.

The stock market's value, which I shall use to describe the level at which it would be if it were neither over- nor under-priced, varies around a stable mean and, if these fluctuations could be forecast, they would be arbitraged

---

[4] At longer horizons real equity returns exhibit negative serial correlation. Periods of high returns tend to be followed by periods of low returns and vice versa.

away in the pursuit of profit. This has not happened and as the years have passed the fluctuations have not become smaller, indicating that attempts to forecast short-term variations have so far failed. It thus appears that the market's short-term fluctuations are random and unpredictable. Arbitrage would even eliminate the longer-term blips if its rewards were sufficiently sizeable and rapid for those engaging in it to become rich at the expense of other participants. Either the longer-term predictability is not sufficient, regarding the level of mis-valuation and the timing of its correction, to make this worthwhile, or the transfer of wealth from those who mistime these longer-term fluctuations to those who benefit is not sufficient to alter market behaviour—each generation produces a new supply of winners, who do not then become so wealthy that they dominate market behaviour, and a new supply of relative losers to finance the winners.

To understand a complicated system, it is not sufficient to describe it, we also need to discard its inessential features and show that the resulting simplified model accurately simulates the system's behaviour. To do this I ignore the market's short-term fluctuations and seek to explain its longer-term stabilities. My first step is to show that its key features follow from the risk aversion of investors. I present a model which shows why this determines the long-term stable return on equities around which the shorter-term returns vary, being driven by the unpredictable fluctuations in investor sentiment. The attitudes to risk of investors and the managers of quoted companies determine the relative long-term risk-free real returns on bonds of different maturities (the yield curve), the negative serial correlation of real equity returns, the preferred proportions of debt and equity in household portfolios, and the level of corporate leverage.

Acting in isolation the key variables, such as growth, the proportion of the return paid to shareholders, leverage, and demography, should naturally result in changes to the return on equity but so far as can be observed, this has not happened. It appears that the fluctuations in these variables have offset each other. It is improbable that this has arisen by accident, but rather through a natural process which involves corporate behaviour responding to the stability of equity returns induced by investors' risk aversion. This produces a stable long-term return on corporate equity, the 'hurdle rate' below which companies do not invest, but above which they must, as failure to do so renders them liable to losing market share.

Changes in the proportion of household wealth that investors wish to hold in debt or equity assets must match the wish of companies to be financed by debt or equity—an important identity which seems previously to have been ignored by economists. When there are *ex ante* mismatches between the two, the effect is similar and parallel to *ex ante* mismatches in net savings. It requires changes in monetary or fiscal policy to bring net savings into equilibrium under conditions of full employment, while market-driven changes in long bond yields achieve the balance between corporate leverage and investors' portfolio preference. Variations in the risk-free rate of interest and the yield curve have historically been the main ways through which these two separate equilibria have been realized, though fiscal policy also affects both.

The preferred level of equity held by households can change, not only with short-term swings in confidence but over the longer term, for example with changes in demography, and these need to be reflected in changes in corporate leverage. Household portfolio preferences are insensitive to changes in long-term interest rates, but corporate leverage is sensitive to them. These differences in elasticities result in the required change in leverage being realized through small changes in long-term risk-free interest rates, while the equilibrium return on equities remains unchanged.

This process of adjustment would not be possible if the fluctuations of equity returns were related to those of bonds, or if long-term bond yields changed only in line with short-term interest rates. But bond and equity returns are independent of one another, contrary to assumptions often made regarding their relationship, and while short- and long-term interest rates are related, their changes are partly independent so that the yield curve can vary. The partial independence of short-term rates and long bond yields allows the latter to stimulate changes in corporate leverage so that these can match changes in the preferred portfolio balance of investors. The lack of relationship between bond and equity returns is shown both in the long and the short term. The former is due to the insensitivity of equity returns to changes in bond yields, within the narrow range of their long-term variations. The lack of any short-term relationship is the natural result of the way in which short-term fluctuations in investors' confidence often respond to changes in expectations for profit which tend to offset changes in interest rates, whose fluctuations also affect investors' hopes and fears. High expectations from growth are often, but not always, accompanied by rising interest rates and low expectations by falling ones. The variations, both over the long and the short term, in the yield curve, interest rates, and equity returns ('equity risk premiums'), are thus necessary to allow markets and the economy to rebalance towards the equilibrium conditions needed both for full employment and the debt equity balances in household portfolios and corporate leverage.

The faults in the neoclassical synthesis have been made possible by failures to test assumptions, or to ignore evidence against them: 'one must not fall into the error of supposing that assertions about reality can be derived from *a priori* assumptions. Whether well-behaved homogeneous-and-linear production functions exist or not is a question of fact. They cannot be presumed to exist as a consequence of some basic postulate.[5] I show that such failures include the assumption that leverage does not affect the value of corporate assets, that interest rates and the cost of equity capital are co-determined and that the decisions of corporate managements aim to maximize the present value of corporate assets, rather than the value determined by the stock market.

The resulting explanation of the economics of financial markets raises other important issues, which include the differences in the returns from different international stock markets, the way in which stock markets can be valued, the issue of market efficiency, the rationality of investors' behaviour, and the problems of measuring returns. Expected real returns from different stock markets cannot diverge, as investors would buy those with higher ones, but the portfolio preferences of domestic investors are likely to do so as the demographics of individual countries move independently. Nominal long bond yields, however, differ between countries, and these rather than real yields determine leverage. Because nominal bond yields and leverage can differ internationally between companies and financial markets, expected real returns on equities can be the same despite differences in demographics and the consequent differences in portfolio preferences.

To be valid a model must be testable and prove consistent with the evidence. To test mine I will mostly turn to the United States where the data for equity returns are available for much longer than elsewhere. In addition, the United States has avoided massive capital destruction in wartime and hyperinflation, both of which have created data problems in other major countries which I examine. I show, however, that negative serial correlation of equity returns can be observed in all stock markets whose economies have avoided massive capital destruction, indicating that the risk aversion of households is a universal attribute and not confined to the inhabitants of the United States. Changes in the tax system and interest rates are not trivial, as they can affect the growth rate of the economy, but they do not change the long-term return on equity.

This book's key conclusions are as follows, together with the chapter numbers which particularly address these issues:

(i) The real return on equity is mean reverting at approximately 6.7 per cent p.a. This follows from the risk aversion of the owners of capital (Chapter 15).

[5] Kaldor (1966).

(ii) This applies worldwide, with outturns deviating from it only through major periods of capital destruction in war (Chapter 16).

(iii) Corporate decisions on investment, pay-out ratios, and leverage are made by managers whose behaviour is determined by a utility function which is different from that which determines the portfolio preferences of the owners of capital (Chapter 4).

(iv) Companies seek to avoid equity issues. Their pay-out ratios vary with growth which can thus be financed without needing changes in private-sector savings. The ratio of corporate interest payments to profits is stationary (Chapter 4).

(v) With stable demographics the risk aversion of the owners of capital is stationary. It changes with ageing and the structure of retirement savings, but due to the high elasticity of leverage to long bond yields and the low elasticity of the portfolio preference of the owners of capital, these changes are accommodated by changes in long bond yields leaving the return on equity unchanged (Chapters 12 and 13).

(vi) Corporate capital can be usefully divided into short-term debt ('cash'), long-term bonds ('bonds'), and equity. Their returns are derived independently: savings and investment are equated by movements in the short-term interest rate and corporate leverage is balanced with the preferences of the owners of financial assets by variation in the bond yield: equity returns are stationary (Chapters 7, 8 and 10).

The neoclassical consensus is not necessarily a completely unified or internally coherent body of doctrine, but the conclusions set out above differ sharply from those usually held in the following ways:

(i) Companies do not seek to maximize the present value of their net worth (often termed profit maximization). If they did they would vary their rate of investment with the cost of capital. Because the return on equity is stationary the cost of capital is known, and the rate of corporate investment does not vary with it (Chapters 18 and 19).

(ii) Bond yields and equity returns are derived independently. The gap between them (the equity risk premium) is not mean reverting and bond yields provide no information on future equity returns (Chapter 9).

(iii) The cost of capital varies with leverage. The Miller-Modigliani Theorem (MMT) assumes otherwise and is thus demonstrably false (Chapter 19).

2

Surprising Features of the Model

Economists, like scientists in other disciplines, naturally carry around with them a view of the world which includes many standard assumptions. I am proposing a model for financial markets which diverges in so many ways from the current consensus that, according to those economists who have been kind enough to read and comment on it before publication, it is fundamentally different from the neoclassical synthesis. To prepare readers for the jolts that they may therefore experience when reading this book, I set out below some of my more obvious differences with the standard view. Since these are also explained in detail later, the following points are logically redundant but I hope that they will prove rhetorically helpful by alerting readers to the large differences they will encounter in my model compared with the form which discourse usually takes when these issues are debated.

(i) The independence of the corporate sector

To understand the economy, it is essential to divide it into sectors, as the behaviour of governments differs from that of households, even those elected by them. Economists are agreed that the public sector needs to be considered separately from the private sector but differ over whether a further division needs to be made within the private sector between companies and households. The current consensus often makes no distinction. For this assumption to be valid the corporate veil must be a flimsy construction with the behaviour of companies determined as if they were directly managed by their owners. But the corporate veil is almost impenetrable, with the behaviour of companies driven by the interests of their managements. The behaviour of the same individuals will, as owners of capital, depend on different types of risk assessment to those which determine their actions as corporate managers. Behaviour responds to the relative utility of different benefits, such as income and job security. I agree with many economists who hold that the utility functions of shareholders and managers are sufficiently different to make it essential to separate the private sector between households

The Economics of the Stock Market. Andrew Smithers, Oxford University Press. © Andrew Smithers 2022.
Foreword © Andy Haldane 2022. DOI: 10.1093/oso/9780192847096.003.0002

and companies: 'We start from the proposition that corporate directors may subject corporate policy decisions to utility functions of their own.'[1]

The central concern of managers is their careers. This is reflected in the success of the businesses they manage, the pay they receive, and their security of tenure. As the first two are closely related, the main tension for managers is to balance the rewards of higher short-term profits and share prices against risks to their jobs. In the United Kingdom and the United States, where the business sector is dominated by quoted companies, managements are alert to share prices as their jobs are under threat if theirs are weak compared with their competitors'. Their concern is thus with relative share prices, not with the overall level of the stock market. One consequence is that companies are almost totally indifferent to the cost of equity capital so managements do not raise new equity when shares are cheap. They respond, however, to changes in long bond yields. The Miller-Modigliani Theorem is not a valid hypothesis on which to base a model of the economy. Although the value of an individual company's assets is not perceptibly affected by leverage, it is a fallacy of composition to assume that the same holds for the corporate sector. In aggregate the value of produced corporate assets is raised by increased leverage and falls with declines. The prospective profit stream from their employment is unchanged, but their value alters with the change in the applicable discount rate.

In the short term, due to the bias of the stock market and the relative cost of debt and equity after corporation tax, research shows that increased leverage tends to push up share prices.[2] While this encourages managers to raise debt, leverage is not constrained, as seems usually assumed, by the caution of lenders but rather by the fears of senior executives. While individual managers no doubt vary in their risk aversion, the leverage of companies in aggregate depends on the way managers balance the benefits of higher leverage against the risk of losing their jobs. In a profit downturn, companies may need to raise cash; those that are already highly leveraged must then issue new equity or cut dividends, which are job-threatening activities. The need to boost equity is a threat to the careers of managers and comes earlier than bankruptcy which is the main risk for lenders. Lenders, who will usually own a diversified portfolio of debt instruments, are able to offset the risk of loss through higher lending margins, which increase the risk for borrowers. The worries of managers rather than the risks and fears of lenders thus determine corporate leverage.

---

[1] *'The Economic Theory of 'Managerial Capitalism'* by Robin Marris (1964) Macmillan.

[2] 'The Determination of Financial Structure: The Incentive Signalling Approach' by Stephen Ross (1977) *Bell Journal of Economics* 8.

Cash needs rise with inflation. The shorter the duration of a firm's debt the greater its exposure, as rising inflation has, in the short term, a proportionately greater impact on nominal interest rates than on profits, while over time inflation has an equal impact on both profits and interest payments. The risk that inflation will damage profits and raise the need for equity is strongest if debt is short-dated, companies therefore prefer to borrow long-dated bonds. Corporate leverage is sensitive, not only to the level of real interest rates over sustained periods of time but to changes in nominal rates, which explains the apparent insensitivity of investment to changes in real ones.[3]

(ii) The independence of the level of savings from the portfolio preferences of owners of wealth

The level of national savings responds strongly to the level of investment and thus to the rate of growth. The return on equity is stationary, but its composition varies between the proportion of that return which is paid out in cash as dividends and buy-backs net of new issues ('the broad dividend'), and the rate at which the amount paid out changes. The proportion of the return attributable to each varies and responds to the level of corporate investment, so that corporate savings rise and fall in response to changes in investment and growth. Household savings are not, however, indifferent to interest rates so the risk-free short-term rate, which today is controlled by central banks and historically was market determined, can adjust to keep the balance between *ex ante* savings and *ex ante* investment. Fiscal policy can also be used to do this and the need for rainy day savings also fluctuates in response to changes in unemployment and health benefits. The savings' rate, and the contributions to it from the household and corporate sectors, are thus to some extent exogenous. National savings respond to swings in growth and investment, through changes in the corporate sector's pay-out ratio, to changes in the short-term risk-free rate of interest and to exogenous political decisions.

(iii) The portfolio preferences of wealth owners

Owners of wealth have different portfolio preferences which depend on the purpose of their savings and their risk aversion. Rainy-day savings will have

---

[3] 'Reflections on Macroeconomic Modelling' by Ray C. Fair (2015) *B.E. Journal of Macroeconomics* 15.

short and uncertain time horizons being made to moderate changes in consumption arising from the uncertainties of employment and health. The pleasure resulting from increases in income improves by less than the rise in income and the discomfort arising from falls increases more rapidly. This naturally leads to a low risk-free short rate and a large premium for the returns on debt of longer maturities. The yield curve is thus steep as the horizon lengthens for short- to medium-dated debt. Longer-term savings also serve primarily to protect the saver against falls in consumption, but as the main aim is to preserve consumption in retirement, they have naturally long time horizons. The portfolio decision for such saving is thus between equities and long-dated bonds, rather than short-term deposits. As the shape of the utility function applies here as well, the additional return required to persuade investors to hold equities is large. Over the period for which investors expect to hold their assets, the returns on government bonds of matching duration are risk-free, but those for equities which have an infinite time horizon are not. To offset this risk, the likely but uncertain return on equities must be substantially higher than that on bonds.

The rise in the discomfort that households experience if they must reduce their consumption and the way this grows more than proportionately in the event of its enforced decline, means that saving has closer similarities to paying an insurance premium against falling income than to skimping now to achieve a higher standard of living in the future.

The risk aversion of the owners of wealth varies considerably between individuals, but for a population of stable age the proportions of those who are highly risk averse compared with the less cautious are likely to be stable over time and I assume that they are. The availability of equity (its supply) must match corporate needs (its demand); this will only occur if an adequate number of householders with the necessary wealth are prepared to hold a sufficient proportion of their assets in equities. The marginal suppliers of equities will be more risk averse than the average owner and, as so often in economics, they determine the price, which in this case is the required return, at which demand is satisfied. Equity returns are therefore higher than expected in models which involve a 'single representative investor'.

During periods when the population has a relatively stable age profile, the risk aversion of the marginal wealth owners will be stationary and so will their time horizon when assessing their portfolio preferences. These are, however, subject to exogenous changes in the age composition of the population and to changes in the way pensions are funded. When these occur, household demand for bonds will change relative to the demand for equities, which must be accommodated by alterations in their relative supply through changes in relative returns, involving either equities or bonds or both. Changes in the corporate supply of debt respond readily to small variations in risk-free bond yields, so that without changes in the short-term risk-free rate of interest, bond supply responds elastically to small movements in the yield curve. Households' portfolio preferences are, however, unaffected by small changes in the yield curve. The high elasticity of corporate leverage to long-term bond yields, combined with the indifference of households, results in changes in household portfolio preference being accommodated by small changes in the yield curve and none in the required return on equities. Households are not, however, the only source of demand for bonds and equities, nor are companies the only source of debt supply. Changes in foreign capital flows and in the fiscal deficit will also lead to changes in the yield curve. The return on equity is thus stable despite changes in the age structure of the population or in the structure of pension-fund savings and is historically determined by the long-term risk aversion of those investors who are needed to supply the marginal amount of equity capital needed to match demand. The yield curve is also affected by changes in foreign capital flows and the fiscal balance.

The risk aversion of wealth owners fluctuates in the short term with their optimism but is stable over time, not only in terms of the average level of risk aversion but also in terms of the distribution of degrees of risk aversion between individuals. Over time there appears to have been no evolutionary advantage in having the mix of risk aversion in the population change. We presumably benefit from the existence of such a range. As with blood groups, whose distribution remains stable over time, the inherited level of risk aversion appears to be polymorphic.

(iv) The time horizon of business investment results in a flat yield curve at the long end

The average life of the economy's total produced capital stock is twenty years and has been very stable, with the corporate portion being shorter than that of housing or public-sector infrastructure and averaging around sixteen years. By borrowing for twenty years companies reduce the risks arising from fluctuations in profits and inflation but have no incentive to pay more for longer debt. The yield curve is thus steep from one to ten years' duration, then flattens and is flat beyond twenty years.

(v) There are different equilibria for short-term interest rates, long dated bonds, and equities

While both the risk-free short and long bond rates vary over time within relatively narrow limits, their fluctuations within these limits are effective in balancing *ex ante* savings with *ex ante* investment and in balancing the supply and demand for equities. There are at least three separate equilibria, that for short risk-free rates which is needed for the *ex ante* net savings balance, the long bond rate which is needed to balance the supply and demand for equities, and the long-term return on equity which is stationary. Over the longer term bond yields are able, within their respective and quite narrow historic limits, to diverge from the short rate through changes in the yield curve. The neoclassical synthesis is at fault in assuming, contrary to the evidence, that returns on these three different asset classes are co-determined. As George Akerlof has observed it has oversimplified Keynes's work by restricting the equilibria needed for a stable economy to one, namely the balance between *ex ante* savings and investment: 'Neoclassical supply had resolved the determination of the price level and assets prices (as the inverse of the interest rate).'[4]

Although both long and short rates vary within narrow ranges and the equity return is stationary, both short and long interest rates need to be able to move independently from one another and from the return on equities. The equity risk premium, however measured, is not therefore mean reverting and this absence of stationarity is a requirement for economic stability in a world in which the level of savings and wealth owners' portfolios preferences move independently. As savings are to some extent exogenous and equity returns are stationary, the current level of the equity risk premium contains no information about future levels of short interest rates, long bond yields, or equity returns.

(vi) Equity returns are determined at the margin by the desire to maintain consumption

The model[5] in which returns on the risk-free rate of interest and its relation to equity returns depends on a single representative investor who saves to improve future living standards was shown by its authors to be incompatible

[4] 'What They Were Thinking Then: The Consequences for Macroeconomics during the Past 60 Years' by George Akerlof (2019) *Journal of Economic Perspectives* 33.
[5] 'The Equity Premium: A Puzzle' by Rajnish Mehra and Edward C. Prescott (1985) *Journal of Monetary Economics* 15.

with the data. Others have sought to resolve the puzzle while maintaining these two key assumptions.[6] I show that the historic data on risk-free short-term interest rates, long bond yields, and equity returns are compatible with the assumptions that savings are primarily made to mitigate falls in future consumption rather than raise them, and that they depend on the risk aversion of the marginal holder of equities rather than that of a single representative one. These assumptions fit the evidence that a significant proportion of savings are made to preserve consumption in retirement rather than for enhancing it and that individuals differ in their attitudes to risk. This model should therefore be preferred to that derived from a single representative investor who saves to improve his future consumption because of its inherent probability as well as its compatibility with the data. With this model there is no equity premium puzzle.

The model explains many of the stock market's features, rather than concentrating on one aspect, such as the relative returns on bonds and equities. Compared with more narrowly based approaches it is thus open to a wider range of objections and needs to be compatible with a greater range of data. But if, as I claim, it is coherent and its parts stand up to testing, they provide evidence in favour of each other and for the whole model.[7]

---

[6] e.g. 'Rare Disasters and Asset Markets in the Twentieth Century' by Robert Barro (2006) *The Quarterly Journal of Economics* 121.

[7] 'The more a theory forbids, the better it is' and 'Thus conformability (or attestability or corroborability) must increase with testability' *Conjectures and Refutations* by Karl Popper (1963) Routledge and Kegan Paul.

3

The Model in Summary

(i) Basic approach and structure of the economy

In terms of the economy's structure I make a clear distinction between the household and business sectors, rather than treating the private sector as a unified whole in which the utility function of managers is assumed to be the same as that of households.[1] I draw equally sharp demarcations between the value of companies' equity based on their assets ('net worth') and that shown by the stock market value ('market capitalization') and between households' behaviour as savers and as owners of equities and bonds. In both respects I follow James Tobin,[2] though I show that both the ratio of net worth to equity market capitalization ('equity q') and the ratio of the total value of companies (net worth plus net debt) to the total stock market value of companies' equity and debt (Tobin's Q) are mean reverting. The cost of equity is stationary but not the cost of capital, as debt is cheaper than equity and leverage varies over time. In general, I simplify my model by dividing financial assets into three asset classes, cash (short-dated debt), bonds (long-dated debt), and equities, rather than by treating bonds as having a range of maturities.

(ii) Short- and long-term fluctuations in asset prices

Central banks through their control of short-term interest rates and governments through their management of fiscal balances usually aim to minimize fluctuations in unemployment and inflation. In the absence of these often exogenous changes and in addition to them, fluctuations in short-term interest rates, bond yields, and the stock market vary with the ebbs and flows of investors' confidence, particularly over the outlook for profits and interest rates. Investors could profit from these swings if they could forecast them

---

[1] In this respect my view is that set out in Marris (1964) and in *Reconstructing Keynesian Economics with Imperfect Competition* by Robin Marris (1991) Edward Elgar.

[2] 'A General Equilibrium Approach to Monetary Theory' by James Tobin (1969) *Journal of Money, Credit and Banking* 1.

The Economics of the Stock Market. Andrew Smithers, Oxford University Press. © Andrew Smithers 2022.
Foreword © Andy Haldane 2022. DOI: 10.1093/oso/9780192847096.003.0003

and, as they have failed to do so and their efforts show no signs of causing the fluctuations to diminish, it seems clear that short-term swings are random and unpredictable. But this does not apply to longer-term swings in equity returns which exhibit negative serial correlation and are thus mean reverting. The longer-term predictability of these returns has not, however, been eliminated by arbitrage either because the returns are insufficient to offset the risks involved, given the uncertainty of the level or the speed with which mis-valuations are corrected, or because those who suffer from mis-timing still prosper and only lose compared to those who gain. They can thus continue to contribute to those who benefit, with each generation producing a new supply of relative winners and losers.

(iii) Long-term returns are determined by the risk aversion of owners and managers

The longer-term real returns of cash, bonds, and equities ('the separate asset classes') are not derived randomly and are primarily determined by the risk aversion of managers of companies who use capital and households who provide it. Most households own financial assets, and they allocate these between asset classes in response to their assessment of their risks and return. As asset owners, corporate managers act in the same way, but when making decisions for their companies they have different risks to balance. The utility preferences which determine the behaviour of households and companies are thus different and the private sector must therefore be divided between the household and business sectors.

The effect of these differences is that the equilibrium levels of the separate asset classes are independently derived, and I thus agree with George Akerlof that the neoclassical consensus is wrong to hold otherwise.[3] That the returns of these asset classes are not co-determined is shown by their lack of relationship. Real equity returns are stationary, while those for cash and bonds are not. Although the short and long free rates of interest are not mean reverting their long-term averages have varied only between quite narrow limits as has the ratio between them (the yield curve). Under the equilibrium conditions of full employment, and in the absence of changes in the monetary policies of central banks, the fiscal balances of governments and capital flows from abroad, the identity of *ex post* savings and *ex post* investment and of *ex post* corporate leverage with *ex post* household portfolio preference must be determined by endogenous changes in short-term interest rates and long bond

---

[3] Akerlof (2019).

yields. As these two identities are determined separately by the different utility functions of managers and asset owners, they must be independent.

While the ratio between returns on cash and bonds (the yield curve) cannot be stationary, it does not need to vary much because corporate leverage responds elastically to small changes in long bond yields. This characteristic is extremely important. If leverage responded strongly to changes in bond yields then portfolio preferences would also have to do so. In the absence of such elasticity for leverage, it would be unlikely for the return on equities to be stationary. The elasticity of corporate leverage to bond yields is thus an essential condition for the stability of the real return on equities and provides a test for the validity of my model, which it passes.

It is equally important that household portfolio preferences are indifferent to small changes in bond yields. This indifference is the result of the strong negative correlation of equity returns at the time horizons of the owners of equity and the large difference between equity and bond returns over these time periods. Both short- and long-term interest rates are affected by exogenous variables. In their absence endogenous changes in the risk-free short and long rates enable the economy to achieve equilibria, with the former adjusting to allow *ex ante* savings to balance *ex ante* investment and the latter changing to ensure that *ex ante* corporate leverage matches *ex ante* wealth owners' portfolio preferences. These equilibria are also achieved when there are exogenous changes in fiscal policy and foreign capital flows, but these can affect the risk-free yield on long-dated bonds and the growth rate of the economy. Endogenous changes in monetary policy are designed to achieve full employment and are therefore assumed to have no independent longer-term impact on the returns from financial assets.

(iv) The risks and returns for owners and managers

The users and providers of capital take on different risks for cash, long-dated bonds, and equities, which are reflected in their returns and costs. The relative returns on these asset classes depend on both their risks and the nervousness ('risk aversion') of those who own or employ them. Risk aversion is part of our genetic inheritance. It appears to be polymorphic in that it varies widely between individual members of a population while remaining stable in its distribution.[4] The risk aversion of a population with an unchanged age

---

[4] 'It is *populations* that evolve … Individual members of the population differ from one another, but the population itself has a stable genetic structure, i.e. a stable pattern of genetic inequality' *The Threat and the Glory* by Peter Medawar (1990) Oxford University Press (Medawar's italics).

distribution is stable in terms of both its average and the distribution of individuals' attitudes around that average. Risk aversion changes if the age structure changes and portfolio preferences are also affected by changes in the sharing of risk by investors if, as has happened in recent years, the structure of pension funds change. Changes in cash returns facilitate the achievement under conditions of full employment of the *ex post* savings and *ex post* investment balance while those of bond returns enable the required balance to be achieved between *ex post* corporate leverage and *ex post* household portfolio preference.

The risk aversion of corporate management is not necessarily the same as that of the total population, as it may attract less or more risk-averse people than other activities such as civil or military service, but the form of the utility preference of the population of corporate managers is assumed to be stable over time and this determines corporate leverage and its elastic response to small changes in bond yields. The risk aversion of managers also determines their companies' investment decisions and the level of corporate savings. Jobs are at risk for those who publish poor profits, or are forced to raise new equity, or whose companies lose market share. As investment tends to depress short-term profits and boost longer-term success, these are competing objectives and the results have historically been determined by risk aversion. In recent years the level of investment at which shorter-term profits balance the longer-term risks of underinvestment has been reduced by changes in incentives, which have thereby had an adverse effect on labour productivity and growth.[5]

(v) The stability of the real return on equity

The stability of risk aversion has resulted in steady historic responses to the returns available on corporate equity. Managements have authorized spending on new produced capital when the expected return on equity (the hurdle rate) has matched the long-term return required by investors; both have therefore been stationary and necessarily so as the return on corporate equity must equal that received by shareholders.

Managers have ignored the fluctuations in the stock market and thus the cost of capital, which is dominated by them, because new equity issues tend to depress share prices. Shareholders are rationally more concerned with share prices than with corporate net worth, they thus dislike new issues and corporate managements do not therefore usually take advantage of high

---

[5] *Productivity and the Bonus Culture* by Andrew Smithers (2019) Oxford University Press.

share prices to make new issues. It follows that companies' level of investment does not respond to the cost of capital as neoclassical consensus models assume.

(vi) Corporate savings vary with growth

The level of corporate savings is determined by the 'broad dividend'. This has become the accepted phrase among economists for the cash pay-out ratio, which is the proportion of profits after tax needed to finance dividends, buy-backs including debt-financed takeovers, net of new equity issues. Reducing this ratio, and thus increasing savings,[6] does not have the same negative impact on share prices as raising new equity, so corporate managements have a different attitude to raising new equity through varying the pay-out ratio to that of raising new equity through share issues. Companies therefore adjust their pay-out ratios to their level of investment, so that corporate savings rise and fall in line with the rate of growth of produced capital and output. Major changes in growth do not therefore require changes in interest rates, while the *ex post* savings' balance can be preserved in the face of fluctuations in the savings of the household sector by changes in short-term interest rates. The return on equity is stationary but independent of the contribution from dividends per share and their growth rate. The savings' rate thus adjusts to the growth of the economy, without having any impact on the return on equity.[7]

(vii) The shape of the yield curve

The same individuals respond to different utility preferences when they take decisions as corporate managers or as investors. Their careers are not usually at risk when they decide the asset allocation of their wealth but are of great importance when they make decisions on behalf of the companies they manage. The impact of these decisions also differs, as it is the aggregate risk aversion of corporate managers which determines average corporate leverage, while the required return on equity will depend on the risk aversion of the

---

[6] Savings, defined as the amount of profits not distributed to shareholders, change with the ratio of the broad dividend to profits after tax. A different definition is, however, used in national accounts where buy-backs are treated as capital rather than income transfers and corporate savings thus vary with changes in the ratio of the narrow dividend to profits after tax.

[7] The duration of equities is thus conceptually different from that of bonds as explained in Appendix 1.

marginal investor needed to provide an adequate supply of equity to match corporate demand. The average life of corporate assets affects the shape of the yield curve as the risk to corporate profits, and thus to the security of managers' tenure, is increased if companies borrow short term, but this risk does not fall if their debt has a longer maturity than the average life of their fixed produced assets, which is sixteen years. As can be seen from the importance of pension funds and other retirement savings, the major purpose of savings is to mitigate future reductions in consumption and not, as has been often assumed, to increase it.[8] This purpose, which applies both to rainy-day and to pension savings, combined with the shape of the utility function for the owners of financial assets, leads to risk-free short-term rates being low, to a steep yield curve for bonds with durations of up to twenty years and to the average return on equities being large compared with bond yields. The flatness of the yield curve after twenty years reflects the average life of produced assets.

(viii) The differences in return on equities and risk-free bonds

Where the purpose of savings is to avoid reductions in future consumption, a small annual reduction in current consumption results in a much smaller drop in future consumption than would otherwise occur and, as large falls are many times more painful than small ones, no real return on savings is needed to reward the saver and, for the holders of risk-free bonds which match their expected time horizon, the returns are small. Equally, such savers need a high return to reward them for any risk that endangers their future consumption, so the additional return needed to tempt risk-averse households to hold equities (the equity risk premium) is large.

Equity returns are volatile and have an infinite duration. Even for savings which are expected to be held for a long time, they are thus riskier than bonds. Savers therefore need a large reward for holding equities compared with bonds whose duration matches the length of time before the asset is expected to be sold to pay for consumption. When these time horizons are short, as they are for rainy-day savings, equities are unsuitable assets because of their high volatility. Equities, however, exhibit strong negative serial correlation so that the risks of holding them fall sharply as the time horizon

---

[8] e.g. Mehra and Prescott (1985) and Barro (2006).

lengthens.[9] The probability that savers would match or exceed the average long-term return on equities thus rises sharply with the time horizon of savers. If the yield curve were steep for bonds of over twenty years' duration, the rapid improvement in the ratio of risk to reward could be offset by an improvement in this ratio for bonds. However, the yield curve flattens after twenty years, because the average life of the produced capital assets of companies is around sixteen years, and companies have no incentive to pay for longer-dated debt. The benefit of holding shares rather than bonds thus rises sharply with the time horizon and the return on equities needed to justify their place in savers' portfolios changes little as the horizon lengthens.

(ix) Changes in portfolio preference

Portfolio preferences are likely to change with the age structure of the population and with different ways of pooling risk through pension funds. The relationship between bond and equity returns and corporate leverage must alter to offset such exogenous changes in portfolio preferences, and this could occur either through changes in the returns on bonds or the expected return on equities. Leverage is elastic in its response to small changes in bond yields. Changes in portfolio preference thus result in matching changes in corporate leverage through small changes in the bond yield and require no alteration in the long-term expected returns on equities. The demand for equity by companies must match its availability which is determined by the time horizon of the marginal supplier, who will be more risk averse than the average one. The high return on equities relative to bonds is thus due to their infinite time horizon and the risk aversion of the marginal supplier.

It is often, and not at first sight unreasonably, assumed that changes in portfolio preference due to aging will affect the return on equities. That they do not, and that equity returns and the hurdle rate are unaffected by such changes, is due to the high elasticity of corporate leverage to bond yields and the relative indifference of investors with long time horizons to them.

[9] As investors have a choice between holding bonds and equities they will be influenced by the difference, at any one time, in the returns they expect from either asset class. This does not mean, as is usually assumed by those who place emphasis on this difference—the equity risk premium—that it is mean reverting or has any predictive power with regard to future returns on either class of assets.

4

Management Behaviour, Investment, Debt, and Pay-out Ratios

People make decisions not companies. It is therefore the behaviour of managements that determine the savings, investment, and the debt levels of the corporate sector. The main concerns of managements are the success of their businesses, their pay, and tenure. The first two tend to move together so it is only over issues that involve pay and tenure that difficult choices must be made.

Investment tends to lower profits in the short term but protect companies over the longer term by improving labour productivity and thereby supporting profit margins, which would otherwise fall with the rise in real wages. Managements therefore balance their short-term prospects for higher pay against the longer-term security of their careers. Investment depresses profits if the increases in depreciation, capital, and maintenance costs are greater than the increases in output per employee and this is the regular short-term cost of the long-term benefits of investment.

While for the corporate sector in aggregate the level of investment is quite stable, it tends to swing more sharply for individual companies, for whom increases in output capacity are often lumpy while rises in sales and output are not. Thus, after a period of heavy investment profits, or at least the return on equity, tend to fall initially before rising. As new equipment is more efficient than old, it should be profitable even at a lower capacity utilization rate and more profitable at the same level. As real wages rise the old equipment will cease to be profitable and new investment is thus essential for survival. So long as businesses can increase output with their existing capital, the decision when to install new equipment is flexible. Delay usually has problems and incurs costs—as potential output from existing capital can also be lumpy if it involves putting on an extra shift and, if output cannot be raised, it will mean loss of market share as demand rises: 'the competitive strength of any one enterprise…varies with the enterprise's share of the market—it declines

The Economics of the Stock Market. Andrew Smithers, Oxford University Press. © Andrew Smithers 2022.
Foreword © Andy Haldane 2022. DOI: 10.1093/oso/9780192847096.003.0004

with any decrease in that share and improves with an increasing share.'[1] The decision to invest will often be good for long-term profits and essential for survival, but often caries the cost of a short-term reduction in the return on equity. As the stock market seldom welcomes this, managements have historically treated investment decisions with caution and this has been aggravated by remuneration contracts in which they are well rewarded for short-term results. The bonus culture has shifted the balance against investment.

The long-term real return on equity to shareholders is stationary at around 6.7 per cent, so that on corporate equity ('net worth') must be also. While the return on new investment is uncertain, managements' investment decisions are based on their expectations and they must therefore have in effect a target return of 6.7 per cent on the equity needed to finance new investment ('the hurdle rate'). Investment decisions are key to managements' jobs. If the return on equity is below average, they risk their companies being taken over and, if they fail to invest when such returns are available, their companies will have higher production costs than their competitors, who will then be able to gain market share at their expense through lower pricing or greater expenditure on marketing.

The long history of stable returns on equity (RoE) must have tended to 'hard wire' the hurdle rate. While this has been affected by the bonus culture, the impact is unlikely to be lasting as it acts more strongly on the management of quoted companies than on others and is thus much more important in the United Kingdom and the United States than in other major countries where a lower proportion of companies are quoted, takeovers less of a threat, and the business culture consequently less short-term. The impact of the bonus culture, while currently very damaging to the UK and US economies, is thus likely to prove to be a temporary phenomenon, as quoted companies will lose out to unquoted companies including foreign-owned ones. As expectations and outcomes differ over the short and medium term, corporate returns on equity fluctuate around their long-term level and neither these nor the impact of the bonus culture are likely to change the long-term stationarity of the expected return on equities nor its counterpart in the hurdle rate.

The supply of equity and its demand from companies must be in equilibrium. In a two-sector economy the ratio of debt to equity in the assets of the household sector must be the same as the ratio in companies' balance sheets. If the portfolio preferences of investors vary, the relative returns available on

---

[1] Kaldor (1966).

bonds and those expected on equities must alter to reflect this and there must also be an offsetting change in corporate leverage. The change in returns could involve both equities and bonds or be limited to either, but as expectations on equity returns reflect their long-term stationarity and those available on bonds are observable, it is likely that exogenous changes in household portfolio preferences will be accommodated by changes in bond yields. This expectation is fulfilled as a result of the relative elasticities of leverage and portfolio preferences to changes in bond yields.

For companies, debt is substantially cheaper on average than equity. This encouragement to higher leverage is offset by the risk that interest payments will amount to an overly large part of the income available to meet them. Even if the excessive debt does not result in bankruptcy, adverse changes in profits or inflation will require highly leveraged companies to refinance their debt with additional equity at a time when their share prices will be depressed, thus threatening the jobs of their senior management.

Inflation increases both the risks and the rewards of being financed with debt. It tends to increase short-term financing needs more rapidly than profits, because the costs of raw materials and wages need to be paid before the resulting output can be sold and the real burden of corporation tax rises as depreciation allowances are seldom increased to allow for the rising cost of new equipment. If short-term debt then becomes needed, its cost rises much faster than the nominal value of output, as the latter rises proportionately to the rate of inflation whereas the cost of a rise in interest rates is far greater. For example, an increase in interest payments if rates rise from 5 per cent to 6 per cent to allow for a one percentage point rise in inflation, is twenty times greater than the change in inflation. The rewards of those leveraged companies which survive bursts of inflation are also great since the value of the companies' assets rises relative to the nominal liability of the debt.

If the risk aversion of company managements were stable over time we should expect leverage to reflect the cost of debt with companies being willing to increase their borrowings if interest rates fall and for the increase to be such that interest payments will have the same ratio as before to profits.

We lack very long-term data with which we can test this assumption, but those for the past ninety years, set out in Figure 1, provide support for it. The figure shows that there was a major rise in the ratio of pre-tax profits to net interest payments during World War II, when access to the long bond market was restricted to government debt, then fell sharply and has remained relatively stable, at least since the 1980s after which inflation stabilized.

The risks that managements will wish to avoid are the exteme one of bankruptcy and the less extreme one of having to tap the market for additional

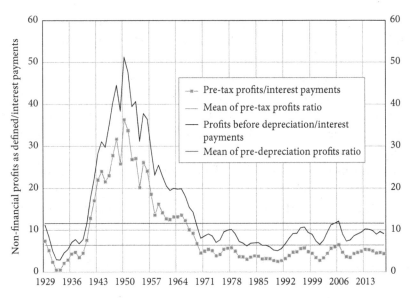

Figure 1. United States: Non-financial interest cover, profits before tax, and profits before depreciation

Data source: NIPA Table 1.14.

equity finance. A failure to cover interest payments with profits, measured after depreciation but before interest and tax payments, will cause net worth to fall which increases the risk that the company will have to raise new equity; it is therefore the ratio that should determine the degree of leverage. I show in Figure 1 two ratios, but the logical one for management to choose is that in which profits are measured after depreciation. Since 1970 this ratio of interest to profits has revolved around its average.

The slow rate at which corporate interest payments respond to changes in long-term bond yields, and the complicated impact on both risks and rewards that result from inflation, means that the equilibrium level of leverage at any one time is only known within a broad range. Within this range, however, we can calculate its sensitivity. Currently interest payments amount to 4.5 per cent of non-financial corporate net output. A fall of 0.1 per cent[2] in the debt interest payments would thus allow a rise in the ratio of debt to net output of 2.1 per cent. The current debt to output ratio is at an all-time peak of 69 per cent (Figure 2), so a fall of 0.1 per cent in the bond yield would

---

[2] In Figure 2 and in my comments on it, I use log percentages, so that changes in the ratios of debt and output are proportionate to changes in the percentages and a fall of a given percentage followed by a rise restores the ratio to its starting level. This does not occur if ordinary percentages are used. For example, a fall of 50 per cent, followed by a rise of 50 per cent, leaves a ratio 25 per cent below its starting point as normally calculated. The use of log percentages is my usual practice in other figures and comparisons.

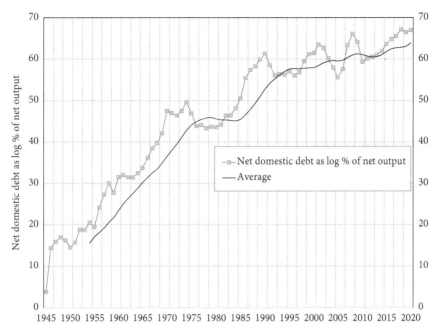

Figure 2. United States: Non-financial companies' leverage
Data sources: Z1 Table B. 103 and NIPA Table 1.14.

allow the equilibrium level to rise by 3 per cent, with proportionately greater rises when leverage was lower. Figure 2 shows leverage using a ten-year trailing average; the maximum difference in this average for one year to another has been 1.74 per cent. Small changes in corporate interest costs will thus allow for large changes in leverage over time.

To mimimize risk, companies should match the duration of their debt to the average life of their produced capital stock and Figure 3 shows the latter has averaged sixteen years, while for the economy as a whole it has been twenty years.

Figure 4 shows that over thirty years the average real yield on long-dated government bonds was between zero and 5 per cent and beween –2 per cent and +6 per cent when measured over sixteen years. Bond yields averaged over sixteen years should then be long enough for their changes to affect corporate leverage and, as Figure 4 shows, these have swung sharply. Corporate leverage is thus likely to respond elastically to changes in long bond yields and, as I will show later, this is not offset by any changes in household portfolio preferences which are unaffected by small changes in bond yields. Given their stationarity, it seems unlikely that expected returns on equity will readily alter and they don't, even when changes in demography alter the relative demand from households for equities or bonds. This is due to the high

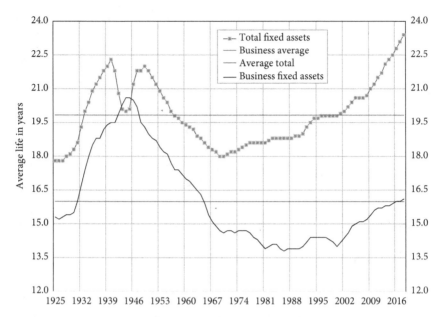

Figure 3. United States: Average life of fixed produced assets
Data source: BEA Fixed Asset Table 1.9.

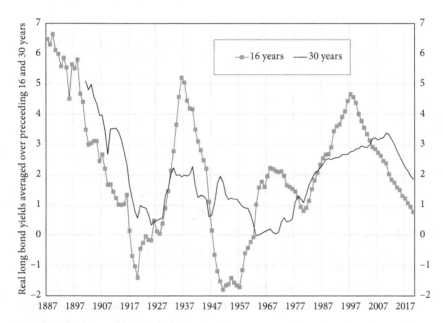

Figure 4. United States: Real bond yields rolling averages over sixteen and thirty years
Data source: Shiller (2000).

elasticity of corporate leverage to changes in bonds yields and the low elasticity to them of portfolio preferences. Changes in household risk aversion are thus accommodated by changes in leverage with no impact on equity returns.

Companies increase their level of investment when opportunities are available which give prospective returns which match the hurdle rate. If, on these occasions, there is no change in household portfolio preferences, leverage will be unchanged and as corporate capital must grow as fast as output so must corporate equity. Companies must therefore increase their equity to match the faster growth of the economy and to do this they must either raise new equity or reduce their cash pay-out ratios and, because shareholders usually dislike new equity issues, the latter route will dominate. If, however, household portfolio preference does alter, corporate leverage will change and faster growth can be accommodated without pay-out ratios changing.

Cash can be distributed to shareholders through dividends or through reductions in equity capital by buy-backs, net of new issues, and takeovers financed by debt—the sum of these being the broad dividend. Output, as Figure 5 shows, changes in line with the value of the net stock of produced fixed capital. Rising output requires a fall in the broad dividend pay-out ratio, i.e. a rise in the retention rate, unless long-dated bond yields are favourable to an increase in leverage.

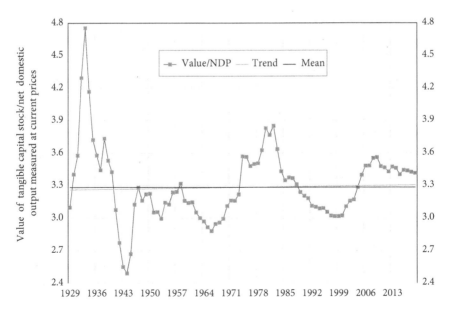

Figure 5. United States: Mean reversion of value of produced tangible capital stock/NDP
Data sources: BEA Fixed Asset Table 1.1 and NIPA Tables 1.1.5 and 5.1.

Figure 6. United States: Corporate pay-out ratios and GDP % p.a., change over previous thirty years

Data sources: Angus Maddison Historical Statistics of the World Economy: 1–2008 AD (2010) and Shiller (2000).

If leverage is unchanged the dividend and the broad dividend will be the same, so the growth of net worth will be lower and more of the total return to shareholders will come in the form of dividends rather than capital gains. We only have data on buy-backs from Q1 1963, but before then they appear to have been small in relation to narrow dividends. So it is possible to compare, as set out in Figure 6, the growth of the economy with that of corporate equity (net worth), using thirty-year averages. I have inverted the scale for the change in GDP to make the relationship clearer. The figure shows a strong relationship between the two series which is confirmed by the R^2 correlation which is 0.380 for 1871 to 1963.[3]

While buy-backs, which include the impact of debt-financed takeovers, had little impact on the broad dividend before Q1 1963 they have since become important and with the data for buy-backs being available it is possible to estimate the proportion of EPS paid out as dividends and buy-backs. I compare in Figure 7 the balance, which is the proportion of cash retained from profits after tax with the growth of GDP, averaging both profit retentions and growth over ten years. Like the longer-term data the recent data

---

[3] The correlation between corporate savings and corporate investment was apparently noted in *The Investment Decision: An Empirical Study* by J. R. Meyer and E. Kuh (1957) Harvard University Press as this is mentioned in Kaldor (1966). I have, however, not yet been able to check the original source.

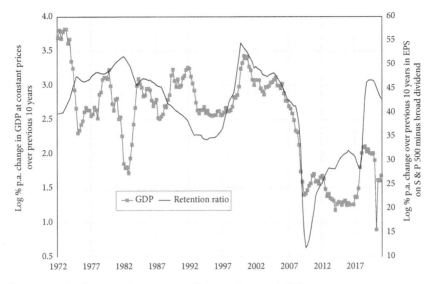

Figure 7. United States: Corporate profit retentions and GDP

Data sources: Shiller (2000), NIPA Tables 1.1.6 and 1.14, and Z1 Tables B. 103 and F. 103.

Table 1. US percentage of the population over 65

1950	8.56	1985	12.06
1955	9.07	1990	12.58
1960	9.49	1995	12.68
1965	9.80	2000	12.43
1970	10.10	2005	12.40
1975	10.83	2010	13.09
1980	11.55	2015	14.88

Data source: Bureau of the Census.

also show a strong relationship between growth and the corporate profit retentions, which is confirmed by the R^2 correlation which is 0.372 for Q1 1963 to Q1 2021.

From 1871 to around 1953 changes in the growth rate of the economy did not affect changes in the return on equity, being offset by changes in the pay-out ratio of corporations, so that changes in the growth of equity have matched changes in the growth of the economy. In the post-war period, however, changes in leverage, possibly combined with the large current account deficits, have resulted in the growth of corporate equity being significantly slower than that of the economy.

The post-war rise in leverage fits with changes in the structure of the population, which seems to have been relatively stable until after World War II but has since changed with the numbers of those over sixty-five growing more rapidly than the total population, as shown in Table 1. The time horizon of the financial assets of the population is likely to shorten as its average age rises. In the model I am proposing this results in a change in leverage rather than in equity returns. Another feature of the model is that equity returns are stationary despite changes in the growth of the economy, with national savings adjusting to them largely through changes in corporate pay-out ratios.

5

Corporate Leverage and Household Portfolio Preference

In an economy in which there are only two sectors, corporations and households, the ratio of debt to equity must be the same in both. If households wish to hold more debt, companies must become more leveraged. Because there are large differences in price elasticity the adjustment occurs through changes in bond yields, rather than in equity returns.

The requirement for the ownership of equity to match the net worth of companies remains true in an open economy with a government sector, but bond yields are affected not only by changes in the portfolio preferences of domestic households but also by fluctuations in the fiscal balance of the public sector, the current account, and foreign portfolios' preferences. In the absence of such exogenous changes, corporate leverage is endogenous and equilibrium is achieved, when fiscal policy and portfolio preference alter, by its response to them via changes in bond yields.

I show, in Table 2, the direction of change in bond yields and corporate leverage that would follow from increases in the fiscal deficit and in domestic and foreign investors' desires to increase the bond portions of their portfolios. The overall effect will, however, depend partly on the extent to which one change is offset by others, as fiscal deficits and capital flows from abroad are not independent variables, and the degree to which a rise in domestic bond demand can be satisfied by supply from either the public or the corporate sector.

Fiscal deficits vary with the cycle, but the possibility of different secular levels rests on the assumption that the economy has more than one possible equilibrium. One, for example, with the government budget in balance and another with a deficit and higher bond yields. This seems implicit in the neoclassical consensus though, due to the failure of that model to recognize the need for the balance between portfolio preference and leverage, there is no analysis on whether the output of economies operating under these different equilibria will grow at different rates. Although I am proposing a model to explain how this balance is achieved, it does no more than indicate that an

The Economics of the Stock Market. Andrew Smithers, Oxford University Press. © Andrew Smithers 2022.
Foreword © Andy Haldane 2022. DOI: 10.1093/oso/9780192847096.003.0005

Table 2. Direction of the impact on bond yields, corporate leverage, and output growth in response to changes in the fiscal deficit and investors' portfolio preferences

		Bond Yields	Corporate Leverage	Output Growth
↑	Fiscal deficit	↑	↓	↓
↑	Domestic bond preference	↓	↑	↑
↑	Foreign bond demand	↓	↑	↑

Source: Author.

economy with a fiscal deficit and higher interest rates will grow more slowly than the alternative,[1] it does not provide a way of quantifying the difference. One uncertainty arises because government bond yields affect leverage and thus the cost of capital and the level of investment and these can differ for several reasons in addition to differences in fiscal policy. While arbitrage should ensure that real short-term risk-free interest rates are similar between different currencies, uncertainties about inflation or within the eurozone about payment, mean that yield curves and real government bond yields can and do vary.

The impact of fiscal policy on broad dividend pay-out ratios is uncertain. Slower growth encourages higher ones and falling leverage lower, as this requires a higher level of retained profit, but pay-out ratios depend on growth, which is determined more by variations in the speed at which technology changes than by secular changes in fiscal policy. The impact of fiscal policy can also be magnified or offset by changes in domestic portfolio preference and foreign capital flows. Both are likely to be exogenous, but it is generally agreed that fiscal policy often affects the exchange rate and thereby foreign demand for bonds. Shorter-term models for the response of the trade balance and exchange rate, such as the Mundell-Fleming Model[2] and that of Rüdiger Dornbusch,[3] do not appear to provide models which can be used to compare the implications of different long-term equilibria. As the table shows, bond yields will be higher if there is a fiscal deficit and if real short-term rates are closely allied through arbitrage there will be pressure for the yield curve for countries running fiscal deficits to steepen. But there are other

[1] This is subject to the proviso that the deficit is not purely the result of public-sector investment and, if so, that this is not matched (crowded out) by a reduction in private-sector investment.
[2] The Mundell-Fleming Model was set out independently in 'Capital Mobility and Stabilization Policy under Fixed and Flexible Exchange Rates' by Robert A. Mundell (1963) *Canadian Journal of Economics and Political Science* 29 and in 'Domestic Financial Policies under Fixed and Floating Exchange Rates' by J. Marcus Fleming (1962) *IMF Staff Papers* 9.
[3] 'Exchange Rate Expectations and Monetary Policy' by Rüdiger Dornbusch (1976) *Journal of International Economics* 6.

factors which determine the steepness of yield curves in different countries, as investors' assessment of the default or inflation risks will also reflect experience, reputation, and institutional structures and regulations. It is, nonetheless, reasonable to conclude that countries with budget deficits, which are not required to ensure full employment, are likely to have steeper yield curves than would otherwise be necessary, lower corporate leverage, and slower growth rates.

Figure 6 and Figure 7 show that corporate savings, defined as profits after tax minus the broad dividend,[4] respond to changes in growth and more precisely to the growth of net worth, which equals growth adjusted for changes in leverage.

---

[4] Corporate savings as defined in the national accounts are profits after tax minus the narrow dividend.

6

The Growth of Corporate Equity

The return on equities may be disaggregated into the dividend yield and the growth of the dividend as set out in the Gordon Growth Model. Equities have thus the characteristics of a bond whose coupon increases each year in line with the growth of the corporate equity. The value of equity (P) is equal to the dividend (D) growing in line with the growth of the corporate equity (G) discounted at the required rate of return on equity (R):

$$P = D\left(\frac{1+G}{1+R}\right) + D\left(\frac{1+G}{1+R}\right)^2 + D\left(\frac{1+G}{1+R}\right)^3 + \ldots..$$

Which simplifies to:

$$P = \frac{D_{t+1}}{R-G}$$

(The return R remains constant independent of changes in the contribution from the dividend D or its growth rate G. It is $D+G$ that is constant.) [1]

In a closed economy there is no net debt, as every creditor is matched by a debtor. The creation of debt therefore requires neither savings nor investment and equally all savings and investment result in an increase in the net worth of the economy which is its total equity component. The corporate sector can be in debt to the household sector, but the former is owned by the latter and if the assets and liabilities of the two are consolidated the net worth of the economy is equal to its accumulated net savings.

The total capital of the economy is divided between produced capital, which is that created by savings and investment, and the natural endowments of land and other resources. Produced capital is divided between fixed capital

---

[1] I explain in Appendix 1 that such a bond would be likely to behave slightly differently from that assumed in the Gordon Growth Model for equities. I showed earlier the evidence, which supports the model, that the return on equities has been unaffected by the pay-out ratio.

The Economics of the Stock Market. Andrew Smithers, Oxford University Press. © Andrew Smithers 2022.
Foreword © Andy Haldane 2022. DOI: 10.1093/oso/9780192847096.003.0006

and inventories and in addition companies need to provide trade credit. The latter has no aggregate value, since the debtors match the creditors, but is needed by the business sector and usually provides credit to the house-hold sector.

The ratio of output to the value of the fixed produced capital stock is mean reverting as I illustrate in Figure 5.[2] Over time, therefore, output rises in line with the rate of change in the net worth of the economy. The equity of the corporate sector will also rise at this rate if the value of other forms of corporate capital, which include inventories, trade credit, and land, has a constant ratio to the value of fixed produced capital and there is no change in corporate leverage. If these conditions are met, the return on equity will be the growth of the economy plus the broad dividend yield.

The broad dividend cannot grow unless it is positive, so for equities to give a return they must in aggregate have a positive broad dividend. (A zero cou-pon perpetuity has no value.) Unless leverage rises, the return on equities must therefore be greater than the growth of the economy, and as leverage is likely to have its limits, the return on equities will be greater than the growth rate of the economy. (It follows that sustained world growth cannot exceed the long-term real return on equity, which is about 6.7 per cent p.a., and that prolonged growth for individual economies at a greater rate than this is also improbable. Growth is disruptive and its marginal utility falls as it rises. The long-term return on equity could therefore be explained as the rate at which the utility of growth, net of its disruptive impact, falls to zero.)

For the whole economy output growth must be matched by the growth of equity, which must be financed either from abroad or by households either directly by subscription to new issues or indirectly via the retained profits of companies. Both foreigners and households can provide finance in debt form thus enabling corporations to increase their leverage and expand their equity more slowly than the growth of the economy. The total return on equities is determined by risk aversion but the distribution of this return between the broad dividend yield and the growth of corporate equity can vary and will depend partly on the growth of the economy, partly on changes in leverage, and partly on the extent to which equity finance is provided from abroad.

The real long-term return on equity, for which we have data from 1801 to 2018, has been 6.7 per cent and over this period the growth of the US economy

---

[2] For the theoretical explanation of why the produced capital value/output ratio is mean reverting, see Smithers (2019: 59 n. 3) and in 'The NTV Model for Total Factor Productivity' by Andrew Smithers (2019) *World Economics* 20.

has been 3.4 per cent p.a. In the absence of changes in leverage or any equity flows across borders the cash dividend would have averaged 3.3 per cent p.a. The United States is not, however, a closed economy; neither has corporate leverage been stable nor do we know the past levels and changes in net equity issues and buy-backs. The gap between the long-term return on equities and the growth of the economy indicates, however, that the broad dividend is likely to have been nearer to 3 per cent than to 1 per cent and this is confirmed by the average dividend yield, as normally defined, which has averaged 4 per cent since 1871.

7

The Yield Curve

Long-term interest rates have a different impact on the economy to short-term ones, and the yield curve, which is the relationship between them, varies greatly in the short term, as Figure 8 shows, but within relatively narrow limits over longer periods as shown in Figure 9.

We have daily data for interest rates on US government debt for a variety of maturities since 1962 and over this period the gap between the yield on one-year and ten-year debt has varied between ±3.5%. While the yield curve varies sharply in the short term it has a more settled shape when averaged over time.

I show in Figure 10 the average differences over the periods for which data have been available on a daily basis and I derive an average from these data to provide an estimate of what the average long-term yield curve would be if such data were available. Figure 10 shows that the additional yields, required by investors to persuade them to hold bonds of longer maturity, rise sharply as they lengthen from zero to ten years then slow until they reach twenty years and are probably flat thereafter.

The shape of the yield curve reflects the preferences of borrowers and lenders. Companies, for example, prefer to borrow for around twenty years to match the life of their fixed produced capital assets, which has averaged sixteen years with a maximum of 20.6 and a minimum of 13.8, as I illustrated in Figure 3. Companies face refinancing risk when borrowing at terms shorter than the life of their investments and they have no incentive to pay a higher rate for longer ones. Households seeking for certainty in the amount they can spend in retirement are natural buyers, both directly and via pension funds, of long-dated bonds but will not be able to obtain any extra income by extending the maturity of the debt purchases beyond the natural time horizon of corporate borrowers.

Compared with its high short-term volatility, the average shape of the yield curve over the medium to long term appears, as Figure 9 indicates, to vary over time within a much narrower range.

The Economics of the Stock Market. Andrew Smithers, Oxford University Press. © Andrew Smithers 2022.
Foreword © Andy Haldane 2022. DOI: 10.1093/oso/9780192847096.003.0007

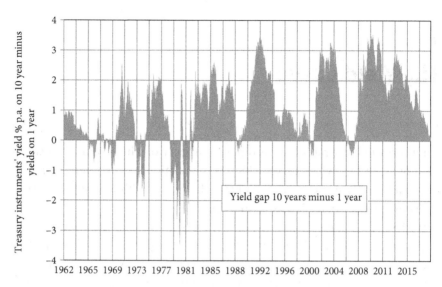

Figure 8. United States: The yield spread ten years minus one year
Data source: Federal Reserve.

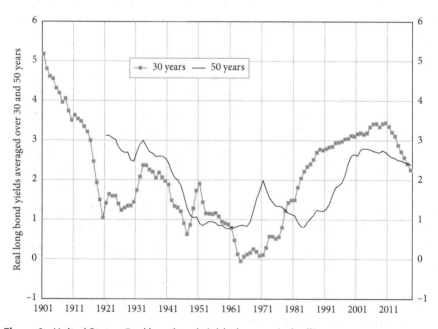

Figure 9. United States: Real long bond yields, long period rolling averages
Data source: Òscar Jordà, Moritz Schularick, and Alan M. Taylor. 2017 updated from Federal Reserve and BLS.

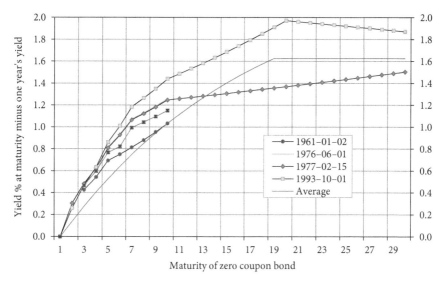

Figure 10. United States: Yield curve for risk-free interest rates
Data source: Federal Reserve Series H15 from inception in 1961.

Table 3. Long-term yield curve (average yields on risk-free return minus one year on bonds of different maturities)

Bond maturity in years	Risk-free return over 1 year	Bond maturity in years	Risk-free return over 1 year	Bond maturity in years	Risk-free return over 1 year
2	0.14	12	1.19	22	1.62
3	0.28	13	1.27	23	1.62
4	0.41	14	1.34	24	1.62
5	0.53	15	1.40	25	1.62
6	0.64	16	1.46	26	1.62
7	0.75	17	1.52	27	1.62
8	0.85	18	1.57	28	1.62
9	0.94	19	1.62	29	1.62
10	1.03	20	1.62	30	1.62
11	1.12	21	1.62	31	1.62

Data source: Author.

By averaging these data series, I have derived estimates of the long-term average yield curve and I show in Table 3 the excess return for risk-free bonds of different maturities above the one-year risk-free rate.

As longer-term bonds mature, they rapidly become less risky and the return on them falls. The yield curve is steep for early years as households hold short-term reserves for short-term expected needs, such as holidays and Christmas, and as a cushion against unexpected shocks, such as illness and unemployment. As the timing of these is uncertain, savers need to be well paid for the risk of holding assets which are not immediately realizable at full value. Given this liquidity preference of households, the yield curve is usually upward sloping through twenty years, at which point it flattens out given the lack of need by corporations for longer-dated finance.

8

The Risk-free Short-term Rate of Interest

Figure 11 shows data on short-term ('cash') returns dating back to 1871, and these indicate a long-term tendency for the rate to fall. They are, however, based on deposits with banks which in the early years, being subject to loss through bankruptcy, were not risk-free. Because the prospective rate of inflation is unknown, a certain real return over any given period can only be provided by a zero coupon bond whose final value is protected against inflation, the return being provided by the discount at which the bond is offered for sale.

Since the Federal Reserve was founded at the end of 1913, the risk that owners of bank deposits will face losses has fallen and fell again to near zero for most depositors after the Federal Deposit Insurance Corporation was founded in 1933. I show in Figure 12 the real one-year interest rate since 1913.

The total return to maturity on bonds with a coupon is uncertain as it requires an assumption about the returns available when the interest is paid. We now have Treasury Inflation Protected Bonds (TIPs) but all those issued so far have had coupons and we do not yet have long-term data for their returns. We must therefore make some assumptions to estimate investors' historic expectations for the real returns on bonds over different time horizons.

The short-term risk-free real interest rate has averaged 0.78 per cent with a trend which is very close to that average. It is nonetheless unlikely to be mean reverting because it is partly determined exogenously, but the limits within which it varies are narrow. As earlier data are not risk-free, the long-term average of the short-term interest rate is uncertain. The long-term averages measured over fifty years have been between 2.80 and –0.19 since 1883 and between 2.09 and –0.19 since 1895.

By adding the average risk-free rate of return of 0.78 per cent to the average premium over the one-year risk-free rates shown in Table 3, I have the estimated average long-term risk-free rates for bonds of different maturities as shown in Table 4. The estimates in the latter table show an

The Economics of the Stock Market. Andrew Smithers, Oxford University Press. © Andrew Smithers 2022.
Foreword © Andy Haldane 2022. DOI: 10.1093/oso/9780192847096.003.0008

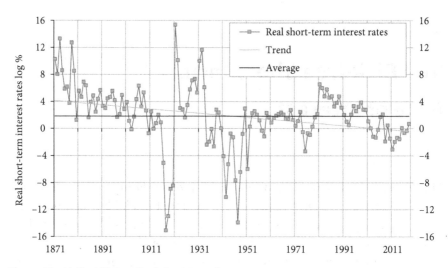

Figure 11. United States: Real short-term interest rates
Data source: Jordà, Schularick, and Taylor (2016), updated from Federal Reserve and BLS.

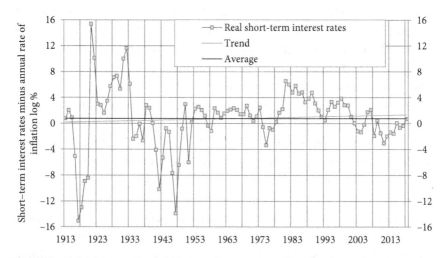

Figure 12. United States: Real short-term interest rates since 1913
Data source: Jordà, Schularick, and Taylor (2016), updated from Federal Reserve and BLS.

average for long bonds which is slightly higher but very similar to the average long bond return from the data on US nominal long bonds since 1871 after deducting the annual rate of inflation. This gives an average real return of 2.16 per cent compared with 2.41 per cent shown in Table 4.

UK data for long bond yields are available since 1703 and these have averaged 2.49 per cent. I show the US data in Figure 13 and that for the United Kingdom in Figure 14; they both show a mild downward trend which

Table 4. Average risk-free return on bonds of different maturities

Maturity in years	Average risk-free return	Maturity in years	Average risk-free return	Maturity in years	Average risk-free return
1	0.79	11	1.90	21	2.41
2	0.93	12	1.98	22	2.41
3	1.06	13	2.06	23	2.41
4	1.19	14	2.13	24	2.41
5	1.32	15	2.19	25	2.41
6	1.43	16	2.25	26	2.41
7	1.54	17	2.31	27	2.41
8	1.64	18	2.36	28	2.41
9	1.73	19	2.41	29	2.41
10	1.82	20	2.41	30	2.41

Data source: Author.

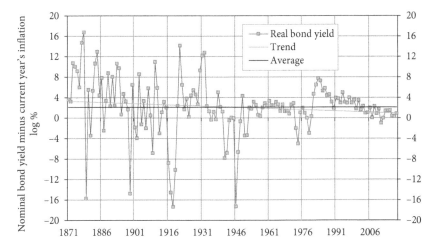

Figure 13. United States: Real long-term bond yields
Data source: Shiller (2000).

is close to the average and, as Figure 15 shows, the fifty-year averages since 1871 for both the United Kingdom and the United States have never exceeded 2.7 per cent. The UK averages for earlier years are higher, but holders of government bonds will not necessarily have then been considered as being free of any default risk: 'Indeed, England did not truly cast off its status as a serial defaulter until 1688.'[1]

---

[1] *This Time is Different: Eight Centuries of Financial Folly* by Carmen M. Reinhart and Kenneth S. Rogoff (2009) Princeton University Press.

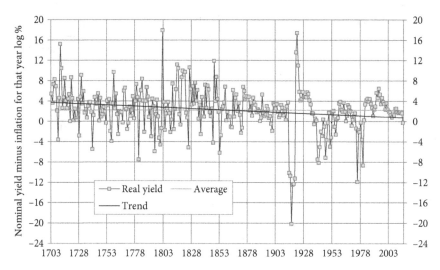

Figure 14. United Kingdom: Real consols/long bond yields 1703 to 2016
Data source: Bank of England (2016).

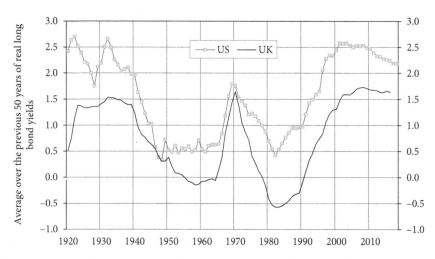

Figure 15. United Kingdom and United States: Average real long bond yields since 1871
Data source: Bank of England (2016) and Jordà, Schularick, and Taylor (2016), updated from Federal Reserve and BLS.

It thus appears that long-dated bond yields and short-dated interest rates, while volatile in the short term, vary within quite narrow limits over longer time spans. The same considerations apply to the shape of the yield curve and the steepness of its slope.

9

Equity, Bond, and Cash Relative Returns

It is often assumed that the expected returns on equities should rise and fall with changes in the return on bonds. It is one of those ideas that seem inherently reasonable but are shown to be false when tested. The difference between the return on bonds and that on equities is termed the equity risk premium (ERP), though the term is used imprecisely being sometimes defined using historic data and sometimes using expected future returns.

The ERP fluctuates but, as it has not been historically mean reverting, it has no stable average and its level at any one time therefore provides no information about its future level or about the prospective returns for either equities or bonds. Despite this evidence, papers are regularly published on the ERP which assume that its level does provide information on one or other of these variables. It is an example of a common unwillingness among economists to discard an assumption which seems reasonable despite the evidence against it.

Figure 16 shows the returns on cash, bonds, and equities over the preceding thirty years. Equity returns have been stationary, but those on cash and bonds fell until around 1970 and have since risen. The lack of any stability in the ERP is confirmed in Figure 17 which shows that it was on a rising trend in the periods ending 1831 to 1972 and has then fallen.

Investors have choices, one of which is to invest either in bonds or in equities, and it is reasonable to assume that they will be readier to hold equities if bonds' yields are low than if they are high and that this readiness will depend on the level of real bond yields: while reasonable, the assumption proves to be wrong in practice. As illustrated in Figure 17, the long-term trends in the ERP, first to rise and then to fall, show that if there is a relationship it is not a stable one, even when measured over the past 217 years.

This is confirmed when the returns are measured over different time periods. As Table 5 shows, there have been periods over which bond and equity yields have shown significant correlations, but such relationships seem accidental as they do not persist over time. There are no significant correlations over any period when measured since 1801, over the whole period since 1801, or since 1943.

The Economics of the Stock Market. Andrew Smithers, Oxford University Press. © Andrew Smithers 2022.
Foreword © Andy Haldane 2022. DOI: 10.1093/oso/9780192847096.003.0009

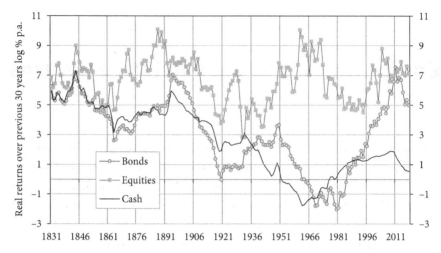

Figure 16. United States: Cash, bonds, and equities real returns over previous thirty years

Data sources: Siegel (1994), Dimson, Marsh, and Staunton (2002), S&P 500, and BLS.

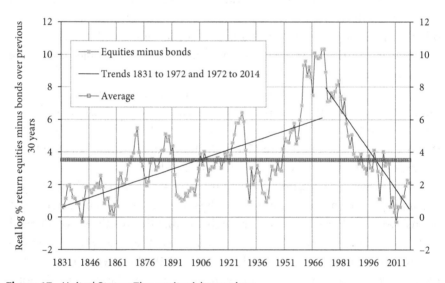

Figure 17. United States: The equity risk premium

Data sources: Siegel (1994), Dimson, Marsh, and Staunton (2002), S&P 500, and BLS.

As equity returns are stable over the long term their prospective returns vary with the level of the stock market. If investors' eagerness to hold equities were influenced by bond returns, the stock market would be cheap when expected real bond returns are high and vice versa. This has not, however, been the case in the past. There have been no correlations between the level

Table 5. R^2 correlations between US real log % equity and bond returns

Time period in years	1801 to 2014	1801 to 1872	1872 to 1943	1943 to 2014
1	0.08	0.35	0.11	0.01
10	0.13	0.05	0.37	0.10
20	0.12	0.24	0.51	0.05
30	0.09	0.18	0.53	0.00

Data sources: Siegel (1994), Dimson, Marsh, and Staunton (2002), S&P 500, and BLS.

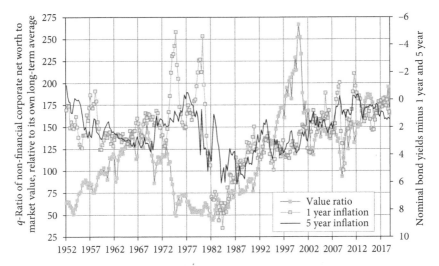

Figure 18. United States: Real bond yields and equity value
Data sources: Shiller (2000) and Z1 Table B. 103.

of the equity market, and thus its prospective return, with long bond yields whether inflationary expectations are based on current inflation (R^2 0.164) or when measured over five years (R^2 0.199), as I illustrate in Figure 18.

The lack of any past relationship between real returns on bonds and equities could have been the result of poor forecasting by investors. We can now begin to test this because bonds which protect investors, both in terms of their income and principle, from the ravages of inflation, called Treasury Inflation-Protected Securities (TIPS) were first issued in 1997. Their real returns have varied between −1.43 per cent and 4.36 per cent.

The same lack of relationship between real bond yields and equity value is shown if TIPS are used for the comparison, as Figure 19 illustrates. Since 1997 there has been a low but not significant perverse relationship with the bond yields fallling and the over-valuation of equities trending down from its 1999 peak. Twenty-year TIPS were introduced in 2004 and there has since been a significant correlation (R^2 = 0.43) but as bond yields have steadily

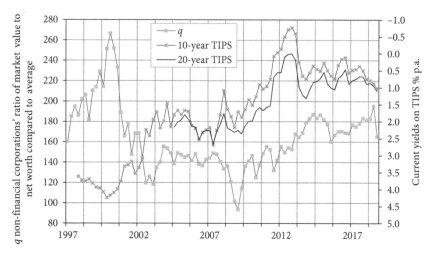

Figure 19. United States: Yields on TIPS and *q*

Data sources: Federal Reserve interest rates and Z1 Table B. 103.

fallen and equities' valuation risen this is likely to reflect only their accidental serial correlation over this limited period.

Over the very long term, real returns on both bonds and equities fluctuate within a narrow range and equities appear to be mean reverting. It follows that the longer the period over which the two averages are measured the less volatile the differences in the two returns will be, but this is not evidence that the relationship is stationary. That it is not is shown by the fact that there is no mean reversion of ERP even when measured, as in Figure 16, over the past 218 years.

While there is no relationship between the level of the stock market and bond yields, changes in interest rates have a short, but not long-term, effect on equity prices: 'Given the likely co-dependence of (share) prices, earnings and interest rates, it is necessary to study their relationship simultaneously rather than separately or on a bilateral basis. This can be carried out via multiple regression analysis, specifically using so-called Vector Auto Regressive (VAR) models...In the long run, defined forecast horizons of five years or greater, interest movements do not appear to affect stock prices. This is consistent with the absence of a long run relationship between interest rates and stock prices.'[1]

[1] 'Interest Rates, Profits and Share Prices' by James Mitchell (Appendix 3) *Wall Street Revalued: Imperfect Markets and Inept Central Bankers* by Andrew Smithers (2009) John Wiley & Sons Ltd.

The absence of any relationship between bond yields and equity returns is not evidence that investors are irrational, but that preferences follow rationally from their assessment of risk rather than changes in relative returns. It is exceedingly rare for the prospective real returns on long-term bonds to match those on equities as the long-term average of the former is 2.2 per cent and 6.7 per cent for the latter. It is not therefore the relative returns that determine investors' preferences, but those returns adjusted for the risk of receiving a below-average return over their time horizon.

I showed earlier that investors' preferences are insensitive to changes in the long-term average risk-free rate of interest and Table 5 shows that they are also insensitive to short- and medium-term changes. The explanations for these insensitivities are, however, different over longer- and shorter-term periods. Over the longer term real interest rates fluctuate within a narrow range, but they do not do so in the shorter term. But over short periods investors' risk aversion is also volatile, and the fluctuations appear to depend partly on the degree of confidence that profits will rise. As rising interest rates and improving profits tend to move together, the two frequently offset each other.

Consumer and business spending decisions are independent of one another as are their portfolio decisions. The decisions made by companies on their level of investment are independent from their decisions to finance their existing capital with debt or equity and the decisions by households to save or consume are independent from their decisions to hold their assets in debt or equity. There can be an *ex ante* disequilibrium between intentions to save and invest, but *ex post* savings must equal investment. *Ex post* equilibria can be achieved painfully by falls in income depressing savings or through inflation, and without either through skilful policy changes in short-term interest rates or fiscal deficits. Households' portfolio preferences on whether to hold their assets in equity or debt have also to be in equilibrium with corporate leverage and this occurs without any change in the long-term return on equity. Changes in long-term interest rates is one way in which this balance is obtained with changes in fiscal policy and the foreign investors' portfolios preferences being the other. The decision to use fiscal or monetary policy to balance *ex ante* net savings at full employment depends on political decisions. They affect the level of the long bond yield which is needed to achieve the necessary balance between corporate leverage and household portfolio preference and as political decisions are exogenous so must be changes in the yield curve, but for any given fiscal policy or flow of funds from abroad, long bond yield is derived endogenously.

Savings and investment are sensitive to changes in short-term interest rates, but long-term equity returns are not. Changes in short-term interest rates can thus be used to avoid potential mismatches between *ex ante* savings and investment from causing imbalances in the economy. Savings and investment appear to be much less sensitive to changes in long-term than short-term interest rates, but corporate leverage over time is largely determined by long-term rates. Mild changes in long-term interest rates therefore allow the required balance between household portfolio preferences to be achieved with stable long-term returns on equity. Small variations in the yield curve, independent from the level of short-term interest rates, thus allow the required balance in household portfolio preferences and corporate leverage to be achieved without impinging on the ability of changes in short-term rates to influence *ex ante* intentions to save and invest.

10

Stock Market Returns Do Not Follow a Random Walk

For many years there was widespread agreement among economists that stock market returns are distributed in a random manner around a long-term positive upward trend. This is termed a random walk with drift and was well explained in a best-selling work on the stock market.[1] The hypothesis was that owning shares gave you a positive real return in the long run, but that the expected return at any one time was the same: prospective returns did not increase when the market fell or decline when it rose. The theoretical basis for this hypothesis was set out by Paul Samuelson[2] and is based on the reasonable assumption that investors seek to maximize their returns so they will buy the market when it's cheap but not when it's expensive, and this will have an effect like arbitrage so that the market will always be priced fairly.

Hypotheses can, however, be reasonable without being right and the Random Walk is one example. This is now accepted by nearly all economists and by going over the ground I can be accused of flogging a dead horse. But the horse is still alive and kicking, as the consequences that follow from the falsification of the Random Walk model have not yet been assimilated into any general understanding of the way financial markets behave.

The Random Walk Hypothesis is a testable hypothesis and one that is incompatible with the evidence. As the return on equities to shareholders rotates around a stable mean, investors will get a higher-than-average return after a sustained period when returns have been below average and a lower-than-average return after a period of high ones.

The ability to value the stock market depends on equity returns not being random but mean reverting. This can be demonstrated not only by the history of those returns, which I set out later, but also by the way in which the volatility of real equity returns declines over time much faster than would result simply from being measured over a longer period. This is shown in

---

[1] *A Random Walk down Wall Street* by Burton G. Malkiel (1953) W.W. Norton & Co.
[2] 'Proof that Properly Anticipated Prices Fluctuate Randomly' by Paul Samuelson (1965) *Industrial Management Review*.

The Economics of the Stock Market. Andrew Smithers, Oxford University Press. © Andrew Smithers 2022.
Foreword © Andy Haldane 2022. DOI: 10.1093/oso/9780192847096.003.0010

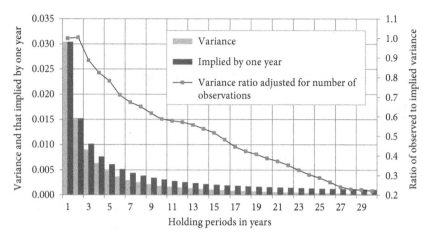

Figure 20. US equities: Annual volatility and returns 1801 to 2018

Data sources: Siegel (1994), Dimson, Marsh, and Staunton (2002), S&P 500, and BLS.

Figure 20 where volatility is measured by the variance which is the square of the standard deviation.[3] The variation in the returns, and thus the risk of receiving poor ones, is not just because the same degree of short-term volatility would have less impact on the total return the longer an investment is held, but because volatility declines over time This shows that stock market returns do not follow a random walk with drift since, after periods when they have been high, real returns tend to fall and, when they have been low, to rise.

Figure 20 shows that the negative serial correlation takes time to be effective and there has been an initial period of very low positive serial correlation. This is shown by the slight rise in the ratio of the observed to the implied variance when the market is held for two years. This short-term positive correlation is more pronounced when returns are measured quarterly.

Figure 20 shows that the market has exhibited negative serial correlation over the 217 years for which we have data. I also show in Figure 21 that this is a persistent feature of market behaviour over time. Negative serial correlation continues to increase as the period for which the investment is held up to thirty years. This means that we need at least seventy years of data to have enough periods of thirty years over which to measure the changes in variance. Even over 217 years of data we only have three of these and I show in Figure 20 the ratios of observed to implied variance for each of these

---

[3] If we had an infinite number of observations and returns followed a random walk, the ratio between the actual and implied variance would always be one. If we have T observations, then the expected sample variance ratio for n-year horizon returns would be $(T - n + 1)/T$. I have therefore adjusted the ratio for the number of observations.

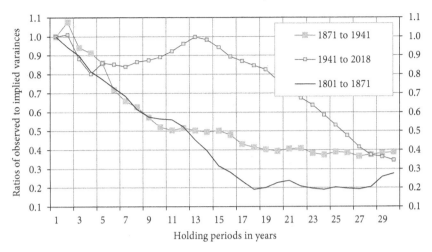

Figure 21. US equities: Negative serial correlation shown by non-overlapping periods of circa seventy years

Data sources: Siegel (1994), Dimson, Marsh, and Staunton (2002), S&P 500, and BLS.

seventy-year periods. The most recent period, which covers 1941 to 2018, has a different profile compared to the two earlier ones. Although the reduction in variance, and thus of risk, is the same over thirty years for all periods, it has been much less over fifteen years since 1941.

The evidence of negative serial correlation shown in Figure 20 is based on overlapping time periods and where sufficient data are available it is better from a statistical viewpoint to use data covering time periods which are discrete and non-overlapping and I do this in Figure 21.

We only have enough data for three non-overlapping periods which are long enough to test over twenty years, but we can also calculate the strength of negative serial correlation for the shorter time periods. We have for example forty-two non-overlapping periods of five years and twenty-one for ten years and I compare the results for these time periods.

As Table 6 shows, the evidence for the negative serial correlation of real equity returns is robust when non-overlapping time periods are used although somewhat less strong than when overlapping time periods are used.[4] Even with ten-year periods the number of non-overlapping periods is small for testing and the comparisons cannot sensibly be used for longer periods.

---

[4] The variances for non-overlapping periods differ with the starting date and those shown in Table 6 are the averages for all possible starting dates.

Table 6. Comparison of data on negative serial correlation comparing non-overlapping and overlapping time periods for five and ten years

	Five-year non-overlapping average	Five-year overlapping	Ten-year non-overlapping average	Ten-year overlapping
Standard deviation	0.0694	0.0587	0.0450	0.0421
Implied by one year	0.0779	0.0779	0.0551	0.0551
Variance	0.0048	0.0034	0.0020	0.0018
Implied by one year	0.0061	0.0061	0.0030	0.0030
Variance ratio	0.7936	0.5681	0.6657	0.5848

Data sources: Siegel (1994), Dimson, Marsh, and Staunton (2002), S&P 500, and BLS.

11

The Risks of Equities at Different Time Horizons

It follows from the negative serial correlation of equity returns that they must have been mean reverting around a stable long-term average. The realization that the real return on equity capital is stable over time is a relatively recent development in financial economics. It needs to be incorporated into macroeconomic models if they are to include finance. Constants are rare in economics but the stability of the real return on equity capital appears to be one.

Thanks to the work of Jeremy Siegel, we have data on the time-weighted returns in the United States dating back to 1801.[1] I show in Figure 22 the annual fluctuations in these returns and in Figure 23 when measured over thirty-year periods from 1801 to 2020. As the closeness of the trend to the average in Figure 22 shows, the returns are mean reverting around a long-term stable average, my best estimate for which is 6.7 per cent.[2]

Equities have no maturity, and their returns are volatile over all time periods, though the volatility declines the longer investors expect to hold them. Although the composition of the stock market changes as companies are liquidated and new ones take their place, in aggregate equities are irredeemable. To be compensated for the risk that this involves investors need a higher return and its extent depends on their aversion to risk.

If the risk aversion of investors has been historically constant, the required return on equities for different time horizons will have been also because the volatility of equities has been mean reverting as Figures 24 and 25 illustrate.

Not only are these volatilities stable over time but although their distribution is not quite normal it has been approximated closely enough, as Figure 26 illustrates, for the probabilities of returns to be calculated as if it were. The

---

[1] I am grateful to Jeremy Siegel for sending me his annual data which he used for his tables of longer period returns in *Stocks for the Long Run* (1994) Richard D. Irwin.
[2] I explain later the details involved in deriving this estimate.

The Economics of the Stock Market. Andrew Smithers, Oxford University Press. © Andrew Smithers 2022.
Foreword © Andy Haldane 2022. DOI: 10.1093/oso/9780192847096.003.0011

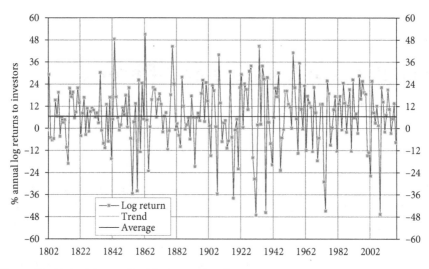

Figure 22. United States: Equities' annual real returns
Data source: Siegel (1994), Dimson, Marsh, and Staunton (2002), S&P 500, and BLS.

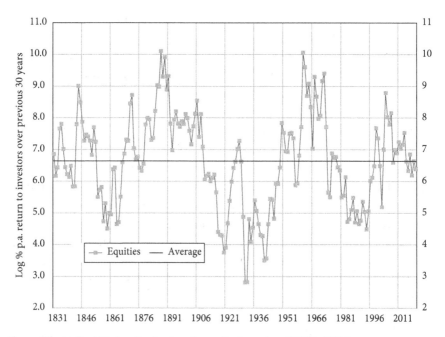

Figure 23. United States: Real return to equity investors 1801 to 2020
Data source: Siegel (1994), Dimson, Marsh, and Staunton (2002), S&P 500, and BLS.

average returns are 6.4 per cent and 6.8 per cent, thus being greater or lower than my best estimate of the long-term return of 6.7 per cent, with the higher figure matching the actual return from 1801 to 2018.

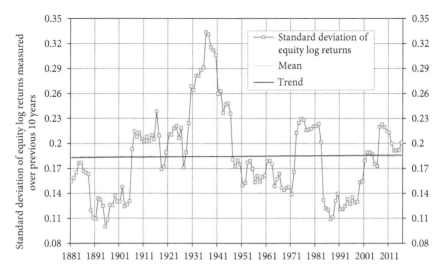

Figure 24. United States: The long-term stability of volatility of one-year real equity returns

Data source: Shiller (2000).

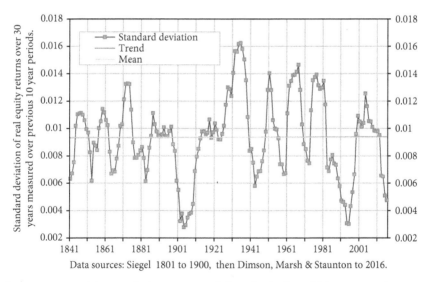

Figure 25. United States: The long-term stability of volatility of thirty-year real equity returns

Data source: Shiller (2000).

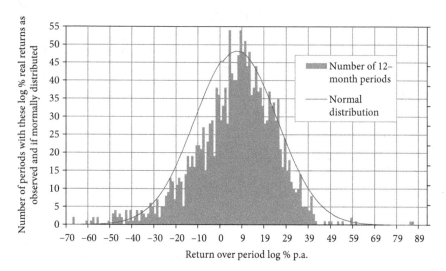

Figure 26. United States: Distribution of equity log returns 1871 to 2019

Data source: Shiller (2000).

12

The Time Horizon at Which Investors Will Prefer Equities to Bonds

By combining the risk-free return on bonds of different maturities (Figure 10) with the minimum likely return on equities at different probabilities (Figure 27) we can calculate the time horizon (T) at which investors will prefer equities to bonds.

The combination of stable volatility with a near normal distribution of the returns allows the time horizon of investors with different levels of risk aversion to be calculated. The risk aversion that determines this time horizon is that for the marginal supplier of sufficient equity and thus at the high end of the spectrum of individual attitudes. T is thus likely to be considerably longer than if the time horizon was determined by the average willingness to accept risk.

Figure 27 shows the returns on equities which have probabilities of 83.5 per cent and 95 per cent of being exceeded, which are those within 1.00 and 1.67 standard deviations of the average, based on average long-term returns of 6.8 per cent p.a. (A) and 6.4 per cent p.a. (B). Figure 28 compares the risk-free real returns on bonds, using my estimate of the long-term average yield curve and a steeper curve (A) in which the twenty-year bond return is increased by 0.1 per cent. If an 83.5 per cent probability of matching or exceeding the equity return is required by the marginal investors, their holding period will be nine years and twenty-one years if a 95 per cent probability is required.

Because the probability of any given minimum return on equity rises so quickly with time, T is insensitive to small changes in the yield curve. I showed earlier, however, that corporate leverage is highly sensitive to changes in risk-free twenty-year bond yields. Because corporate leverage responds elastically to changes in the yield curve and investors' time horizons do not, changes in leverage will occur readily in response to changes in the yield curve and accommodate required changes in households' portfolio preferences without any change occurring in the returns on equity.

The Economics of the Stock Market. Andrew Smithers, Oxford University Press. © Andrew Smithers 2022. Foreword © Andy Haldane 2022. DOI: 10.1093/oso/9780192847096.003.0012

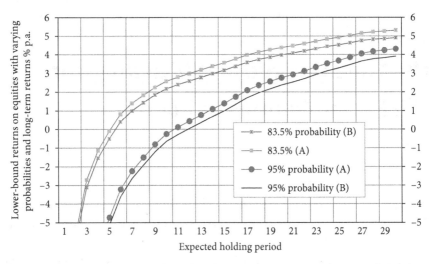

Figure 27. United States: Lower-bound real returns on equities with two probabilities with two average returns
Data source: Author.

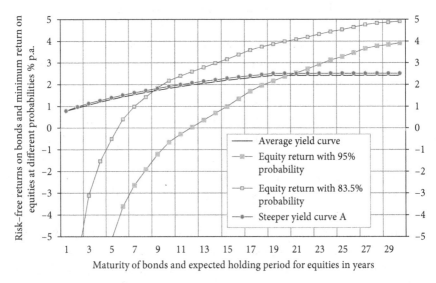

Figure 28. Time horizon (T) at which US investors will prefer equities to bonds
Data source: Author.

13
Changes in Aggregate Risk Aversion

It is reasonable to assume that individuals' risk aversion will, considered in total, fluctuate in the short term around a stable long-term average. It seems likely, however, that risk aversion in aggregate will vary with changes in demography.

With stable risk aversion the minimum return that investors will accept on equity will be 6.7 per cent. Companies will respond by having the same equity hurdle rate, which is the minimum expected rate of return on the equity finance needed for new investment. If they invest in new capital which gives a lower return their share prices will suffer. If their return on equity is below the acceptable level for investors, the company will sell at a different level than others relative to its net worth and will then be vulnerable to being taken over. (Even if a company is selling above its net worth it will be vulnerable if its ratio is lower than that of others, because the even more highly valued shares of the aggressor can be used to finance the acquisition.) If opportunities to invest at 6.7 per cent are not taken, then companies risk having higher costs of production than their competitors. The return that investors require of 6.7 per cent thus becomes the return that companies obtain on their equity capital.

If risk aversion rises, for example, through a rise in the retired proportion of the population, then the demand for debt will rise and that for equity fall. To restore equilibrium there will have to be changes in their cost. If corporate risk aversion is stable, leverage will rise as interest rates fall. The required return on equity is insensitive to changes in the long-term level of long bond rates (Figure 28), whose average measured over fifty years has fluctuated within relatively narrow limits (Figure 14). Changes in interest rates can therefore occur without changing the required return on equities and allow changes in aggregate risk aversion to take place without having any effect on the required return, provided that leverage changes significantly in response to a small change in interest rates which, as I showed in Chapter 4, they do. It follows that a change in the aggregate risk aversion of households has no impact on the required return on equity thus allowing the return on equity to remain constant over time. The adjustment to changes in aggregate risk

The Economics of the Stock Market. Andrew Smithers, Oxford University Press. © Andrew Smithers 2022.
Foreword © Andy Haldane 2022. DOI: 10.1093/oso/9780192847096.003.0013

thus takes place through changes in the long bond yield, either through changes in the short-term rate with an unchanged yield curve or through the stability of the former and a change in the steepness of the curve.

The required return on equities depends on the long-term risk aversion of investors in aggregate. The model assumes that the average individual will have over time a stable level of risk aversion, but the rational policy for an investor will nonetheless change over time. Demographic and other changes are likely to affect the aggregate level of risk aversion and this will determine the proportions of debt and equity assets that households will wish to hold.

The total *ex post* levels of savings and investment must be equal, but their level is partly determined by the decision over the combination of fiscal and monetary policy used to keep *ex ante* net savings at zero. As equity returns are insensitive to their changes, short-term interest rates can be altered to achieve the optimum level of output and employment without affecting the equity/debt balance desired by households. Changes in household portfolio preferences will usually need to be matched by changes in the desired level of corporate leverage. Leverage is, however, sensitive to the long-term interest rate so this equilibrium can be achieved at different levels of the risk-free rate of interest through small changes in the yield curve.

At least two equilibria are thus needed for a stable economy; one is for *ex ante* net savings to be zero, the other is that the portfolio preference of households must match the desired level of corporate leverage. This avoids the criticism levelled about the neoclassical synthesis by George Akerlof.[1]

It seems likely that changes in short-term interest rates have a greater impact on private sector savings than on long-term bond yields, while the opposite is true for corporate leverage. Equilibrium conditions for the balance between *ex ante* savings and investment and the preferred portfolio balance of households can thus be obtained through small independent changes in the risk-free interest rate and the yield curve.

The principal reasons for saving are to have funds available to limit the fall in living standards that would otherwise arise from adverse changes in unemployment and health and to pay for a comfortable retirement. The driving principle behind both these forms of savings is to avoid sharp falls in future consumption. This has a profound effect on the required returns from savings. Large reductions in consumption are proportionately many times more painful than small ones. A 10 per cent fall is more than ten times more painful than a 1 per cent one. Investors will therefore require a high return with a high probability of it being met if they are to invest their retirement

---

[1] Akerlof (2019).

savings in risky assets and they will be loath to suffer losses in the value of savings they are making either for their retirement or to protect them from the shorter-term falls in income due to unemployment or ill health. These requirements will mean that they will accept low returns on risk-free invest-ments with maturities matching their investment time horizons and will require much higher average returns from more risky assets. The pain for investors of having to cut their consumption determines their aversion to risk and thus the risk-free rate of interest and the differences (equity risk premiums) between the average returns on equity and the risk-free returns on bonds of varying maturities. These equity risk premiums will not, how-ever, be stable or mean reverting, as they must be free to adjust so that they achieve the required balances between *ex ante* savings and investment and in the desired portfolio balances of the household and corporate sectors.

Economists have found that models that assume that the purpose of sav-ing is to increase future consumption are incompatible with the equity risk premium as measured over many years between the average risk-free return at zero maturity and the average return on equity.[2] The utility of a rise in future income is, however, asymmetric to the negative utility of a fall and that disutility increases more than proportionately with the decline in income. Those who save regularly in order to improve their future consump-tion or to prevent a fall will have to cut back their current consumption by a small amount in the initial year when they start saving but no more there-after and will have a substantial reward from their accumulated savings in the future, even if they receive no return on them, through the protection it will give them against having to cut back on their future consumptions. But the reward for those seeking to raise consumption will be small compared with those who aim to prevent a fall. Those seeking to enhance their spend-ing will want a much bigger risk-free reward and be less risk averse with their choice of investment assets, than those who save to prevent or at least mitigate falls in their future consumption.

The return on equities depends therefore on the requirements of the mar-ginal providers of this form of capital. Individual savers will no doubt have a variety of motivations but if those who save for retirement are necessary to provide sufficient equity to meet corporate needs, they will provide these marginal supplies and will determine the return necessary for them to pro-vide the funds needed in equity form. The assumption in the Mehra and Prescott and similar models of a 'single representative investor' will give a lower required return than the more realistic assumption that the risk

[2] Mehra and Prescott (1985).

aversions of individual investors will cover a range and that the marginal supplier of equity will be more risk averse than the average.

It is also likely that the dominant forms of savings will be those for rainy days and for retirement rather than those being made by people whose desire for wealth outweighs other motives. Short-term fluctuations in the confidence and risk aversion of all types of investors will no doubt occur, but there will also be variations of a more considered type. For rainy day savings these are likely to arise from changes in unemployment and health insurance and for retirement savings from demographic change and the arrangements for the provision of pooled pensions.

The impact of demography is complicated. If the age at which people retire rises with their expectation of life, without any increase in the time taken for their education, then the expected time horizon for retirement savings will lengthen and aggregate risk aversion will fall. But if the average age of retirement is unchanged the increased expectation of life will have the opposite effect. There is also a major difference in the time horizon of defined benefit and defined contribution pension schemes. In a demographically stable world a defined benefit fund which paid all pensions would grow forever and have an unchanged and infinite time horizon for its investments. Defined contribution funds have the time horizon of their individual members and, if they were the only type of pension scheme, the time horizon of pension funds would be much shorter than those of defined benefit plans.

The overall impact of these changes is uncertain but the post-war changes which seem likely to have been most important are the increase in the proportion of the population which is over 65, which I illustrated in Table 1, combined with a tendency for the age of retirement to be unchanged, the initial growth and subsequent retreat of final salary pension funds and the reduced need for rainy-day funds as the memory of the slump recedes and unemployment and health insurance have improved. The overall effect of these changes will have been to increase the importance of retirement savings and to shorten their time horizon.

14

Monetary Policy, Leverage, and Portfolio Preferences

In a two-sector economy, corporate leverage and household portfolio preference must match under equilibrium conditions when the equity market
value of companies equals their net worth. In practice the relationship is
complicated by several factors including changes in government debt levels,
foreign capital flows, and fluctuations in land prices which affect the value of
corporate net worth but not the sectors' produced capital stock. Another
complication is that the value of equities, as perceived by the household sector is represented by their market value, which swings around net worth. The
wish of households to hold equity will, under equilibrium conditions, decline
as the time horizon shortens, but in the short term their eagerness to own
shares seems to rise rather than fall as prices rise.

There is, therefore, no simple narrative to account for the relative changes
shown in Figure 29, which compares household ownership of corporate
equity measured at net worth and market value. The sensitivity of corporate
leverage to changes in long bond yields is, however, a crucial factor in the
way monetary policy operates and thus important for the short-term management of the economy.

Without changes in growth and investment conditions for stable employment at the non-accelerating level of unemployment (NAIRU) there will be
two equilibria. One being the *ex ante* levels of savings and investment, the
other will be that between the leverage of the corporate sector and the ratios
of equities and debt in the financial asset portfolio of the household sector.
The neoclassical synthesis assumed that both would respond to one policy
tool, through changes in short-term interest rates,[1] but finding these inad-
equate central banks have now introduced another policy tool in the form of
quantitative easing (QE). Insofar as neoclassical theory provides a coherent
and self-consistent model it holds that central banks can control short-term
interest rates, and these determine the cost of long-term debt and equity and

---

[1] Akerlof (2019).

The Economics of the Stock Market. Andrew Smithers, Oxford University Press. © Andrew Smithers 2022.
Foreword © Andy Haldane 2022. DOI: 10.1093/oso/9780192847096.003.0014

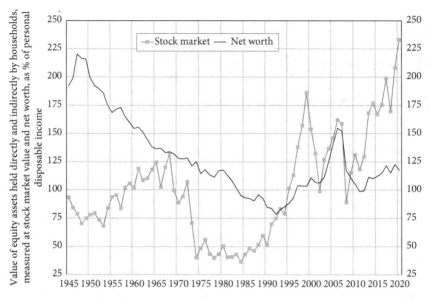

Figure 29. United States: Household ownership of equity assets
Data sources: Z1 B.101e and NIPA Tables 1.1.5 and 5.1.

thus the cost of capital. As Figures 16, 17, and 18 show, this assumption conflicts with the evidence and the introduction of QE is in practice an admission that this aspect of the neoclassical model is clearly wrong. When short-term interest rates were the only policy tool, central banks were using it to maintain the *ex ante* equality of savings and investment and the balance between leverage and household financial assets was either assumed to be unchanged or unimportant. QE, however, involves altering the monetary base and, as Figure 30 shows, this has changed the yield curve. Monetary policy has therefore changed from being solely concerned with the management of short-term rates to involving long-term rates as well and thus recognizing their independence.

When central banks buy bonds, they are reducing their supply but also encouraging higher corporate leverage which reduces the supply of equity and net worth. If household portfolio preference is unchanged the prices of both must increase. The *q* ratio, which is mean reverting, will rise. Using QE to preserve *ex ante* net savings at zero thus increases the disequilibrium between market value and net worth.

An *ex ante* savings mismatch can, however, also be addressed by an easing of fiscal policy. If the impact on demand matches, the difference is that bond yields rise rather than fall and leverage and share prices decline. Keeping both the savings/investment and the *q* ratio in balance requires, therefore, a

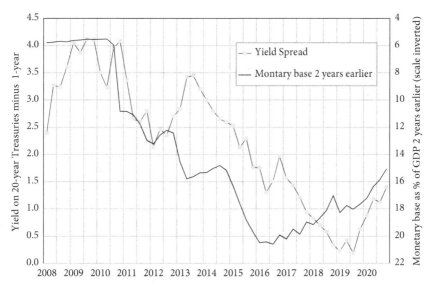

Figure 30. United States: Monetary base as % of GDP and Treasury yield spread (twenty-year minus one-year)

Data sources: Federal Reserve H6 and H15 and NIPA Table 1.1.5.

judicious use of both monetary and fiscal policy, or the use of some other policy tool.

Another assumption of neoclassical economics is that in the absence of a liquidity trap all private sector *ex ante* net savings surpluses must be cyclical. Provided that fiscal policy is used sufficiently to allow monetary stimulus to preserve full employment, it is assumed that the need for such stimulus must be temporary. The persistence of near zero interest rates plus QE since its introduction in 2011 shows that this is unlikely to be justified. The current mismatch between the savings and investment intentions of the private sector thus appears to be structural rather than cyclical.

If this is correct the need for another policy tool has become urgent. A prolonged continuation of QE will at some stage be incompatible with the extremely elevated level of q that it has produced, and this seems likely to produce another financial crisis. The problem would remain, although in a less acute form, if fiscal stimulus had been used in place of QE: while government debt ratios can rise without causing great economic damage well above their current level, they must in time be brought under control.

15

Valuing the US Stock Market

As the returns from US equities fluctuate around a stable average, they must give poor ones after sustained periods of high returns and good ones following times when returns were low. A market which gives poor returns must be an expensive one and vice versa so we should, given this pattern of returns, be able to value the US stock market. In 2000 two books were published which showed how this could be done.[1]

The method used by Robert Shiller depends on the mean reversion of long-term equity returns. If the current return on corporate equity was always the same as its long-term average, we could measure the value of the market by comparing the current PE with that average. But profits rise and fall cyclically so we need to smooth these fluctuations to arrive at an estimate of what the current PE would be if profits were at their average level. Shiller proposed doing this by averaging EPS, measured at constant prices over the past ten years. The resulting cyclically adjusted PE (CAPE) is then compared to its average to give the market's value.

Stephen Wright and I based our approach on the fact that shares represent a title to the ownership of companies and thus to their assets. In a reasonably competitive economy, the price of those assets cannot deviate for long from their replacement value. The extent to which value deviated from price was therefore shown by the ratio (q) between the stock market value of companies and the value of their assets after deducting debt (net worth). Value defined in this way would not, however, necessarily be the same as value based on relative returns. If the return at net worth, i.e. at fair value, was say 9 per cent on one occasion and 6 per cent at another, the relative return would be higher in the first instance than the second, even though the market was fairly valued on both occasions. For q to be a useful measure of value, defined in terms of relative returns, the long-term real return on equity must be mean reverting. In a reasonably competitive economy q would still be a valid measure of value even if the real return on equity were not mean reverting,

---

[1] *Irrational Exuberance* by Robert Shiller (2000) Princeton University Press and *Valuing Wall Street* by Andrew Smithers and Stephen Wright (2000) McGraw Hill.

The Economics of the Stock Market. Andrew Smithers, Oxford University Press. © Andrew Smithers 2022.
Foreword © Andy Haldane 2022. DOI: 10.1093/oso/9780192847096.003.0015

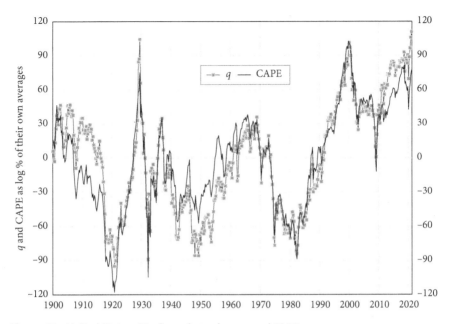

Figure 31. United States: Stock market value—*q* and CAPE
Data sources: For *q* Wright (2004) and Z1 Table B. 103 and for CAPE Shiller (2019).

but in the absence of a stable long-term return it would not be possible to use *q* to define value in terms of relative returns.

Both *q* and CAPE therefore depend in practice on the mean reversion of equity real returns. The similarity of the market's value shown by both metrics is therefore additional evidence for the stationarity of real equity returns. An interesting and important feature was that the two approaches are very different and rely on different datasets. This means that as the two separate methods produced similar results, as Figure 31 shows, they reinforce the validity of each other.

The potential importance of the relationship between market value and net worth had been familiar to economists since James Tobin wrote about it fifty years ago and showed that the market value of companies and the replacement cost of their assets must on average be equal.[2] Tobin termed the value of this ratio *q*, which must on average equal one. Stephen Wright and I were, however, concerned to show the value of the equity market and to do this our definition needed to be slightly different from Tobin's and we called the ratio of stock market value of corporate equity to that of the companies' net worth as *q*. It is therefore different from Tobin's ratio, which I will call Q

---

[2] Tobin (1969).

Table 7. Comparison between implied and observed growth in US quoted company dividends

Average retained profit ratio 1871 to 2018 (A)	38.84%
Real returns to investors should equal average earnings' yield (current price/the next 12 months EPS) (B)	7.66%
Implied real growth of dividends (B) × (A) ÷100	2.98% p.a.
Observed real growth of dividends	1.61% p.a.
Actual pay-out ratio in 2018 was below average, had it been average, growth of real dividends would have been	1.80% p.a.

Data source: Shiller (2019).

to differentiate it from that used for valuing the stock market. Tobin's Q compares the total assets including debt with the total value of debt and equity.

Both CAPE and q are compared with their own long-term averages. If the profits of US companies were correctly calculated, CAPE could be compared with the long-term return on equity as the average prospective earnings' yield (next year's EPS × 100 ÷ current share price) would then be same as that return. But US companies habitually overstate their profits and, as the data we have on the net worth of companies are derived from their past profits, these data on net worth are also overstated. Provided that the degree of overstatement is reasonably constant over time we can still measure value by comparing CAPE and q with their average ratios.

We know that US companies habitually overstate their profits because the geometric average earnings' yield on US stocks from 1871 to 2018 was 7.66 per cent and the arithmetic average 7.70 per cent, both of which are significantly higher than the total real return to investors over the same period which was 6.6 per cent p.a. The overstatement of profits is also shown by the data on the proportion that is paid out in dividends (the pay-out ratio). The published pay-out ratios imply a more rapid rise in dividends per share than the observed change, as shown in Table 7. This could have been the result of overstated profits, a fall in the pay-out ratio, or some combination of the two. I show that it must have been partly the result of the former by demonstrating that the real growth of dividends would have been much slower than that implied by the profit data even if there had been no fall in the pay-out ratio.

By defining value, as it is generally understood, to be a measure of the returns that will subsequently be derived by an owner, relative to their long-term average, we can tell, if we have enough subsequent data, whether equities were priced fairly in the past and their degree of mis-valuation. The validity of CAPE and q as valuation metrics can therefore be tested by

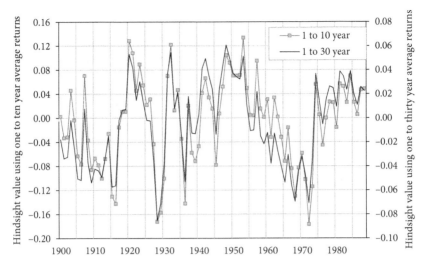

Figure 32. United States: Hindsight value using one to ten and one to thirty years' data
Data sources: Siegel (1994), Dimson, Marsh, and Staunton (2002) updated from S&P 500.

comparing them with values based on hindsight. As returns are stable over the long term there is a stable average return with which subsequent returns can be compared and a cheap market will give above- and an expensive market below-average returns. Short-term results are no use for this test as the return is determined by the level of the market at the end as well as the beginning of the period. A market is not necessarily cheap because it goes up next year, even if it rises strongly. Returns need therefore to be measured over many different time periods, such as the next one to ten years, and these returns averaged. Using this method, the measure of cheapness is not overly influenced by the value at the end of the set period.

This approach, however, raises the question of what is the minimum number of years needed to test for the correlation of returns against the value metrics of CAPE and q? It is desirable to use the minimum number as the longer the period we use the less information we will have to check the results.

Hindsight value is the return achieved over a given range of time periods compared with the average return over the total time span of these periods. We can measure this over different periods and the minimum useful number of years is shown when the inclusion of more years ceases to have any significant impact on the results. Figure 32 compares hindsight value when measured over ten and thirty years and Figure 33 makes the comparison between thirty and fifty years. It is clear from the Figures that using ten years can give misleading results but that this is improbable if thirty-year data are used.

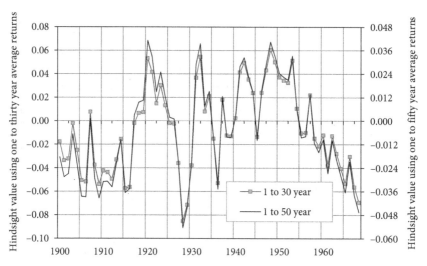

Figure 33. United States: Hindsight value using one to thirty and one to fifty years' data
Data sources: Siegel (1994), Dimson, Marsh, and Staunton (2002) updated from S&P 500.

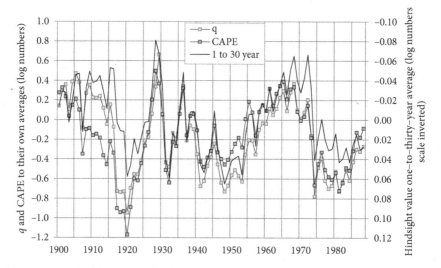

Figure 34. United States: Hindsight compared with *q* and CAPE
Data sources: Siegel (1994), Dimson, Marsh, and Staunton (2002) updated from S&P 500.

With the benefit of hindsight, the accuracy of *q* and CAPE as valuation metrics can be tested. (Both Figures 32 and 33 cover the years for which we have data on *q* and CAPE.) I compare the three methods of valuing the equity market in Figure 34.

Both *q* and CAPE track the fluctuations in value shown by hindsight though *q* does so more closely, as is shown by the R^2 correlations which is 0.80 for *q* and 0.52 for CAPE. An interesting feature of Figure 34 is that CAPE and, to a lesser extent, *q* usually overestimate the cheapness of the

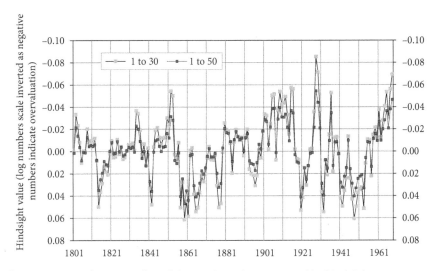

Figure 35. United States: Value of the stock market measured by hindsight 1801 to 1968

Data sources: Siegel (1994), Dimson, Marsh, and Staunton (2002) updated from S&P 500.

market, as shown by hindsight, when it was low and underestimate its over-valuation when it has been high.

In Figure 35 I use hindsight value to calculate the long-term real return on equities more accurately than we can do by measuring the return over the whole period for which data are available. Measured from 1801 to 2018 the return has been 6.83 per cent p.a., but even when measured over thirty years the swings are pronounced as Figure 32 illustrates. To assess the level of the long-term return around which the observed returns have fluctuated we need to adjust the levels in 1801 and 2018 for the degrees to which they were misvalued.

Figure 35 shows that the market at the end of 1801 was slightly cheap, but not by enough to have had any significant impact on the long-term return. Figure 31 however, shows that the stock market was 2.13 times overvalued at the end of 2018. If it had been at fair value, the return from 1801 to 2018 would have been 6.7 per cent p.a. This is therefore the best estimate available for the level of the long-term mean-reverting real return on equities.

The return on capital for the economy is profits (Π) divided by the value of the capital stock (V). The capital/output ratio is (V/Y) and the profit share of output is (Π/Y) where output is (Y).

V/Y is stationary (Figure 42) as is Π/V (Figure 5) so the return on capital for the whole economy Π/Y must be also. In aggregate everything belongs to the household sector: in a closed economy, there is no net debt when sector balance sheets are consolidated and this is the net position for households who own the business sector and receive the benefit of government services. All capital is past savings and consists only of equity; the creation of debt does not involve any addition or reduction in total savings.

Government investment requires no equity and the return on it must be the same for business and residential capital because investment will flow to any sector which gives an above-average return. In addition the total return on capital for the economy could not be stationary as the distribution of total capital between government, business, and housing is not. The return on capital for the whole economy must therefore be the return on equity, which is the same as that on business. The returns on equity and bonds must be the same for all sectors, but as leverage and tax incidence varies the return on capital will differ between sectors.

The national per cent p.a. return on equity Π/V = must be:

$$\Pi/Y \times V/Y = (100/3.27) \times 0.2187 = 6.6688\%$$

This is also the real return on corporate equity derived from the real return on corporate equity to shareholders. The consistency of the results for the three ratios Π/V, Π/Y, and V/Y, is necessary for them to be mean reverting and thus strong evidence that they are.

16

The Real Return on Equity Capital Worldwide

The intended real return on net worth for companies and shareholders will be the same worldwide for two reasons: arbitrage and our common humanity. Given freedom, at least for marginal capital flows, shareholders will choose the country with the highest expected return, driving up share prices in that equity market. Intended equity is also likely to be equal as the pattern of risk aversion among different nations is likely to be the same and small differences due to demographic age distribution and institutional arrangements for pension savings are reflected, as shown in Chapters 12 and 13, by changes in long bond yields in different currencies rather than by changes in real returns on equities. This is due to the high elasticity of corporate leverage to bond yields and the relatively low elasticity of household portfolio preference to changes in equity returns. Nominal bond yields can and do vary in different currencies without being equalized by arbitrage due to differences in institutional structures and expectations for inflation.

The long-term real return on equities in any country is:

$$\sqrt[n]{\Pi}[(1+r)_{t+1} \times (1+E)_{t+1} \times (1+r)_{t+2} \times (1+E)_{t+2} \dots (1+r)_{t+n} \times (1+E)_{t+n}]\dots\dots\dots\dots\dots 1$$

where r is the US return and E is the error in expectations for periods starting at time t, i.e. t + 1, t + 2, etc.

Because returns can be negative but value cannot be, E > –1 and if errors are random $1 < E > -1$ and $\sqrt[n]{} \Pi [(1 + E)_{t+1} \times (1 + E)_{t+2} \dots \times (1 + E)_{t+n}] \to 1$.

If errors in expectations sum to zero over time the real return on equities will be the same in all countries, provided that there are no exogenous shocks such as government expropriation of assets, as occurred in Russia in 1917, and for Germany by wartime legislation in the United Kingdom and United States for the appropriation of enemy property. Differences in growth rates

The Economics of the Stock Market. Andrew Smithers, Oxford University Press. © Andrew Smithers 2022.
Foreword © Andy Haldane 2022. DOI: 10.1093/oso/9780192847096.003.0016

between different countries will have no impact on returns unless expectations for such growth rates were persistently misguided.

In this chapter I test out this model for international returns and show that the data support the model, indicating that barriers to capital flows do not seem to have affected relative returns and that risk aversion is probably similar between different nationalities.

The United States is unique in that it is the only country for which we have data for equity returns over 217 years. Reliable data on other markets are generally available only since 1900 and we have complete data for fifteen of these, which exclude Finland, Ireland, and Norway, countries which obtained their independence after 1900, or Sweden and Austria, whose economies changed drastically in size through the break with Norway[1] and the collapse of the Austro-Hungarian Empire, respectively.

These fifteen countries fall into two groups. Eight of them, Belgium, Denmark, France, Germany, Italy, Japan, the Netherlands, and Spain suffered major losses of capital destruction, either through being defeated and occupied in one or both of the two World Wars or from civil war. The other seven, which are Australia, Canada, New Zealand, South Africa, Switzerland, the United Kingdom, and the United States, largely avoided such losses. I have included the United Kingdom in the second group as it was never occupied though it suffered extensive capital losses of shipping and through bombing. Excluding South Africa, for which we lack early twentieth-century data for GDP, we have reliable data on growth and market returns for all fifteen countries.

Table 8 shows the growth rates and equity returns for the stock markets of those countries which had suffered major losses of capital equipment during either or both the two World Wars and the Spanish Civil War. The returns differ when measured in local currency or US dollars, while the latter, by measuring all countries in a common currency, is better for comparing relative returns. If expectations coincide with the outturn, the returns in all markets should be the same in a common currency, but not necessarily the same when measured in their domestic currencies. Over any given period, the more rapidly growing countries will, according to the Balassa-Samuelson effect, have rising real exchange rates so their returns expressed in domestic currencies will be below average.

---

[1] Norway obtained its independence from Sweden in 1905: in that year the real return on the Swedish stock market is recorded by Dimson, Marsh, and Staunton as 93 per cent. No other country showed an anomalous return in that year, which therefore seems to have been affected by the independence of Norway and makes it doubtful that year-on-year comparisons can be properly made from the corporate share price data.

Table 8. Comparisons between growth of GDP and equity returns for countries experiencing capital destruction 1899 to 2019

	Change in GDP % p.a.	Real equity returns in local currency % p.a.	Real equity returns in US $ % p.a.
Belgium	2.05	2.92	3.44
Denmark	2.54	5.55	6.03
France	2.19	3.48	3.39
Germany	2.12	3.45	3.71
Italy	2.38	2.15	3.71
Japan	3.49	4.20	4.52
The Netherlands	2.77	5.17	5.50
Spain	2.76	3.56	3.63
Average	2.54	3.81	4.24

Data sources: Angus Maddison (2010) and Dimson, Marsh, and Staunton (2002, updated 2013), then updated from National Share Indices and Data via Bloomberg (2020).

Table 9. Comparisons between growth of GDP and equity returns for countries experiencing little or no capital destruction 1899 to 2019

	Change in GDP % p.a.	Real equity returns in local currency % p.a.	Real equity returns in US $ % p.a.
Australia	3.29	7.34	7.46
Canada	3.56	5.71	5.82
New Zealand	2.95	6.41	6.22
South Africa	N/A	7.10	4.68
Switzerland	2.13	4.56	5.80
United Kingdom	1.78	5.32	5.29
United States	3.12	6.64	6.64
Average	2.81	6.00	6.20

Data sources: Angus Maddison and Dimson, Marsh, and Staunton (2002, updated 2013), then updated from National Share Indices and Data via Bloomberg.

Table 9 shows the same data as Table 8 but for the relatively fortunate countries which escaped massive capital destruction in wars. The returns are again similar whether measured in local currencies or US dollars, but the returns on equity are significantly higher in Table 8 than in Table 7, while the difference in the growth rates of GDP are much smaller. It appears that the countries which suffered major losses through capital destruction have largely caught up in terms of growth but suffered permanent losses of capital which reduced their returns on equity.

In Table 10 and Table 11, I show the differences in returns for each group of countries comparing the period 1899 to 1955 with that from 1955 to 2019. In

Table 10. Comparisons between periods 1899 to 1955 and 1955 to 2019 for equity returns for countries experiencing capital destruction

	US $ real return 1899 to 1955	US $ real return 1955 to 2019
Belgium	1.44	5.22
Denmark	3.44	8.35
France	1.16	5.38
Germany	−0.11	7.18
Italy	−0.11	4.45
Japan	1.69	7.06
The Netherlands	1.45	9.18
Spain	2.00	5.08
Average	1.37	6.49

Data sources: Angus Maddison (2010) and Dimson, Marsh, and Staunton (2002, updated 2013), then updated from National Share Indices and Data via Bloomberg.

Table 11. Comparisons between periods 1899 to 1955 and 1955 to 2019 for equity returns for countries not experiencing capital destruction

	US $ real return 1899 to 1955	US $ real return 1955 to 2019
Australia	7.70	7.24
Canada	6.49	5.23
New Zealand	3.02	9.10
South Africa	2.94	6.22
Switzerland	2.62	8.66
United Kingdom	3.41	6.95
United States	6.74	6.74
Average	5.00	7.32

Data sources: Dimson, Marsh, and Staunton (2002, updated 2013), then updated from National Share Indices and Data via Bloomberg (2020).

the second period the returns for the two groups are similar, averaging 6.49 per cent and 7.32 per cent respectively, but in the first period the difference is large, with the average returns for countries which suffered major capital losses being 1.37 per cent compared with 5.00 per cent for the relatively fortunate countries.

I compare in Tables 12 and 13 the growth rates of the two groups for all the years 1899 to 2019 and for 1899 to 1955 and 1955 to 2019. Growth was adversely affected in those countries which suffered losses through capital destruction, but they were catching up after 1955 and, by growing more rapidly than the others, averaging 2.90 per cent p.a. compared with 2.83 per cent.

I have taken 1955 as the year for dividing the two periods for comparing growth and returns for countries that suffered major capital losses from others because stock markets were depressed in wartime due to fears for the future as well as due to actual capital losses and did not recover quickly in

Table 12. Comparisons between periods 1899 to 1955 and 1955 to 2019 for growth of GDP for countries experiencing capital destruction

	Growth of GDP at constant prices 1899 to 1955	Growth of GDP at constant prices 1955 to 2019	Growth of GDP at constant prices 1899 to 2019
Belgium	1.49	2.55	2.05
Denmark	2.68	2.43	2.54
France	1.52	2.79	2.19
Germany	1.73	2.47	2.12
Italy	2.21	2.53	2.38
Japan	2.91	3.99	3.49
The Netherlands	2.74	2.80	2.77
Spain	1.77	3.64	2.76
Average	2.13	2.90	2.54

Data source: Angus Maddison (2010) updated from 2008 to 2011 from national data.

Table 13. Comparisons between periods 1899 to 1955 and 1955 to 2019 for growth of GDP for relatively fortunate countries

	Growth of GDP at constant prices 1899 to 1955	Growth of GDP at constant prices 1955 to 2019	Growth of GDP at constant prices 1899 to 2019
Australia	3.01	3.54	3.29
Canada	3.95	3.23	3.56
New Zealand	3.19	2.75	2.95
South Africa			
Switzerland	1.96	2.28	2.13
United Kingdom	1.27	2.22	1.78
United States	3.31	2.95	3.12
Average (excl. South Africa)	2.78	2.83	2.81

Data source: Angus Maddison (2010) updated from 2008 to 2011 from national data.

real terms in the immediate post-war years. As shown in Figure 36, the stock markets of six countries which suffered most from major capital losses in the two World Wars and the Spanish Civil War halved on average in the three years immediately following World War II.

The collapse in share prices from 1945 to 1948 cannot be sensibly ascribed to capital destruction, and to judge its effect we therefore need to use as a base year one by which share prices had to some extent recovered. 1955 was the first year in which these markets had given a small positive real return (1.0 per cent) since the outbreak of World War II in 1939. This return of 1.0 per cent was low enough to allow for new investment net of massive capital

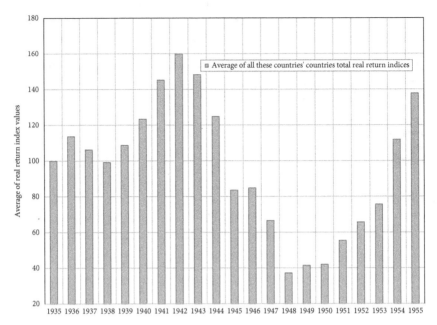

Figure 36. Belgium, France, Germany, Italy, and Japan: Average of real total return indices

Data source: Dimson, Marsh, and Staunton (2002).

destruction. Basing the comparison on the years before and after 1955 has the additional advantage that, as Table 12 illustrates, the relatively 'lucky' countries grew at the same pace, on average, over the two sub-periods.

Measured in constant prices, markets have usually fallen when there were sharp rises in consumer prices, and the post-war surge in inflation, which is illustrated in Figure 37, provides a likely explanation for the accompanying precipitous fall in these markets.

The international data indicate that the loss of return through capital destruction is not made good by higher subsequent returns, but that the loss of output is. It appears that returns on equity capital, and probably therefore on capital in total, were not significantly higher after 1955 when there was no capital destruction, but the higher growth achieved in the second compared with the first period was the result of faster growth in the capital stock, which could have been the result either of a low pay-out ratio by domestic companies or of inflows of capital from abroad.

Output seems to have recovered because of the use of more capital rather than through a lower capital/output ratio. It seems that expectations that the recovering countries would grow rapidly were correctly anticipated and the ability of capital to flow ensured that returns were kept down to the general international level, even if such flows were not needed due to a low pay-out

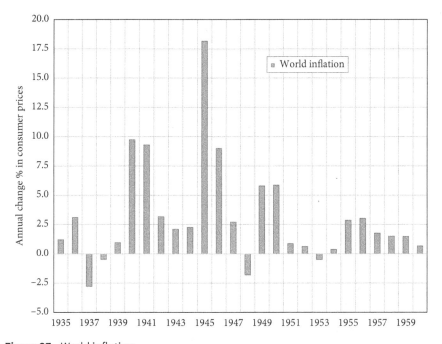

Figure 37. World inflation
Data source: Elroy Dimson, Paul Marsh, and Mike Staunton (2002).

ratio by domestic companies. It therefore appears that the tendency for the long-term return on equity to be stable can be taken as applying internationally and not just as being unique to the United States. This is the expected result in a world in which capital can flow between countries. In these circumstances money will flow to equalize the expected returns everywhere and these returns will not therefore depend on actual growth rates, unless such growth is to some extent unexpected. This hypothesis can be tested by considering the historic returns on individual stock markets compared with the growth rates of those countries.

Figure 38 compares growth with equity returns and shows that there is no apparent relationship between them. The return for the United Kingdom (5.3 per cent) is slightly above average (5.1 per cent), despite having suffered some loss of capital due to bombing and in overseas investments during World War II, while it has been the country with the slowest growth rate. The two countries with the fastest growth rates, Canada and Japan, have, respectively, mildly above and below average returns.

In Figures 39, 40, and 41 I show that the real equity returns for all these markets exhibit negative serial correlation, though in the case of Japan only barely, showing that this is a worldwide phenomenon, rather than something peculiar to the United States.

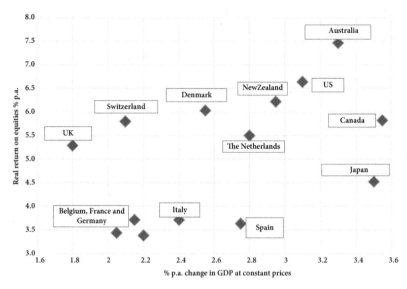

Figure 38. International growth and equity returns

Data sources: Angus Maddison (2010) and Dimson, Marsh, and Staunton (2002, updated 2013), then updated from National Indices and Data via Bloomberg (2020).

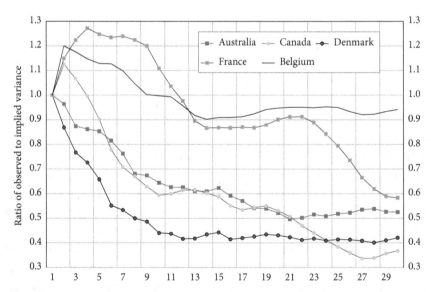

Figure 39. Australia, Belgium, Canada, Denmark, and France: Serial correlation of equity returns in local currency

Data source: Dimson, Marsh, and Staunton (2002, updated 2013).

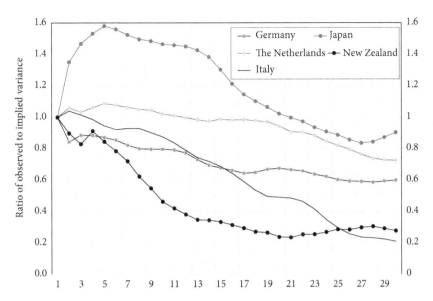

Figure 40. Germany, Italy, Japan, the Netherlands, and New Zealand: Serial correlation of equity returns in local currency

Data source: Dimson, Marsh, and Staunton (2002, updated 2013).

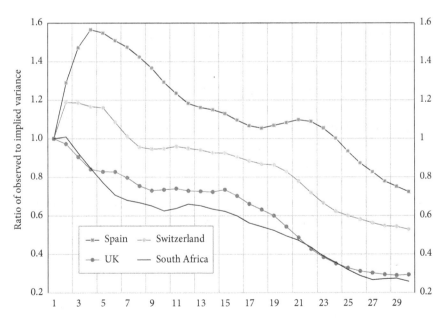

Figure 41. South Africa, Spain, Switzerland, and the United Kingdom: Serial correlation of equity returns in local currency

Data source: Dimson, Marsh, and Staunton (2002, updated 2013).

17

Money- and Time-weighted Returns

The return to shareholders in aggregate must be the same as the return on corporate equity. But this return will be the money-weighted not the time-weighted return. The latter is the figure we have from the published data on shareholder returns. It is calculated from the value that an investment in the stock market would have at the end of the period, allowing for the dividends received on the investment being reinvested in the market. The rate of return is that at which an initial investment of 1 (one) would have been invested to equal the final value of the investment. Where the final value is (V_t), the time-weighted rate of return is (r_t) and the number of years over which the investment is held is (n):

$$\left(1 + r_t\right)^n = V_t \dots\dots\dots\dots\dots\dots\dots\dots\dots\dots\dots\dots\dots\dots\dots\dots\dots\dots\dots\dots\dots\dots\dots\dots\dots\dots 2.$$

In practice, however, the cash distributed to shareholders cannot be reinvested mainly because the return on equity, which has been around 6.7 per cent, has been greater than the growth of the economy, which has been around 3.4 per cent p.a. If all cash distributed to shareholders had been reinvested in equity the net worth of companies must also have grown at 6.7 per cent p.a. and, if the share of output going to profits after interest and tax had been stable, the profitability of that net worth would have had to fall at 3.3 per cent p.a.

Only by having the share of output taken by profits after tax rising at this rate would it have been possible for the long-term return on equity to have been stable and this has not occurred, nor would it be feasible in practice as wages would have had to be a constantly falling proportion of output. (As I show in Figure 42, profit margins have been stable, so this is also true of the labour share of output since the labour and profit shares add up to 100 per cent of output after capital consumption.)

To know the return on corporate net worth we need to calculate the money-weighted rate of return. This is the rate of interest which equals the present value of all past cash distributions to shareholders plus the change in the capital value of the stock market at the end of the period. The initial value

The Economics of the Stock Market. Andrew Smithers, Oxford University Press. © Andrew Smithers 2022.
Foreword © Andy Haldane 2022. DOI: 10.1093/oso/9780192847096.003.0017

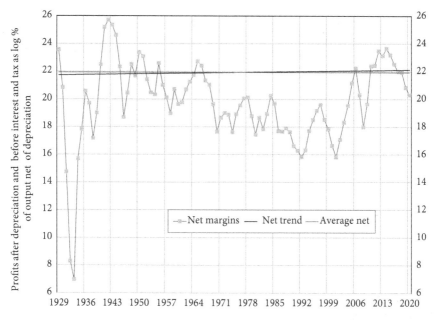

Figure 42. United States: Corporate profit margins
Data source: NIPA Table 1.14.

of the market is (1) broad dividends are (C) when received at times $(t_1, t_2,...)$ discounted at the money-weighted rate of return (r_m) plus the value of the stock market without reinvested income (V_m) at the end of the period (n) years discounted to give its present value at the money-weighted rate of return:

$$1 = \left(\Sigma \left[Ct_1 / \left(1 + \left(r_m\right)\right) + C\, t_2 / \left(1 + \left(r_m\right)^2\right)... \right] \right) +$$
$$V_m / \left(1 + \left(r_m\right)^n\right)..................................3.$$

Unfortunately, for the stock market we do not have data for broad dividends (C) only for dividends as normally defined. We do, however, know from the national data that the difference between broad and normally defined dividends, which is net new issues, has changed sharply as Figure 43 shows.

If these data were available on a per share basis for the S&P 500, it should be possible to produce accurate data on corporate RoE. This would enable the value of the stock market to be determined from past returns, on the lines proposed by Donald Robertson and Stephen Wright.[1] Unfortunately my

---

[1] 'Testing for Redundant Predictable Variables' by Donald Robertson and Stephen Wright (2009) working paper downloadable from http://www/econ.bbk.uk/faculty.wright.

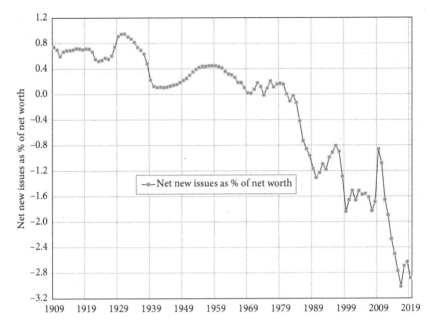

Figure 43. United States: Non-financial companies' net new issues as % of net worth
Data sources: Wright (2004) 1900 to 1945, then Z1 Tables B. 103 and F. 103.

attempts to persuade Standard & Poor's to do this have so far proved unavailing. If money-weighted returns were to become available, it would add another useful check on the values given by q and CAPE. The results published by companies have become increasingly volatile and thus suspect, so the need for another method of assessing market value is growing.

18

The Behaviour of the Firm

As the corporate sector produces more than half total output (Figure 44), the performance of the economy depends on those who run companies. The observation that their motives and incentives are likely to diverge from those of owners dates back at least to 1776, when Adam Smith pointed out that company directors 'being the managers rather of other people's money than of their own, it cannot well be expected, that they should watch over it with the same anxious vigilance.'[1] As pointed out by James Burnham,[2] the possible divergence between the interests of owners and managers has grown in importance as business has become dominated by quoted companies.

Economists are, however, divided on the consequences. Some hold that the distinction is unimportant in practice as companies run by managers have the same aims and behaviour as those run by entrepreneurial owners: 'The neoclassical theory of investment starts from a firm's optimisation behaviour. The objective is to maximise the present discounted value of net cash flows subject to the technological constraints summarised by the production function.'[3] Others hold that 'the practical distinction between management and shareholders is a valid one, and the two groups may be properly regarded as separate elements in the corporate structure.'[4]

Businesses are of three different types: if incorporated they can be either quoted or unquoted, or they can be unincorporated. On the assumption that quoted companies are run by managers while the interests of owners determine the behaviour of both other groups, the practical differences can be examined by comparing the behaviour of quoted companies with that of the other two types of business.

Investment in the United States is dominated by non-financial companies who account for 50 per cent of the total and 75 per cent of that by business, as I illustrate in Figure 45.

---

[1] *An Inquiry into the Nature and Causes of the Wealth of Nations* by Adam Smith (1776) London.
[2] *The Managerial Revolution* by James Burnham (1941) John Day NY.
[3] 'Tobin's Marginal *q* and Average *q*: A Neoclassical Interpretation by Fumio Hayashi (1982) *Econometrica* 50.
[4] Marris (1964).

The Economics of the Stock Market. Andrew Smithers, Oxford University Press. © Andrew Smithers 2022.
Foreword © Andy Haldane 2022. DOI: 10.1093/oso/9780192847096.003.0018

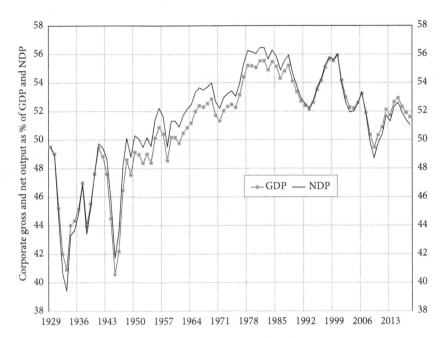

Figure 44. United States: Corporate sector's share of total output

Data sources: BEA Asset Table 1.3 and NIPA Tables 1.1.5 and 1.14.

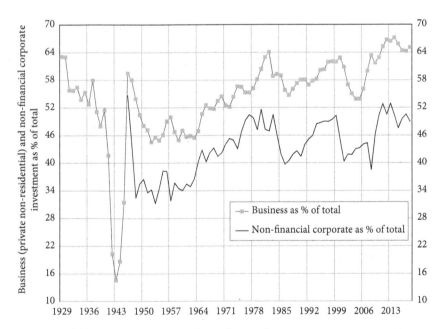

Figure 45. United States: Business and non-financial corporate investment as % of total

Data sources: BEA Asset Table 1.5 and Z1 Table F. 103.

The Financial Accounts of the United States (Z1) show that unincorporated companies account for 44 per cent of non-financial-business net worth but only 17 per cent of investment.[5] The market value of US-owned incorporated businesses is divided between publicly quoted (82 per cent) and closely held (18 per cent). The latter are, however, valued by the Federal Reserve at a discount of 25 per cent[6] and, if allowance is made for this, the split is 77 per cent publicly quoted and 23 per cent closely held. We do not have data on the proportions of either output or investment attributable to US- and foreign-owned companies, but as the subsidiaries of foreign-owned companies are run by managers, we can estimate the proportions of US corporate investment in which decisions are made by managers rather than more directly by owners from the market value data. I do this in Table 14, having adjusted upwards the value of closely held incorporated companies to offset the discount accorded to them in the Z1 data.

Table 14 ascribes 64 per cent of total investment to publicly quoted companies and 36 per cent to closely held and unincorporated ones: the easier access of quoted companies to capital, no doubt contributing to this difference. If the behaviour of the two groups differs, it will therefore be the behaviour of companies run by managers which predominates. The different ways in which the actions of the two groups can diverge include leverage, pay-out ratios, investment, and a willingness to raise new equity when it is cheap.

If there is no change in leverage, net worth must grow in line with output. Figure 5 shows that from 1871 to the end of World War II, when leverage is assumed to have been low and relatively stable, the published dividend pay-out ratios of quoted companies fluctuated with changes in growth. In the absence of any changes in leverage this will also have been true for broad dividends. The decisions by managers on the pay-out ratios of quoted

Table 14. United States: Relative importance of quoted, unquoted, and unincorporated non-financial business in 2018, by net worth and fixed non-residential investment

	Net worth $bn	% of total	Fixed Investment $bn	% of total
Total	30,361	100	2,490	100
Quoted incorporated	16,903	43	1,583	64
Unquoted incorporated	3,907	13	476	19
Unincorporated	13,458	44	431	17

Data sources: Z1 Tables L. 223, B. 103, B. 104, F. 103, and F. 104.

---

[5] Z1 Tables B.103 and B. 104.   [6] Appendix 2 sets out the details of the valuation method used.

companies appear, therefore, to have been made without reference to the preferences of shareholders for either income or capital appreciation, as it is unlikely that these would have changed in line with growth rates. This supports the view of Nicholas Kaldor when he wrote, 'I have always regarded the high savings propensity out of profits as something which attaches to the nature of business income, and not to the wealth (or other peculiarities) of the individuals who own property. It is the enterprise, not the particular body of individuals owning it at any one time, which finds it necessary…to plough back a proportion of the profits earned.'[7] I explained in Chapter 4 that decisions on pay-out ratios followed from companies' need to finance enough investment, but only just enough, to maintain market share, without tapping the market through new equity issues. Paying out too little and too much are both strategies which threaten managements' security of tenure.

Unquoted companies are also reluctant to raise new equity as this weakens the owners' control and thus threatens their role as managers. They differ, however, about leverage. They have the same need to invest enough to preserve their market share and will prefer retentions to new issues for providing the necessary amount of equity finance but, being immune to the threat of being taken over, they have no fear of being underleveraged. The owners of unquoted companies have the freedom to decide how much income they will receive in pay and dividends and how much profit they will retain in the business. The result will depend on their utility preference between current income and future wealth, whose balance will depend partly on the incidence of tax.

Both quoted and unquoted companies will invest when the expected returns on equity match the hurdle rate. Unquoted companies will invest sufficiently to avoid losing market share but will be less concerned if their return on equity falls below the hurdle rate of quoted companies, either through being less leveraged or by being willing to invest in projects which have a lower return on equity.

As explained in Chapter 4, the hurdle rate for quoted companies does not change in line with the cost of equity. As the long-term return on equity is stationary the current cost of raising new equity varies with the valuation of the stock market and the difference between the price at which new shares can be sold,[8] and their price prior to the announcement. Figure 31 illustrates

---

[7] Kaldor (1966).

[8] It should be noted that the cost of new equity is less than the subscription price of a rights issue, as the right to subscribe has value and that value rises as the subscription price falls. The cost of equity in rights issues is not therefore determined by the subscription price but by the extent to which the value of a shareholder's stake in the company has fallen assuming that the shareholder sells enough rights to pay for subscribing for new shares for which he has retained the rights.

the large fluctuations that have occurred in the stock market's value. As a result the current cost of equity has varied between 12.8 per cent and 3.2 per cent. I am not aware of data on the extent to which share prices fall in response to the announcement of new equity issues, but it is clearly a trifling matter compared with the impact on cost of market fluctuations. If the level of corporate investment responded to the cost of capital, it would fluctuate with the stock market but, as I show later in Figure 47 and Figure 48, it does not.

Expected returns on different projects vary and those that are rejected will be lower than those implemented. Investment by quoted companies would thus rise in response to falls in the cost of capital if it were not for the constraint on their managers from exploiting its fluctuations. This constraint comes from the fact that managements are concerned with the price of their companies' shares, rather than the overall level of the stock market. It is the share price of their individual company relative to those of other companies that managements worry about. Companies can use their own shares to acquire others. A company whose share price is high in absolute terms is not thereby protected from takeovers if it is low in relative terms. This explains why, as the data show, quoted companies do not invest more when capital is cheap and why the assumption made by neoclassical consensus growth models that they do is fallacious. Since managers wish to prevent their companies from being taken over, they are indifferent to the variations in the cost of capital that arise from fluctuations in the stock market.

The cost of new equity for unquoted companies is higher but otherwise determined by the same factors which apply to quoted companies. The higher cost is due to the discount from the equivalent price for quoted companies that investors require to compensate them for the loss of liquidity. This is slightly indeterminate, as the equivalent price if quoted is unknown, but judging from my own experience the discount for lack of quotation is usually around 25 per cent and this is also the discount used by the Federal Reserve to value unquoted companies.[9] While significant, this is small compared to the impact arising from stock market fluctuations. The fear of weakening control is likely to be at least partially price sensitive, so unquoted companies respond more than quoted ones to changes in the cost of equity and are more likely to raise new equity and become listed when the stock market is overpriced. Being unconcerned with their share price, they will also be less affected by the impact of the bonus culture on the hurdle rate. Relative to quoted companies they are likely to invest more when the stock

---

[9] For details see Appendix 2.

market is overvalued and this expectation is supported by the evidence.[10] As may seem counter-intuitive, one result of being quoted is to reduce the response of companies to the cost of equity shown by the market's fluctuations.

It thus seems that Robin Marris was too mild when he claimed that management and shareholders may be properly regarded as separate elements in the corporate structure.[11] It is rather that the distinction is essential. Quoted companies do not behave as if they were run by shareholders and because, as Table 14 shows, they dominate business investment, the corporate veil must not be ignored. The behaviour of the private sector can only be properly analysed and understood if it is separated into the household and business sectors. Similarly the latter can only be sensibly modelled if it is recognized that its behaviour is dominated by quoted companies, run by managers with their own interests and utility preferences in mind.

The stock market has a major impact on the growth of the economy as it stops fluctuations in the cost of capital from affecting the level of investment and this invalidates models which assume otherwise. When combined with Tobin's model the stock market has a place in the neoclassical consensus, but only if investment and growth vary with the cost of capital. This is testable and when tested is shown to be wrong, thereby confirming the validity of the widespread concern which I set out in the opening paragraph to this book, that a major weakness of the neoclassical consensus lies in its failure to incorporate finance into its economic models.

Investment does not rise and fall with fluctuations in the cost of capital. If it did, rises in the stock market would be constrained by a growing flood of new issues as share prices rise and their falls would be limited by their absence in weak markets. Smaller fluctuations in the stock market would seem naturally to follow. Corporate issues and purchases of equity would be negatively correlated with periods of under- and overvaluation of share prices rather than positively as seems recently at least to have been the case.[12]

The managements of quoted companies do not ignore the stock market. Their survival requires them to avoid takeovers and this constrains them from issuing new equity even when equity capital is cheap. The stock market does not behave as if it were represented by a single company.

Because they are immune from the threat of takeovers, unquoted companies are freer to hold substantial cash balances, although the extent to which they do is likely to be limited by shareholder pressure as, unlike quoted

---

[10] As shown by Asker, Farre-Mensa, and Ljungqvist (2013).   [11] Marris (1964).
[12] See Figure 63 in Smithers (2019).

companies, their pay-out policy will respond more directly to their share-holders' utility preferences for current cash or capital appreciation. If the management skills and investment opportunities for quoted and unquoted companies were the same, the former would then have higher returns on equity and shareholders who receive no perks or pay from their role as managers will prefer to have shares in quoted companies in addition to the benefits of greater liquidity. A balance is, however, likely if start-ups have higher returns on equity. As they are initially unquoted their investors require a higher return to offset the reduction in liquidity. After the start-up stage, the investment opportunities and the skills needed to exploit them are unlikely to differ enough to prevent quoted companies dominating the economy's business output and investment.

Economists who accept that corporate behaviour differs between firms that are run by managers and entrepreneurial owners usually claim that this results in a reduction in profit maximization and thus the value of those which are management run. For example P. J. Wiles asserts that 'the Managerial revolution is quite fatal to profit maximisation'[13] and Michael Jensen and William Meckling claim that 'an entrepreneur or manager in a firm which has a mixed financial structure (containing both debt and outside equity claims) will choose a set of activities for the firm such that the total value of the firm is *less* than it would be if he were the sole owner.'[14]

Profit maximization is not synonymous with maximizing this year's profits as this may damage longer-term ones, it is maximizing the present value of the business. Companies do not exploit the fluctuations in the stock market to raise cheap capital when this is possible, which is a failure to maximize the firm's present value. It is a course of action seldom taken by either quoted or unquoted companies because in both cases those who take such decisions place their job security highly. This is not a significant factor in the models of management behaviour which I have encountered. For example, Jensen and Meckling do not specifically include job security among the factors in the utility that managers seek to maximize. It might be considered as part of 'non-pecuniary benefits' and while these are assumed to have a cost, they do not seem to approach the scale of that incurred by failures to exploit opportunities to raise cheap equity.

The failure to raise equity when the stock market is overpriced may be seen as a missed opportunity by an individual company but being constrained from doing so by the dislike that shareholders have for new issues, it

---

[13] *Price, Cost and Output* by P. J. Wiles (1956 and 1961) Basil Blackwell, as quoted by Marris (1964).
[14] 'Theory of the Firm: Managerial Behavior, Agency Costs and Ownership Structure' by Michael C. Jensen and William H. Meckling (1976) *Journal of Financial Economics* 3.

is also overlooked in aggregate. The leverage and thus the capital structure of companies must match the portfolio preferences of investors. The economic models used by adherents to the neoclassical consensus assume that companies ignore the stock market and seek to maximize the present value of their net worth. As this would involve exploiting overpriced stock markets to raise new equity, it is clear from the data that this is not the way that companies behave, and these models are therefore fallacious.

Leverage is encouraged up to the limits of prudence for quoted companies, which is when the threat to their managers' job security is perceived to be greater than any benefit to the share price. The incentive to leverage is thus less for unquoted and unincorporated businesses where managements' jobs are more secure provided that the business is not threatened by bankruptcy. Low leverage depresses the return on equity and the comparison between unincorporated businesses' net worth/investment ratio and that for those that are incorporated shown in Table 14 suggests that managers are, in this respect at least, more adept at maximizing present value than owners. The rise in the importance of quoted companies has therefore the opposite impact to that attributed to it by Jensen and Meckling. It should also be noted that leveraging both encourages more investment by increasing the expected return on equity and makes the economy more prone to financial instability. I discuss these issues more fully later.

19

Corporate Investment and the Miller-Modigliani Theorem

The Miller-Modigliani Theorem[1] states that subject to certain conditions the value of a firm will be independent of how it is financed. This runs against the general perception, supported by evidence, that companies' market values rise if they take on additional leverage.[2] Miller-Modigliani defines value differently, not as that ascribed by the stock market, but as the underlying value of companies' assets, which James Tobin termed their 'replacement cost'.[3] This is not the cost of reproducing such assets, as no one would sensibly go to the expense of manufacturing equipment which is less efficient than that which, due to technical progress, is currently available to do the same job at a cheaper price. It is the cost that would be involved in replacing the same equipment by purchase in the second-hand market. The way the BEA determines these prices is by surveys as explained in Appendix 3. As these surveys show the speeds at which these prices fall, they are also used to determine rates of depreciation.

The prices of equipment in the second-hand market are determined by the profit stream they can generate valued at the appropriate discount rate. Leverage does not alter the profit stream, and the validity of the theorem, as a hypothesis for a model of the economy, therefore depends on whether leverage changes the discount rate. The model assumes that it doesn't, on the grounds that the risk of investing in a company rises with its leverage and that the required return on equity will thus rise with it. The required rate of return is based on the level of risk associated with the investment and is directly proportional to the company's leverage level. It is also assumed that the risk-free rate is unchanged and that this applies to the corporate sector as a whole.

---

[1] 'The Cost of Capital, Corporation Finance and the Theory of Investment' by F. Modigliani and M. H. Miller (1958) *The American Economic Review* 48.

[2] See, e.g. Ross (1977).

[3] The term appears in Tobin (1969) and this has been generally followed, e.g. by Hayashi (1982) and James Chan-Lee (1986) 'Pure Profits and Tobin's *q* in Nine OECD Countries' OECD Working Paper.

The Economics of the Stock Market. Andrew Smithers, Oxford University Press. © Andrew Smithers 2022.
Foreword © Andy Haldane 2022. DOI: 10.1093/oso/9780192847096.003.0019

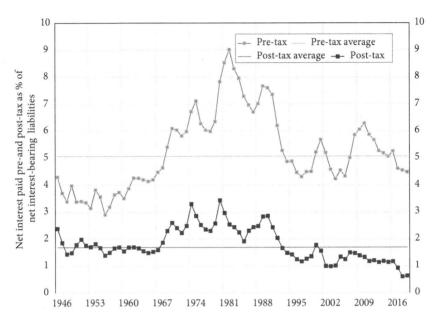

Figure 46. United States: Non-financial companies' interest rate of net debt
Data sources: Z1 Table B. 103 and NIPA Table 1.14.

The value of a company's assets must be equal to the sum of its net worth plus net debt. An increase in debt must match a reduction in equity, so unless such a change alters the value of the assets it cannot alter the value of the firm. The Miller-Modigliani Theorem is therefore a tautology, which must be true if the value of assets is unaffected by changes in leverage. When it is applied to the corporate sector as a whole its validity depends on whether the required return on equity rises with leverage. As equity returns are stationary and have not fallen despite the large post-war rise in leverage, the Miller-Modigliani Theorem is not a valid hypothesis. Even if the model were valid when applied to individual companies it is not when applied to the corporate sector as a whole—it is a fallacy of composition.

Companies take no notice of fluctuations in the cost of equity capital, but they do take note of changes in the return on investment, which rises if leverage increases provided that the cost of debt is less than the hurdle rate of 6.7 per cent after corporation tax. As Figure 46 shows, this has invariably been the case over the period for which we have data, when the interest rate is measured after allowing for tax and on average even when not.[4] Leverage thus raises the value of a given stream of profits without altering its flow, and

---

[4] The post-tax interest rate shown in Figure 46 is based on the tax rate paid in that year. The effective rate is the marginal tax rate which, due to tax credits such as those on R&D investment is higher than the average rate. The effective rate of interest after tax is thus even lower than that shown.

therefore increases the value of the assets measured at replacement cost. The value of an individual company's assets barely changes if it substitutes some of its equity with debt, since its impact on the discount rate applicable for valuing corporate assets is too small to be observable. In aggregate, however, increased leverage can only occur if the discount rate does not alter as it must match the portfolio preferences of the owners of financial assets. Even if the margin over the risk-free rate were to rise, which it does not seem to have done in the past, the risk-free rate would need to adjust to prevent any change in the average cost of corporate debt.

The value of the assets of the corporate sector in aggregate thus respond significantly to changes in leverage. The neoclassical consensus habitually assumes that the Miller-Modigliani Theorem is a valid hypothesis for a model of the economy and is wrong to do so. A recent example was shown by James Bullard, president of the St. Louis Federal Reserve, when dismissing the deleterious impact of buy-backs on investment remarked: 'I'm a little sceptical of this entire argument. The firm has choices about how it wants to fund itself. One is to issue stock, another is to issue debt; it's not all that clear to me that it should matter really one way or the other, as per the Modigliani-Miller theorem.'[5]

Managements can increase both the stock market and replacement-cost value of their companies by leverage, so they would do so without limit unless inhibited by other constraints. The effect of leverage is not only to reduce the cost of capital but to increase the risk that the company will be in financial difficulties should profits fall or a sharp rise in inflation cause cash-flow problems. Figure 1 showed that over time companies balance cost against risk so that the ratio of profits before tax to interest payments is stable. There thus appears to be some long-term stability about corporate risk aversion though it may, like that of investors, be subject to short-term fluctuations. To reduce their exposure to problems arising from inflation and because the average life of fixed produced business capital is around sixteen years, companies prefer long-dated to short-dated debt.[6] Changes in leverage therefore respond slowly to long-term changes in interest rates.

The rate of interest paid by companies on their long-term debt is determined by the risk-free rate and the margin above that rate charged by lenders. These margins will change over the short term if, as seems probable, the attitudes to risk of both investors and managements have short-term

---

[5] 'Interview of James Bullard by Christopher Jeffery' (11 August 2020) published by Central Banking www.centralbanking.com/central-banks/financial-stability/7668906/james-bullard-on-the-feds-policy-review-fsoc-and-forecasting-jobs-data.

[6] I show the statistical evidence to confirm this in Chapter 27.

fluctuations. Over the longer term they will cover the specific risk of default, which will be stationary if there is no change in systemic risk, although this is likely to vary with the severity of recessions. The three factors which are likely to dominate the size of cyclical swings in output are errors in economic policy management, shocks such as Covid-19 and the oil crisis, and corporate debt levels. The reduction in the severity of the trade cycle since the slump of the early 1930s was accompanied by growing confidence that this showed a permanent improvement in economic management. This was reinforced by the reduction in the volatility of both output and inflation, and therefore with their associated risks after 1980 onwards. This became known as 'The Great Moderation'. I have not been able to find data on the average lending margin charged on long-dated corporate bonds over their equivalent risk-free yields, but they do not seem to have changed during the post-war period of rapidly rising leverage. It thus appears that lenders have not seen higher leverage as having increased the systemic risk of lending long-dated bonds to companies, which is easily explained by the reduction in the magnitude of recessions and the widespread confidence that this would continue.

The confidence that skilful economic policy had rendered major recessions improbable reached its peak before the Great Recession. This was illustrated by the comments of Governor Ben Bernanke who claimed in 2004 that 'improvements in monetary policy, though certainly not the only factor, have probably been an important source of The Great Moderation.'[7] The nemesis of the Great Recession of 2008, which followed this hubristic comment, has naturally raised fears that the current high level of corporate debt will no longer be sustainable without increases in the volatility of output and in the systemic risk of bankruptcy. If this occurs then there will be a rise in the cost of long-dated corporate bonds relative to their risk-free return. As it is cost which determines leverage, which has to match the portfolio preferences of the owners of wealth, the impact of a rise in lending margins will, with unchanged portfolio preferences, result in a less steep risk-free yield curve than would otherwise be needed.

This systemic risk could increase with the aggregate level of leverage but does not appear to have done so in the past despite the major post-war rise in corporate debt levels. As the severity of recessions as well as aggregate leverage is likely to affect the systemic risk of bankruptcy and the former have fallen since the slump of the early 1930s, lenders apparent past indifference to aggregate leverage is eminently reasonable.

---

[7] 'The Great Moderation' remarks by Ben Bernanke (20 February 2004) at the meeting of the Eastern Economic Association Washington, DC.

Average lending margins are, nonetheless, likely to change in the future if the systemic risks of bankruptcy rise and may follow from the current high level of corporate debt and the severity of the 2008 recession. While this would increase the cost of debt to companies, it would not constrain their leverage, which must match the portfolio preferences of wealth owners. The high elasticity of corporate debt to changes in long bond yields and the low elasticity of portfolio preference to them, results in changes in portfolio preferences having no impact on equity returns but solely on bond yields. A rise in the systemic risk of bankruptcy would increase the lending margin over risk-free rates and, without other changes, increase the interest rates paid on corporate debt, but if portfolio preferences remained unchanged this would have to be offset by a fall in the risk-free long-dated bond yield. If corporate bonds were priced correctly relative to government bonds, the return to holders would not change as the rise in yields would be offset by an increase in defaults. The return on bonds would thus fall relatively to that on equities, but because of the low elasticity of portfolio preferences they have no impact on equity returns. The interest paid by an individual company covers the risk-free rate and the lending margin, with the latter reflecting its specific risk and the systemic risk of corporate bankruptcy. A rise in the latter would, if the risk-free rate were unchanged, lower leverage, but this cannot occur without a change in the current portfolio preference of wealth owners. A rise in the systemic risk of bankruptcy, should it occur, must therefore be accompanied by a fall in the return on long-dated government bonds. Because of the low elasticity of portfolio preference to changes in risk-free returns, the decline in the return on government bonds will induce no change in their ownership. The rise in the lending margin consequent on a rise in systemic bankruptcy risk will not increase the return to bond holders as it will be offset by more losses from bankruptcy. As the rise in margins will be accompanied by a fall in the risk-free return, the cost of a rise in the systemic risk of bankruptcy will be borne by bond holders not by companies.

The Miller-Modigliani Theorem assumes that the cost of debt rises if lending margins rise. This applies only to a single company considered in isolation, as the borrower will have to pay for the additional specific risk, but in aggregate any rise in the systemic risk will be offset by a fall in the risk-free bond rate. There is no aggregate increase in the cost of corporate borrowing. The cost of a rise in bankruptcy risk is borne by lenders not borrowers.

Corporate capital comes in two forms, equity and debt, and its cost depends on their individual cost, the proportions of each involved (leverage), the rate of corporation tax, and the rules of tax deductibility. The cost of equity in the United States is known over the long term because the

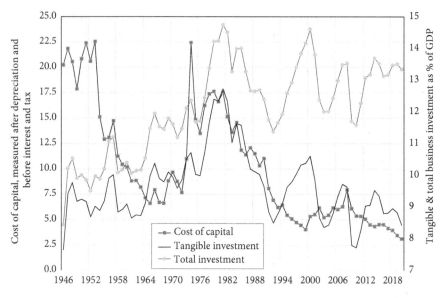

Figure 47. United States: Business investment and the cost of capital, measured after depreciation and before interest and tax

Data sources: Z1 Table B. 103 and NIPA Tables 1.1.5 and 1.14.

real return on equity is mean reverting around 6.7 per cent, and over the short term because the current degree of over or undervaluation of the market is known. At any one time therefore the real cost of equity, after corporation tax, is the long-term return adjusted for the current degree of mis-valuation. Data on leverage, interest, and corporation tax rates are also available. We can therefore calculate the current cost of corporate capital. Our ability to measure the cost of capital depends on the stationarity of the return on equity, our consequent ability to measure the value of the stock market, and in combination to measure the current and long-term cost of equity. The claim that 'the true supply cost of capital is (not) directly observable'[8] is not therefore correct.

Figure 47 illustrates the lack of relationship between business investment and the cost of capital.

Table 15 shows that there is no significant correlation between the cost of capital and neither tangible capital nor total investment, when measured over the whole period. Nor, if the period is divided into two sub-periods, is there any significant correlation between the cost of capital and total investment. There is, however, a significant correlation between the cost of capital

---

[8] Chan-Lee (1986).

Table 15. Correlations between business fixed investment as % of GDP and the cost of capital

	Tangible investment	Total investment including intangibles
	Coefficients of correlation	
1946 to 2020	0.254	−0.425
1946 to 1981	0.011	−0.146
1981 to 2020	0.748	0.297
	R^2	
1946 to 2020	0.065	0.181
1946 to 1981	0.000	0.021
1981 to 2020	0.560	0.088

Data sources: NIPA Tables 1.1.5 and 1.14 and Z1 Table B. 103.

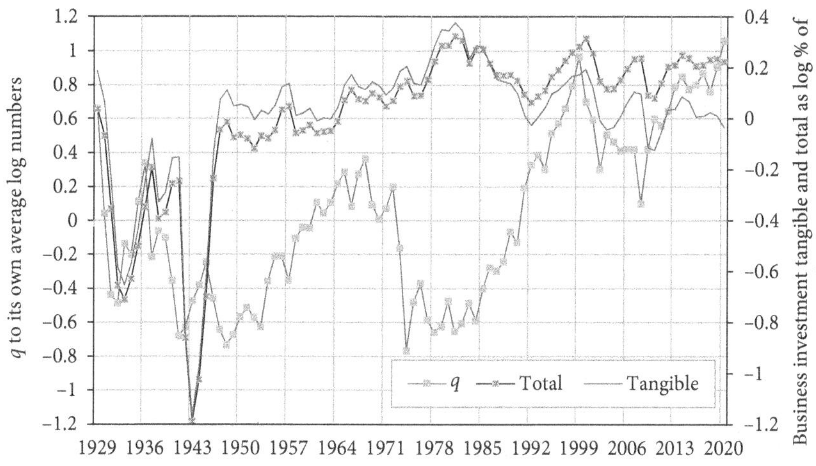

Figure 48. United States: Business investment and the cost of equity
Data sources: Z1 Table B. 103 and NIPA Table 1.1.5.

and tangible investment from 1981 to 2018; but being positive, it is perverse as investment and the cost of capital both fell over this period.

Equity is the main element in the cost of corporate capital and the absence of any connection between investment and the cost of capital is due to the indifference of company managements to the fluctuations in the cost of equity which I illustrate in Figure 48.[9] There are no apparent correlations between the cost of equity and tangible (R^2 0.0110) or total investment (R^2 0.120).

[9] Figure 46 covers 1946 to 2020 and Figure 47 1929 to 2020. This is because B. 103 data, which are required for calculating the cost of debt, start in 1946, whereas earlier data on q and thus the cost of equity are available from 'Measures of Stock Market Value and Returns for the US Non-financial Corporate Sector 1900–2002' by Stephen Wright (2004) *The Review of Income and Wealth* 50.

The indifference of companies to the cost of equity is incompatible with the neoclassical consensus as companies refuse the opportunity provided by cheap equity to increase the present value of their net worth and runs contrary to the assumption in the Miller-Modigliani Theorem that the value of companies should be considered to be their net worth rather than their stock market value. But it is the latter rather than the former with which shareholders are concerned and they do not like new issues which tend to depress share prices. Managements must please shareholders not economists so in the interests of self-preservation they habitually favour buy-backs rather than new issues even when the stock market sells, as it does in June 2021, well above the real net worth of its constituent companies.

As first postulated, the Miller-Modigliani Theorem assumed that there were no taxes, but this was subsequently modified to include them. This method did not, however, allow for the difference between the appropriate discount for valuing the expected profit stream of an investment made by an individual company and that which should apply to the corporate sector in aggregate. It therefore concluded that the advantage of leverage was due only to the allowability of interest as a charge for tax. It made no allowance for the relative cheapness of debt even in the absence of its tax benefits. The revised version allowed for the existence of corporation tax, but not independently for leverage, and it can only be valid if any variations in the return on capital can only be ascribed to changes in the tax rate and not in leverage: 'the tax advantages of debt financing are somewhat greater than we originally suggested...It still remains true, however, that under our analysis the tax advantages of debt are the only permanent advantages.'[10]

By ignoring the swings in the cost of equity shareholders can be accused of myopia, as they thereby forego opportunities to maximize net worth, which over the long term determines stock market value. It should, however, be noted that this does not indicate that investors are irrational. Shareholders are not homogenous; those saving for their retirement have longer time horizons than pensioners and investors are not irrational to prefer share prices to underlying value if they believe share prices are unlikely to fall in the shorter term or that they are unable to time, with sufficient accuracy to improve their returns, when to leave and when to return to the stock market. It would be irrational if the correct timing of the market could be forecast, but it is unlikely that markets would then ever be mis-valued.

---

[10] 'Corporate Income Taxes and the Cost of Capital: A Correction' by Franco Modigliani and Merton H. Miller (1963) *The American Economic Review* 53.

The emphasis placed by shareholders on share prices rather than net worth has been heightened by the growth of the fund management business. The sales of their products are boosted by outperforming the stock market over the short term and, as the profits of these businesses respond sharply to the growth in their assets under management, fund managers are even more concerned with the current share price than are individual long-term investors. It is reasonable to see fund managers as being rationally myopic.

Over the long term, stock market value and net worth are the same as equity q is mean reverting. But the divergence between the two over sustained periods of time means that company managements do not respond to high stock market values by raising new equity and investing more in capital equipment. Shareholders' concern with stock market value rather than net worth does not of course generally apply to unquoted and unincorporated businesses, though it may influence management decisions for those companies which are considering a listing. When modelling the equity market and the economy, it is necessary to separate businesses into quoted companies whose shareholders are primarily interested in the stock market value and others who are concerned with their long-term wealth and thus, as they are less myopic, being concerned with the long-term value of their businesses, which will over time reflect, at least on average, their net worth.

We therefore have two groups of businesses neither of which responds readily to the changes in the cost of equity capital which arise from fluctuations in the level of the stock market. One way in which they differ is in their attention to the underlying net worth of the businesses, which is only a matter of weak interest to both, though of greater interest to unquoted and unincorporated businesses than it is to quoted ones. Over the short to medium term the fluctuations in the stock market will not affect changes in either group's willingness to invest. Over the longer term both will have an incentive to raise equity capital, or at least to have lower cash dividend pay-out ratios, if the prospective returns exceed the cost and do not depress the price of the company's shares. This incentive will apply only in specific circumstances, not simply because the stock market is overpriced. Companies will be able to have low pay-out ratios if they are growing rapidly and raise new equity if the prospective return is above the long-term return on equity. If managements believe that the stock market is overpriced, they cannot use this as an excuse to raise new equity. Broad dividend pay-out ratios are determined by the need to increase net worth, which in turn depends on the availability of investment opportunities where returns exceed the hurdle rate. There is thus, as is to be expected, no relationship between the value of the stock market and pay-out ratios ($R^2 = 0.046$).

If managements realize that shares are generally overpriced, they will need to keep quiet lest investors think that they are commenting on the share prices of their own companies. Remarks on the stock market belong to the large class of statements which, even if correct, should be uttered only with great caution for fear of shocking public opinion.

It is even dangerous for companies to store cash when the market is overvalued in order to have firepower for acquisitions when it falls, as this will expose them to being taken over. Shareholders consider, despite the evidence to the contrary, that they should decide when cash should be conserved to benefit from a future stock market fall.

Contrary to the implied assumption of the Miller-Modigliani Theorem, the level of corporate investment does not respond to changes in the cost of capital and neoclassical models, which assume that the cost of capital is independent of aggregate corporate leverage, are wrong. If companies could in aggregate increase their leverage, they would increase their value. They cannot, however, do so because aggregate leverage is determined by the interest rate on long-dated bonds, which changes with investors' portfolio preferences, fiscal policy, and foreign capital inflows which are independent of individual companies' decisions about their leverage.

Investment does, however, respond to changes in interest rates and leverage, not because companies respond to changes in the cost of equity capital, but because with unchanged technology, the opportunities for investments which will meet the hurdle rate will vary. Lower bond yields increase the expected returns on new investment and thus the level of investment as well as net worth measured at second-hand prices (replacement cost).

In Tobin's model Q = (market value of equity + net debt)/(net worth + net debt) and it is stationary because equity q = (market value of equity)/(net worth) is mean reverting. But the return on Q, unlike that on q is not stationary and cannot be, because the cost of capital would otherwise need to be unchanged as leverage and the level of corporation tax vary. This is generally an assumption of the neoclassical synthesis and must be if it assumes the validity of the Miller-Modigliani Theorem. As I show, the Miller-Modigliani Theorem is testable, but has not been tested by neoclassicists and when tested is not robust.

20
Land, Inventories, and Trade Credit

In addition to tangible fixed produced capital, companies need land, inventories, and trade credit. The greater the proportion of these other assets to their produced capital the faster will be the rate of depreciation. Once installed, the productivity of equipment per person employed is, with some limited exceptions, fixed. It may improve a bit as employees learn on the job and occasional inventions may allow machines to work faster, but with most capital its efficiency is embedded when the investment is made. It is 'hard-baked' rather than 'putty-putty' with the result that 'technical progress and investment are intertwined in a way which growth accounting does not generally recognise.'[1]

As the labour productivity of installed equipment is largely fixed, its profitability and thus value falls as real wages rise.[2] Profit margins are probably stationary in accordance with the Cobb-Douglas production function[3] and so, therefore, must be the labour share of corporate output, as all output is divided between labour incomes and profit income. The rate of depreciation therefore rises with that of labour productivity.

If no other capital were required and equipment did not need maintenance, equipment would be employed until the value of its output minus its scrap value equalled the labour cost. (In practice equipment will not be fully maintained if skimping lowers production costs more than output and this will shorten its remaining lifespan.) To pay for the other capital involved production will halt when the value of the output minus the equipment's scrap value exceeds the labour cost plus the return that can be obtained on those other assets. These will usually have value which, unlike that of equipment, does not primarily depend on the output of the business as they can be readily liquidated, in the case of inventories and trade credit, or in the case of land by sale for some other use. These assets, unlike equipment, have 'alternative use value'.

---

[1] Martin Weale, Forward to Smithers (2019b).
[2] 'Neoclassical Growth with Fixed Factor Proportions' by R. M. Solow, J. Tobin, C. C. von Weizsäcker, and M. Yaari (1966) *The Review of Economic Studies* 33.
[3] For statistical testing of how stationary US profit margins are see Smithers & Co., ADF statistics from James Mitchell at www.smithers.co.uk/page.php?id=59.

The Economics of the Stock Market. Andrew Smithers, Oxford University Press. © Andrew Smithers 2022.
Foreword © Andy Haldane 2022. DOI: 10.1093/oso/9780192847096.003.0020

We have data since 1945 on the constituents of non-financial companies' balance sheets and the total value of those assets, land,[4] inventories, and trade credit, which are needed in addition to produced fixed capital for corporate output. The combined value of these assets, has been quite volatile but fallen slightly, relative to the value of the fixed produced capital stock. The decline will have reduced the rate of depreciation but being modest the impact is likely to have been insignificant.

It is commonly and reasonably assumed that the volume of land is fixed. It is not, however, land which is needed for business but rather floor space in the right location and this, at a price, can be created by investment. The ratio of the price of land to GDP is thus likely to stay constant if the costs of creating floor space are constant.

Figure 49 shows the mild decline in the value of both land and the total of land, inventories, and trade credit relative to total tangible assets and the ratio's short-term volatility which has clearly been due to fluctuations in the price of land. There has been relatively little volatility in the ratios of inventories and trade credit, with that of inventories falling usefully over the postwar period.[5]

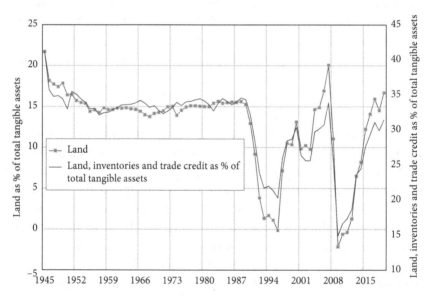

Figure 49. United States: Non-financial companies' land, inventories, and trade credit as % of tangible assets

Data source: Z1 Table B. 103.

---

[4] The value of land is derived by deducting the current cost of structures from the value of real estate.
[5] The data for the value of land shown in Figure 49 and used for Figure 50 are drawn from Z1 Table B. 103 for 2019. They are derived by deducting the lines 40 and 41 which give the current cost of

A fall in the demand for floor space, a sharp change in the geographic position of a desirable location, and changes in planning restrictions, could all cause a change in the land price. Profits after tax as published in company accounts are usually defined as the share of output not taken by labour, minus interest and tax. In a more fundamental assessment, however, they represent the change in the value of a company's assets before the payment of broad dividends. Over time the two should agree but they can diverge and will do so if land prices are volatile or their price relative to those of produced assets changes significantly over time.

In Figure 50 profits after tax, as shown in the national accounts, are adjusted for the changes in the value of land, which is assumed to be due only to changes in price. The impact is on average to increase them by 1 per cent, within a range of +2.3 per cent to –2.6 per cent. The violent swings in land prices do not therefore appear to have significantly affected profits.

A sustained change in the price of land relative to output and therefore to produced asset prices would, however, be important. As the ratio of produced

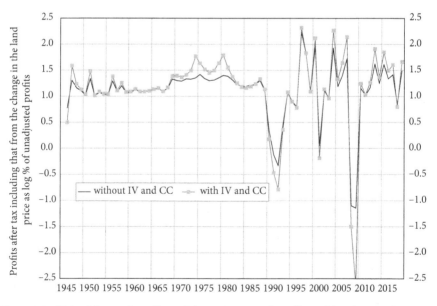

Figure 50. United States: Non-financial corporate profits adjusted for changes in land prices

Data sources: Z1 B. 103 and NIPA Table 1.14.

structures from the value of real estate shown in line 3. In the Table B. 103 for 2020 these data for the current cost of structures are no longer published, so their accuracy is presumably currently in doubt. However I show later by a different approach that the value of land relative to other non-financial corporate assets appears to have been stable over time.

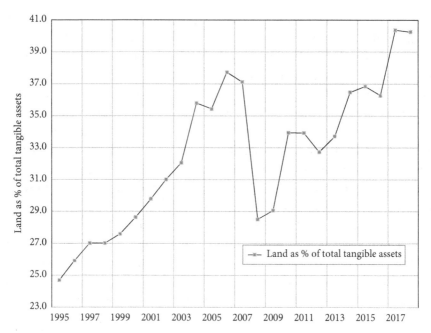

Figure 51. United Kingdom: Non-financial companies' land as % of total tangible assets

Data source: ONS (NG2S and E43J).

fixed assets to output is stationary, a relative fall in the land price would raise the return on corporate equity and, provided that the hurdle rate is unchanged, there would be a rise in investment, which would in turn improve labour productivity and depreciation. Both the capital stock and output would rise leaving their ratio unchanged

We only have UK data since 1995 and since then the land price appears to have shot up (Figure 51). Over this limited period land has amounted on average to 28 per cent of the tangible assets of UK private financial compan-ies compared with 15 per cent in the United States. Land prices can thus vary relative to GDP without affecting the corporate return on equity and can therefore also vary from country to country. A high land price reduces the amount of investment that can produce equity returns above the hurdle rate; countries with relatively low land prices have therefore an advantage.

It seems unlikely that the sharp rise in UK land prices can have any other cause than planning regulations and from the viewpoint of the economy and of prospective home owners, though not from that of current home owners, an easing of restrictions could have significant benefits. In both the United Kingdom and the United States an increase in working from home, which may well be stimulated by the Covid-19 pandemic, could be helpful to economic growth by putting downward pressure on land prices.

21

How the Market Returns to Fair Value

The stock market rotates around fair value, which is when corporate net worth and the market valuation of corporate equity are, when correctly valued, equal. The theoretical case for this was shown by James Tobin[1] and as both Figure 23 and Figure 31 show in different ways, it has proved correct in practice as the q ratio is mean reverting.[2]

The mean reversion of q could occur through changes in net worth or in value or in some combination of both. To fit the assumptions of the neoclassical synthesis the adjustment must come from rises in net worth in response to changes in investment: 'when q, the valuation ratio, exceeds unity there is a clear incentive to invest…If q is less than unity financial investment is more profitable than physical investment. If the market value of existing assets is persistently below replacement costs there are incentives for financial take-overs: "It's cheaper to find oil on Wall Street than in the North Sea".'[3]

Figure 52 compares the level of equity q with net additions to the produced capital stock of the United States. There appears to be no connection and this is confirmed by the R^2 correlation which is 0.0493. Fumio Hayashi[4] and Lawrence Summers[5] have examined whether the apparent incompatibility of the data on q with the neoclassical synthesis can be explained by allowing for tax effects, but it is agreed that neither this approach nor any other has been successful.

The mean reversion of equity q must therefore come from that of share prices and this is the natural effect of the stationarity of equity returns. When the market is cheap future returns from it will be above average and when it is overpriced future returns will be below average, so the risk of loss increases as share prices rise and declines as they fall. The rewards from holding equities thus rise and fall in a way that serves to restrict their swings. Fiscal and monetary policy usually act in a similar way. Profits and shareholders'

---

[1] Chan-Lee (1986).   [2] Chan-Lee (1986).   [3] Chan-Lee (1986).   [4] Hayashi (1982).
[5] 'Taxation and Corporate Investment: A q Theory Approach' by L H. Summers (1981) *Brookings Papers on Economic Activity* 11.

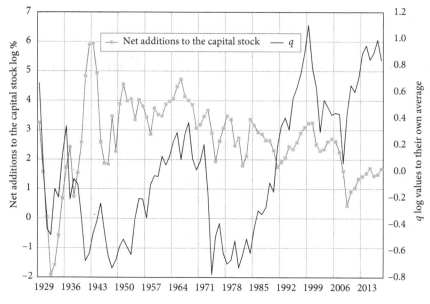

Figure 52. United States: Net additions to the capital stock and *q*
Data sources: Wright (2004), Z1, B. 103, BEA Fixed Asset Tables 1.1 and 1.3.

optimism swing with the cyclical fluctuations of the economy,[6] but cyclical strength induces fiscal and monetary tightening to keep production in line with output capacity and thus avoids unemployment or accelerating inflation and these changes have a negative impact on expectations for profits and raise the discount rate at which it is thought that they should be valued.

Investor optimism about the stock market is not solely related to expected changes in profits; monetary policy, political changes, and taxation are among other factors influencing the fluctuations in both demand and the market's level. The latter's short-term movements are therefore unpredictable even though monetary and fiscal policy should, over the longer term, have a moderating influence on the stock market's valuation.

[6] The R^2 correlation between annual log changes for GDP and profits before interest and tax has been 0.651 when measured annually from 1929 to 2019.

22

Fluctuations in the Hurdle Rate

When companies use debt as part of their capital, their managements are balancing the advantage of the reduction in the cost of capital with the increased volatility of their companies' profits and the consequent risks to their jobs if their companies are taken over or they are forced to raise additional equity capital when it is particularly expensive. There is a considerable difference in the time horizons between the benefit of cheaper capital, which is virtually instantaneous, and the threat to jobs, which is uncertain. The extent to which managements are paid for short-term changes in EPS, share prices, or total shareholder return (TSR) will thus influence their risk aversion and the rise in bonus payments linked to such changes will have reduced managements' concern over the risk to their jobs which arises from underinvestment. They will respond by turning down investment opportunities which they would previously have accepted and take only the limited number which promise to produce a return on equity which is higher than the long-term hurdle rate.

In the 1990s there was, as Figure 53 shows, a very large change in the remuneration of US senior managements and the proportion which was contingent on achieving targets, such as increased EPS and TSRs. In response to this change in incentives, management behaviour has changed and caused the level of investment to fall below what it would otherwise have been.

In the shorter term, the expected return on the equity required to finance new investment will rise when the effective rate of corporation tax falls and this will be maintained until the return on equity falls back to the hurdle rate, in response to the higher level of investment. If the hurdle rate were constant investment would rise in response to a fall in the rate of corporation tax and, as Figure 54 shows, this was the pattern from Q4 1951 to Q4 1999 but has not been the case since 2000. (I have inverted the scale for the tax rate, to make the relationship between it and investment more obvious.) The R^2 correlation between next year's tangible investment as a percentage of output and the effective rate of corporation tax was 0.599 from Q4 1951 to Q4 1999 but 0.01 from Q1 2000 to Q1 2021.[1]

---

[1] The tax rate in Figure 54 is calculated using profits without the IV and CC adjustments for inflation as published and thus apparent profits for management have no such adjustment.

The Economics of the Stock Market. Andrew Smithers, Oxford University Press. © Andrew Smithers 2022.
Foreword © Andy Haldane 2022. DOI: 10.1093/oso/9780192847096.003.0022

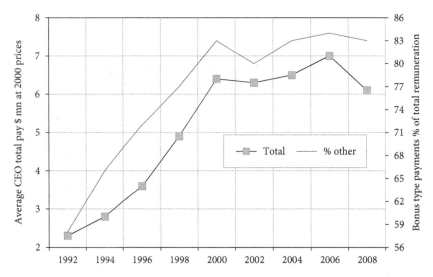

Figure 53. United States: The change in management incentives
Data source: Frydman and Jenter (2010).

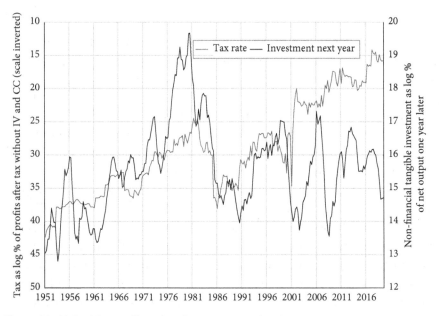

Figure 54. United States: Corporate investment and tax rate
Data sources: NIPA Tables 1.1.5 and 1.14 and Z1 Table F. 103.

It therefore appears that the change in management incentives has raised the hurdle rate. Managements are not approving new capital investment projects for the same expected returns as before but are looking for higher ones. It also seems likely that the change that we have seen this century had not occurred to any significant degree before.

The damage done by the bonus culture is large and it would greatly improve the growth of the United Kingdom and the United States if policies were introduced either to change management incentives or to change corporation tax so that the existing incentives would encourage rather than discourage investment.[2] In the absence of policy action the problem is nonetheless likely to fall away over time. The managements of unquoted and foreign-owned companies have, for the most part, different incentives and there is evidence that they have not cut back investment as has been done by quoted companies.[3]

The bonus culture does not affect all companies. The impact seems to be largely confined to quoted companies in the United Kingdom and the United States and have had relatively little impact on other major economies, such as Germany and Japan, where listed companies account for a much lower proportion of corporate output than in the United States where the incentives to manipulate earnings per share (EPS) and TSRs are estimated 'to determine almost one third of S&P 500 CEO total pay'.[4] The disincentive to

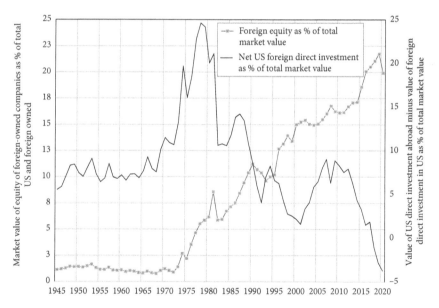

Figure 55. Foreign direct investment in United States

Data source: Z1 Table B. 103.

[2] As explained in Smithers (2019b) and Smithers (2019a).
[3] See Asker, Farre-Mensa, and Ljungqvist (2013).
[4] 'Pay for Destruction: The Executive Compensation Arrangements That Encourage Value Decreasing Stock Buybacks' by Nitzan Shilon Columbia Law School's Blog on Corporations and Capital Markets (15 March 2012).

invest in the United States is thus less for foreign-owned companies than for those which are domestically owned and, as Figure 55 illustrates, the former account for a rapidly increasing proportion of US corporate value and, it must therefore be assumed, of output. While the impact of the bonus culture should therefore weaken over time it has lowered the level of US business investment below that which would otherwise have occurred, given the decline in the rate of corporation tax.

Foreign-owned and unlisted companies have therefore become more important and as this is increasingly realized by the shareholders of quoted companies, the current stock-market fashion for low investment and large buy-backs is being questioned and the risks that such behaviour involve are increasingly understood.

The relative value that corporate managements will rationally place on leverage will also vary with any changes in their time horizons, but this does not affect leverage, which is determined by shareholder portfolio preferences. If there were a rise in the willingness to increase leverage this would be offset by a rise in long bond yields but the impact of such a change would not be seen quickly in the ratio of interest payments to pre-tax profits, due to the delayed impact of new long-term debt on average interest payments. To be observable the impact of the bonus culture on corporate behaviour would need to be long sustained, which fortunately seems unlikely.

23

Tangibles and Intangibles

When Stephen Wright and I first showed that the stock market can be valued by reference to the net worth of its constituent companies[1] many people found this hard to accept as it seemed inconsistent with their understanding of the value of individual companies, which differed widely from their probable net worth. The extra value of those which sold on large premiums to the value of their assets was considered to lie in their goodwill, which reflected various attributes such as brand names, patents, know-how, and management skill. Since those that sold at below-average premiums were not judged to have ill will, it was assumed that companies in aggregate must be worth more than their tangible capital.

If companies are in aggregate worth more than the value of their tangible capital, the calculation of their net worth must understate the true situation and since net worth reflects past retained profits it followed that profits must have been understated in the past. We know this to be incorrect, as profits have been consistently overstated in the past, as I showed in Table 7. This information appears, however, not to have been known to national accountants, and the belief that net worth was understated by the exclusion of intangibles was in due course reflected in a change in the way GDP is calculated, which had the required effect of increasing profits, at least when measured before capital consumption. In 2013 the definition of investment was broadened to include intangible as well as tangible assets and historic data were changed to reflect this decision. The expenditure on intellectual property (IP), which largely reflects research and development (R&D), was added to output so that GDP was increased. In national accounts income must equal output, and income had two sources, wages and profits. The increase in output meant that incomes had to rise and as there was no increase in that from employment, profits were increased, at least as measured before depreciation.

The value of intangible investment was interpreted, for the most part, as being the amount spent on R&D and there were those who considered this too narrow and called for other forms of expenditure such as advertising,

[1] Smithers and Wright (2000).

The Economics of the Stock Market. Andrew Smithers, Oxford University Press. © Andrew Smithers 2022.
Foreword © Andy Haldane 2022. DOI: 10.1093/oso/9780192847096.003.0023

which can boost the value of brand names, to be included.[2] The case for including expenditure on R&D as part of a country's level of investment rests on two assumptions. One is that companies would not spend money on something unless they expected a return from it in the future and that money spent on such expectations is a good definition of investment. The second assumption was that such expenditure was beneficial to future profits, not only for the individual company but in aggregate. It therefore reflected the common assumption of stock market investors that there was no ill will to offset the obvious goodwill that some companies had.

Neither of these assumptions seems to me to be sensible. Companies spend a great deal on advertising and the salaries of senior executives, but the object is as much about staying in business as seeking to improve their future returns. The risk of not spending enough on advertising, or having inferior managers, is a loss of market share, or the need to cut prices and thus lower profits to prevent that occurring. Some companies will win, and some lose, but the expense of both appears to be a zero sum game and thus to have no value in aggregate except that shown in the output of advertising agencies and the income of managers.

Investing in R&D has the same zero sum result. Success leads either to an improved product or to a lower cost of production and thus in either case to a rise in output through higher productivity. Individual winners will temporarily improve their profits, but they will not boost the profits of companies in aggregate. As with any improvement in productivity, real wages and depreciation will rise. The improvement in the profits of the winners will be matched by a fall in those of everyone else. Profit margins are stable over time, as Figure 42 shows when measured after depreciation, despite successful investment in R&D, or other intangibles. Such expenditures do not improve the return on equity. They will, if supported by additional investment to embody the research, boost output and incomes from employment. As profits rise in line with output, it will also boost the total level of profits, but as that rises in line with the capital stock, as Figure 5 shows, the increase in capital that results from the increase in investment will match the rise in profits and there will be no aggregate increase in the return on capital. Depreciation rises with real wages and thus, as the profit share of output is stable, it rises in line with labour productivity. For profits to rise there must therefore be an increase in the amount of new investment which, after allowing for the increase in depreciation, expands the capital stock but leaves the return on it unchanged.

---

[2] See, for example, 'Intangible Capital and Economic Growth' by Carol Corrado, Charles Hulten, and Daniel Sichel (2006) Federal Reserve Board, Finance and Economics Discussion Series 2006–24.

Improved technology and the additional investment needed to finance its realization in new capital does not increase the return on equity, but it changes the contribution to that return from current dividends relative to their future growth. Successful R&D improves growth but not profitability; accelerated growth lowers pay-out ratios but increases the rate at which future dividends will rise, which is the pattern of the past as shown in Figure 6 and Figure 7.

The redefining of investment to include R&D in 2013 was, I think, a mistake. With the important proviso that the data must be reasonably accurate, it would nonetheless be helpful to know how much is being spent on it. The mistakes lie in calling it investment rather than expenditure on R&D and probably in the measurement of the data as it is highly unlikely that the published figures are reliable. Two problems arose from expenditure on intangibles being categorized as investment. The extent to which real investment has fallen, particularly since 2000, has thereby been underappreciated and the idea that expenditure on R&D could produce growth without being supported by additional expenditure on tangible investment has become widespread. The common attitude is that the total level of investment, including money spent on intangibles as well as tangibles, is the key sign of a buoyant economy that should grow in the future. If this were correct, we could grow without any tangible investment. The benefit of successful expenditure on R&D is not because it increases growth but become it provides the opportunity to do so through a rise in tangible investment.

Expanding investment to include intangibles can be compared to a decision to expand the definition of food output to include cutlery on the grounds that both are necessary for eating. A large rise in the output of spoons would still not reduce hunger any more than the large rise in recorded investment in R&D has led to a rise in output.

It is possible for an improvement in technology to allow labour productivity to advance without the need for any additional tangible investment. One way is through 'learning from doing' which occurs when employees become more skilled as they become more experienced. World War II provided some well-known examples of this as the speed with which standard models of ships and aircraft were produced rose as workers learnt on the job, without the need for additional capital. Most improvements in capital and labour productivity, however, require new tangible investment as the technology is embedded in the equipment. The types of capital resulting from these two possibilities have been termed 'putty' and 'hard baked clay'[3] and if, as seems

---

[3] 'Substitution and Fixed Proportions in the Theory of Capital' by Robert M. Solow (1962) *Review of Economic Studies* 29.

virtually certain, the latter is heavily predominant, we cannot, as Martin Weale has pointed out, use the conventional growth accounting framework as a means of determining the contribution of investment to economic growth: 'very stringent assumptions are needed for the growth accounting framework to function—most notably that the labour/capital ratio has to be as flexible on old capital as it is before capital is installed. Such a "putty-putty" proposition seems most unlikely to be true.'[4]

We should recognize this error, discard the conventional growth account-ing framework and distinguish investment, which is tangible, from expend-iture on R&D and advertising, which is not. It would be better if the term investment is never applied to expenditure on intangibles. Calling expend-iture on both tangibles and intangibles as investment is to make a category error, in that one cannot be substituted[5] for the other and for the most part an increase in R&D, even if successful, leads to no improvement in output unless it is supported by tangible investment—a shortfall in tangible invest-ment cannot be offset by an increased expenditure on intangibles. If the latter is successful it can on rare occasions raise productivity without investment, but its usual impact is to produce new opportunities for profitable invest-ment in tangible capital.

Measuring the volume of capital exclusively in terms of tangible assets has the additional advantage of excluding data of dubious accuracy. There is a large tax credit in the United States for R&D which was introduced in 1981. Figure 56 shows that private-sector spending on IP averaged 12 per cent of total investment for twenty-five years before that and has since risen to over 36 per cent. Over the same period total factor productivity (TFP) which measures the contribution to growth from improvements in technology has seriously declined, whether this is measured by the consensus model or my own.[6]

We are therefore left with a choice between believing that companies have devoted more and more resources to R&D over the past thirty-two years for increasingly lower returns or that the rise in the amount attributed to R&D investment in the national accounts does not represent the extent to which expenditure on research has actually increased, but a renaming of spending. Anecdotal evidence points to companies reducing their tax without any real increase in expenditure on IP by categorizing an increasing part of the

---

[4] Foreword by Martin Weale to Smithers (2019b).

[5] There are limits to the extent that one form of tangible capital can be substituted for another. It does not, however, appear necessary to complicate the model of the economy to allow for this, except insofar as housing is treated separately from business investment although there is some scope for substitution between residential and commercial real estate.

[6] Smithers (2019a).

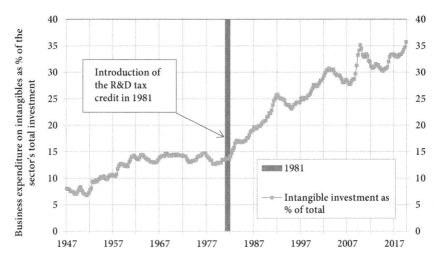

Figure 56. United States: Intangibles as % of total business investment
Data sources: NIPA Table 1.1.5.

salaries and other costs of employees, which were previously treated as general expenditure, as being investment in R&D. There is therefore a strong possibility that investment in IP is mismeasured. The tax credit encourages companies to redefine expenditure which was previously allocated to general management to R&D and if this is done and accepted by the tax authorities and the national accountants as representing a true rise in such expenditure the data will be distorted.

It has been argued that R&D should be treated as a form of investment because it is necessary for technical progress, which is essential for growth in productivity: 'Neoclassical growth models assume that innovation is an exogenous process, with the implication that investments in R&D have no systematic and predictable effect on output growth. But can it really be true that the huge amount of R&D investment was made in recent years without any expectation of gain? A more plausible approach is to abandon the assumption that innovation is exogenous to the economic system and recognize that some part of innovation is, in fact, a form of capital accumulation.'[7] This argument strikes me as naïve. It is sensible to spend heavily on R&D either because it is successful in improving productivity or because it reduces the tax bill, in neither case will it add to the value of corporate produced assets. If successful, it will stimulate tangible investment and productivity. The sponsor of the R&D will benefit, but this will be matched by the reduced

[7] 'Total Factor Productivity: A Short Biography' by Charles R. Hulten (2000) NBER Working Paper 7471.

value of other companies' assets through the rise in depreciation that improved productivity brings. Companies are threatened by the expenditure of their competitors on advertising and on R&D. It is therefore reasonable to argue, as Carol Corrado[8] and others do, that they should be included together as a similar category of expenditure, but it not sensible to include either in the same category as tangible investment. R&D is in practice essential for the growth of productivity, but this does not make it a form of investment. Education is essential for R&D, but it is not a form of it.

Expectation of gain cannot be readily distinguished from anxiety to remain in business, which applies to a broad range of activities undertaken by companies, including advertising and CEOs' salaries. Investment could be defined to include all 'activities undertaken in the expectation of gain or fear of loss', but it is hard to think what this would exclude, and it is not therefore a sensible definition of anything. While R&D contributes to technological advances, it is clear from the rise in the published data on IP investment compared with the trend fall in TFP that it has no systemic and predictable effect on output growth.

It would be helpful to have reliable data on corporate expenditure on R&D, but it seems unlikely that this is what we have. If we had it, it would be better not labelled as a form of investment because of the confusion that this causes. As the published data have been so labelled it is extremely important that they are not bundled together in economic analysis with tangible investment.

---

[8] Corrado, Hulten, and Sichel (2006).

24

Other Problems from Labelling IP Expenditure as Investment

In addition to disguising the extent to which tangible investment has fallen, and thereby delaying the realization among policymakers that this has been the key cause of poor labour productivity, the mislabelling of expenditure on intellectual property (IP) has led to other misconceptions, including those about income distribution. In both the United Kingdom and the United States, the definition of investment used to be confined to the accumulation of tangible assets. This was first modified by the inclusion of expenditure on software, and more fundamentally in 2013 when the measurement of the investment and the capital stock were expanded by including a large amount of other expenditure on IP.

As Table 16 shows, the size of the impact of the revised definition of invest-ment depends on the measure being considered, varying from the insignificant impacts on NDP and GDP to increases of over 50 per cent in business invest-ment and depreciation. The largest rise is for business depreciation and is the combined result of the rise in intangible investment and the rapid rate at which it is depreciated. In 2018 the depreciation rate for IP was 21.3 per cent of its capital stock compared with 3.9 per cent for tangible capital. The impact on the growth of GDP has been only +0.05 per cent p.a. whether this is measured over the past ten or twenty years.

Several economists have questioned this rapid rate of IP depreciation,[1] and if they were correct the impact on the measurement of net output and the capital stock would no longer be limited but would be of major signifi-cance and substantially change the data we use to measure the economy and judge its progress. The changes would not only include a much larger figure for net output but would significantly alter the profit and labour shares of output and substantially increase the size of the capital stock. It would also

---

[1] 'Intangible Capital and the Investment-q Relation' by Ryan H. Peters and Lucian A. Taylor (2017) *Journal of Financial Economics* 123; 'Investment-less Growth: An Empirical Investigation' by Germán Gutiérrez and Thomas Philippon (2016) NBER Working Paper 22897; *The Great Reversal: How America Gave Up on Free Markets* by Thomas Philippon (2019) Harvard University Press; and Corrado, Hulten, and Sichel (2006).

The Economics of the Stock Market. Andrew Smithers, Oxford University Press. © Andrew Smithers 2022. Foreword © Andy Haldane 2022. DOI: 10.1093/oso/9780192847096.003.0024

Table 16. Impact on 2018 data of inclusion of intangible spending in investment

% Increase in NDP	1.84
% Increase in GDP	5.86
% Increase in total capital stock	8.01
% Increase in business capital stock	15.63
% Increase in total investment	35.88
% Increase in total depreciation	43.28
% Increase in business investment	50.17
% Increase in business depreciation	56.54

Data sources: BEA Fixed Asset Tables 1.1 and 1.3 and NIPA Tables 1.1.5, 1.1.6, and 5.2.5.

be important for several economic theories, including the q-relationship between the net worth and stock market value of companies and the Miller-Modigliani Theorem.

If either the rate of depreciation has been overstated or the level of investment under-recorded, profits would have been higher than those published in the national accounts. This would not alter the amounts paid out in dividends or broad dividends and retained profits would thus increase by even more than profits. Net worth would rise faster than profits and the return on equity would thus fall steadily, which is incompatible not only with the data but with a sustainable economy. It follows that neither depreciation nor investment can have been understated in the national accounts.

We also know, from the data on equity returns, that profits have been persistently overstated in the published accounts of companies, as I showed in Table 7, which uses a totally independent source of data. Increasing the assumed level of investment or reducing the rate of depreciation would make this overstatement worse. The claims that the measurement of intangible depreciation has been too high or that of intangible investment too low are thus invalid.[2]

When the division of income between the labour and capital shares of output are being considered it is vital to use a sensible definition of income and that proposed by Hicks eighty years ago has, to put it midly, stood the test of time. As Hicks defined income it is: 'The maximum a man can spend and still be as well off at the end of the week as at the beginning.'[3] While this leaves the definition of 'well off' open to debate, it is clear that spending all profits before depreciation will leave the owner of capital worse off. It is

[2] For a fuller account see *The Debate over the Depreciation of Intangible Capital* by Andrew Smithers (2020) *World Economics* 21.

[3] *Value and Capital: An Enquiry into Some Fundamental Principles of Economic Theory* by J. R. Hicks (1939) Oxford University Press.

therefore important to consider the income shares of business output after and not before deducting capital consumption.

The change in the measurement of GDP has caused particular damage with regard to the measurement of profits, particularly when the shares of labour and capital in total output are being discussed. Including expenditure on IP as investment has sharply increased the disparity between profit margins, measured after capital consumption compared with those measured before. Profit margins for all companies measured after capital consumption are, as I showed in Figure 42, below average at the end of 2020 and are probably mean reverting.[4] In Figure 57 I show profit margins for non-financial companies, as the papers claiming that the profit share of output is high exclude financial companies. However, as Figure 57 shows, non-financial profits are currently at their average level and have been falling since 2013.

The error made by those who claim that the profit share of corporate output is high comes from treating profits as if they included depreciation as Figure 58 illustrates. Overstating profits results in the labour share being

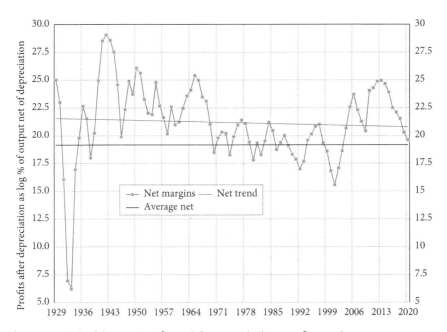

Figure 57. United States: Non-financial companies' net profit margins
Data source: NIPA Table 1.14.

[4] The proportion of total corporate capital employed can vary between financial and non-financial companies; for conformity with the Cobb-Douglas production function, margins need to be measured net for the corporate sector in aggregate.

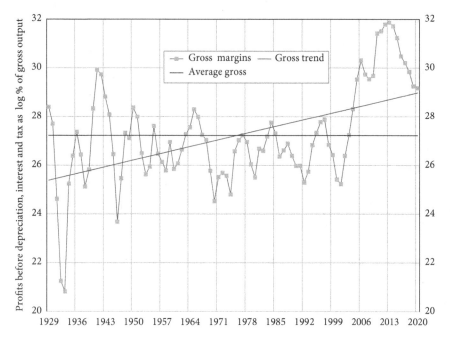

Figure 58. United States: Non-financial gross profit margins
Data source: NIPA Table 1.14.

understated and has been used to give credence to the otherwise improbable claim that monopoly power has risen in the United States in recent years.

The inclusion of IP investment and its depreciation in national income data has also led to confusion regarding the efficiency of new investment as measured by the incremental capital/output ratio (ICOR). When this is measured by the percentage of GDP represented by gross investment divided by the growth rate, it appears that the efficiency of capital has declined badly, in that it takes an increasing amount of investment to achieve a given increase in output. I show this in Figure 59.

However, when the ICOR is measured using net investment and NDP rather than GDP, there appears to be no such deterioration as I show in Figure 60. The assumption that the labour share of output has fallen, has supported several misconceptions about the economy, including the claims of Thomas Piketty,[5] Lance Taylor,[6] Thomas Philippon and others.[7]

---

[5] See 'A Critical Review of Thomas Piketty's *Capitalism in the Twenty-first Century*' by Andrew Smithers (2018) *World Economics* 19.

[6] See my exchange with Professor Taylor over his paper '"Savings Glut" Fables and International Trade Theory: An Autopsy' (2020) available on the website of the Institute for New Economic Thinking at https://www.ineteconomics.org.

[7] See Smithers (2020).

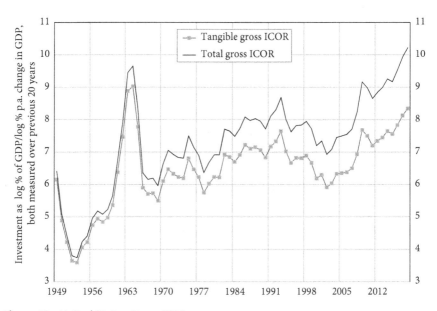

Figure 59. United States: Gross ICOR

Data sources: NIPA Tables 1.1.5, 1.1.6, and 5.2.5.

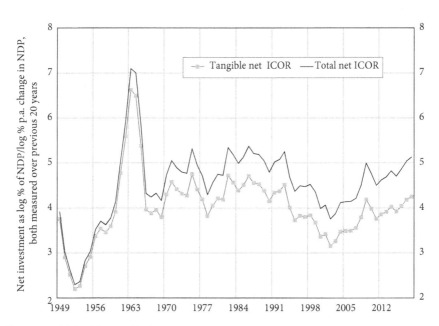

Figure 60. United States: Net ICOR

Data sources: NIPA Tables 1.1.5, 1.1.6, and 5.2.5.

The labour share of output appears to be mean reverting, as Figure 42 indicates[8] and is currently at its average level. This makes it improbable that competition has weakened in the United States in recent years. A stable labour share of output does not require that average wages rise at the same pace as total incomes and output. In the post-2008 recovery the level of unemployment has declined to an exceptionally low level, as the non-accelerating inflation level of unemployment (NAIRU) appears to have fallen. Expectations for both price and wage rises have declined, and employment has risen by even more than that indicated by the fall in unemployment as the participation rate has improved. With an unchanged labour share of output, average wages will have risen more slowly than they would otherwise have done. As it is likely that the additional numbers employed are the less skilled, their employment will have reduced the average wage, but as they would otherwise have been unemployed it has raised the average income of the lower paid. Inequality among wage earners is thus likely to have risen, but inequality of incomes has risen by less than it would otherwise have done.

---

[8] For statistical testing of how stationary US profit margins are see Smithers & Co., ADF statistics from James Mitchell at www.smithers.co.uk/page.php?id=59.

25

Inflation, Leverage, Growth, and Financial Stability

I showed in Chapter 4 that companies' debt levels are determined by the ratio of interest payments to profits. This was sufficient for my immediate purpose which was to show that this element in the behaviour of corporate managements is a vital part of the explanation of how and why the return on equity is stationary.

Corporate leverage is important for financial stability. It is therefore important to consider whether this is threatened by the way that debt has risen relative to output, or whether the ratio of debt to capital employed is more important.

Financial stability is threatened by the responses of both borrowers and lenders to recessions and higher interest rates. In recessions the ratio of pre-tax profits to output falls so companies are less willing to borrow, the extent of the fall depends on the extent to which the profit share of output declines. If the profit share moved with gross output, its current high level, as shown in Figure 58, would be cause for concern, but it moves with net output as Figure 42 and Figure 57 show, and the volatility of the profit share appears unrelated to the ratio of profits to gross output.[1] As interest payments depend on nominal interest, companies would be vulnerable to rises in rates if they borrowed short term, as in general they do not; the willingness of companies to borrow depends mainly on the depth of recessions and the high level of debt to output does not seem to be a cause for concern.

Although it seems sensible not to consider the high debt/output ratio as a threat to financial stability, another ratio of debt/asset values suggests that debt ratios are dangerously high. When companies become bankrupt the liquid assets of other corporations are not available to support highly leveraged companies and their intangible assets have no second-hand value. The risk that lenders have is thus represented by the ratio of gross debt to tangible assets rather than by net debt/net worth or net debt/tangible assets. As Figure 62 shows, gross interest-bearing assets as a percentage of tangible assets are

---

[1] The ratio of net to gross margins is not correlated with the latter's level ($R^2 = 0.001$).

The Economics of the Stock Market. Andrew Smithers, Oxford University Press. © Andrew Smithers 2022.
Foreword © Andy Haldane 2022. DOI: 10.1093/oso/9780192847096.003.0025

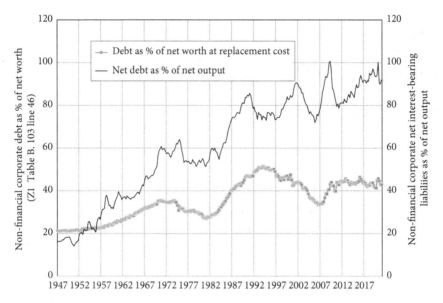

Figure 61. United States: Non-financial corporate leverage
Data sources: Z1 Table B. 103 and NIPA Table 1.14.

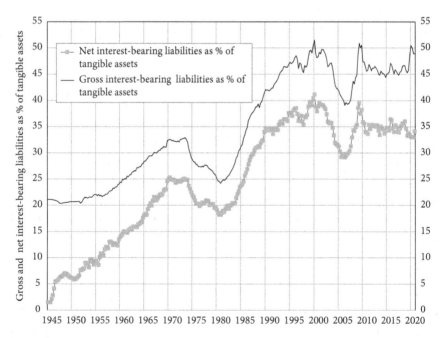

Figure 62. United States: Non-financial companies' debt as % of tangible assets
Data source: Z1 Table B. 103.

currently very near their record highs. Second-hand tangible asset values fall in recessions, but they also fall when the cost of capital rises. Interest rates rise when the Fed seeks to contain the price level, so bankruptcies are likely to be particularly painful to lenders in a recession accompanied by rising inflation.

The supply of long-dated risk-free bonds depends on the government deficit, the extent to which this is funded by long-term bond issues and the extent to which the Federal Reserve buys bonds for Quantitative Easing (QE) and thereby expands the monetary base. As Figure 63 illustrates, QE has flattened the yield curve and a reduction of bond purchases by the Fed will thus raise bond prices even with unchanged short-term rates.

As equity is so much more expensive than debt, companies' low bond yields encourage companies to use less equity and this encourages buy-backs. Household portfolio preference is, however, unchanged so households will seek to maintain their equity ratio despite the lower equity supply. Share prices will then rise and, through buy-backs, net worth will fall. The q ratio is thus pushed up and it is, as Figure 31 shows, extremely high. As q is mean reverting, this renders the US economy highly vulnerable to another financial crisis.

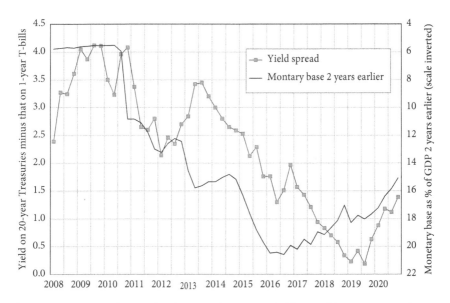

Figure 63. Monetary base as % of GDP and Treasury yield spread (twenty-year minus one-year)

Data sources: Federal Reserve H6 and H15 and NIPA Table 1.1.5.

The difference between the perception of risk by borrowers and that incurred by lenders explains the apparent indifference of lenders to the level of aggregate leverage. This has been amplified by the indifference shown by central bankers to the level of risk caused by high levels of leverage and asset prices.[2] While there has been a growing concern with financial stability since the 2008 recession, the impact of monetary policy on leverage and asset prices has continued to be ignored by central banks.

High debt levels are thus a cause for concern and many economists have therefore suggested that leverage should be discouraged by disallowing interest payments to be an expense when calculating companies' liability to corporation tax. This would reduce the return and thus the level of new investment and thereby slow growth even below the current trend rate. To avoid this the effective rate of corporation tax must fall and, as debt will still be cheaper than equity, if leverage is to fall there must be a fall not only in the rate of corporation tax but also in its revenue.

If leverage is unchanged, post-tax profits will be the same as before if there is no change in interest payments or tax revenue, but as the tax rate will apply to a higher level of pre-tax profits, the rate of corporation tax giving the same

Table 17. Required decline in tax rate for stable RoE if interest is disallowed as an expense for corporation tax on non-financial companies and interest rates unchanged 2019

	Interest allowed	Interest not allowed tax rate unchanged	Interest not allowed RoE unchanged
Capital employed $ bn.	25,896	25,896	25,896
Debt $ bn.	7,655	7,655	7,655
Debt as % of capital employed	29.6%	29.6%	29.6%
Equity $bn	18,241	18,241	18,241
Interest paid on debt $bn	346	346	346
Interest rate on debt %	4.5%	4.5%	4.5%
Profits before tax $bn	1,137	1,483	1,483
Tax paid $bn	160	208	160
Profits after tax $bn	977	929	977
Tax rate %	14.0%	14.0%	10.8%
RoE %	5.4%	4.5%	5.4%

Data sources: Z1 Table B. 103 and NIPA Table 1.14.Notes: The return on equity was above average in 2019. The reason that it appears to be below the long-term stationary level of 6.7 per cent is that assets' values are overstated. The overstatement of profits, which I showed in Chapter 14 results in an even greater overstatement of retained profits and thus of assets. Leverage is increased, if allowance is made for this, and the RoE rises.

---

[2] For a warning and explanation of the folly see 'Stock Markets and Central Bankers: The Economic Consequences of Alan Greenspan' by Andrew Smithers and Stephen Wright (2002) *World Economics* 3.

revenue will be lower. Using 2019 data, Table 17 shows that a decline in the tax rate of less than four percentage points would leave the RoE and tax revenue unchanged. Stopping the tax allowability of interest payments would not therefore pose a problem for fiscal policy unless it succeeded in reducing leverage, which is, however, the purpose of such a change. If we seek to reduce corporate leverage we must therefore be prepared for a fall in the tax rate sufficient to produce a fall in tax revenue.

26

Tax

There was no federal tax on corporate income until 1916. An attempt to introduce it in 1894 was held to be unconstitutional and one could not be enacted until the constitution of the United States was changed by the sixteenth amendment. The effective rate differs from the enacted federal and state ones, as allowances, such as the R&D credit introduced in 1981, have varied. We have data on the effective rate of corporation tax since 1929 and over these ninety years it has varied between 12 per cent and 75 per cent.

There was, therefore, little if any corporation tax during the nineteenth century and a significant and highly variable rate since, while the return on equity has been stationary. It is therefore clear that while the tax is collected by companies the economic cost does not fall on their shareholders. The mean reversion of the labour share of output since 1929 and the absence of any connection with its fluctuations and those in the corporate tax rate show that it did not fall on employees either (Figure 64).

The absence of any direct cost falling on either wages or profits does not, however, mean that corporation tax is costless for the economy. When the level of corporation tax is raised the hurdle rate will not thereby alter but the expected return on new investment will fall, unless the share of output taken by profits rises, or the long bond yield falls so less equity is needed for investment through a rise in leverage. Projects which would previously have been pursued will be cancelled and those that qualify will be fewer than before. The amount of new investment fluctuates with the opportunities provided by improvements in technology, which occur over time at varying speeds. The level of new investment does not therefore rise and fall solely with the level of corporation tax. For any given rate of technological improvement, the amount of investment will also depend on the hurdle rate, interest rates, and leverage. The overall effect of a rise in corporation tax is to shift resources from business investment to government spending. It is, in effect, a tax on investment and not on shareholders or employees.

The immediate effect of an increase in tax is nonetheless to reduce published profits. Its impact on investment is to reduce growth and labour productivity, so real wages rise more slowly and the rate of capital consumption falls. A lower charge for depreciation raises the return on new and past

The Economics of the Stock Market. Andrew Smithers, Oxford University Press. © Andrew Smithers 2022.
Foreword © Andy Haldane 2022. DOI: 10.1093/oso/9780192847096.003.0026

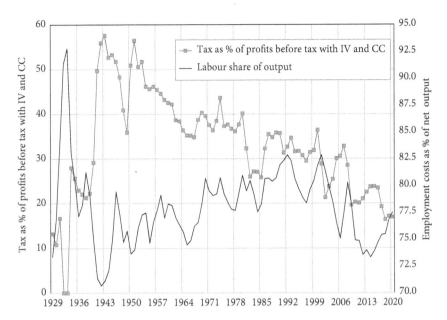

Figure 64. United States: Effective rate of corporation tax and labour share of output
Data source: NIPA Table 1.14.

investment, so the measured return on net worth will return to the hurdle rate after whatever time lag is needed for national data to be adjusted for new information from surveys. Retained profits will fall with lower investment and business savings and national savings will decline. The return on equity will be unchanged but its division will change with the dividend rising relative to the growth of net worth. Profits will grow more slowly in the future, so the short-term rise in income from corporation tax will be followed by lower longer-term receipts.

Produced capital is not the only form of capital that is needed by companies for their output. Land, trade credit, and inventories are also needed, and these have an important impact on the rate at which the value of capital depreciates, and its volume is reduced by scrapping.

In the absence of any need for non-produced capital, as seems to be the case with housing, capital will only be scrapped if it ceases to have any value. Houses are abandoned if they are no longer worth the cost of maintenance, which typically occurs from a decline in the local economy. Ghost towns appear when a mine is worked out, but not in places with varied occupations and rising populations.

For businesses which need non-produced capital, however, equipment will be scrapped if the return on it falls below the hurdle rate on the value of the associated land, trade credit, and inventories required to support output.

Unlike the produced capital embedded in housing, non-produced business capital has alternative-use value. The result is that the produced capital is scrapped before its return becomes negative. If the equipment has some value as scrap, the point at which it will be taken out of production is even earlier.

The higher the value of non-produced capital relative to output, the earlier will old equipment be scrapped. High land values will therefore require more efficient produced capital for returns to pass the hurdle rate. Unless profits are aided by higher margins, the profitability of new investment will decline. International capital flows will result in the expected returns on produced capital being the same in all countries, so high land values will need to be offset either by lower produced capital/output ratios or by higher profit margins.

A comparison of UK and US data supports this. In the United Kingdom produced capital/output ratios measured by value are well below those of the United States as I illustrate in Figure 65. The lower UK ratios do not necessarily indicate that capital is more efficiently employed in the United Kingdom compared with the United States. It is likely that the price of land is higher in

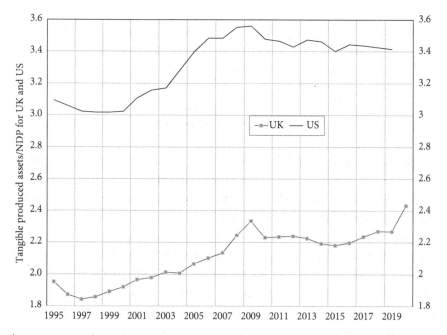

Figure 65. United Kingdom and United States: Tangible produced fixed capital/output ratios

Data sources: ONS (NG22, NG27, CGRD, YBHA, and NQAE) and BEA Fixed Asset Table 1.1 and NIPA Tables 1.1.5 and 5.1.

the United Kingdom, and this causes produced capital to be scrapped earlier than in the United States. As new capital is more efficient than old this will lower the capital/output ratio of the United Kingdom and will do so even if the efficiency with which comparable pieces of equipment are employed in both countries is less in the United Kingdom.

Figure 66 shows that profit margins have been higher in the United Kingdom than the United States since 1995 and may have been one way in which the higher price of land has been offset to produce competitive returns on equity in both countries. The lack of longer-term data, however, makes no definite conclusion possible.

The impact of high land prices on capital scrapping and possibly on profit margins provides a strong argument for the value of land to be taxed. If, as would normally be expected, land prices reflect the comparative returns with other forms of capital, a tax on land will reduce its relative price. The demand for floor space will not, however, change so rental values will be unchanged, shifting the split between the return to the building relative to its underlying land value and more investment in construction. But more floor space will reduce rental values and thus bring down the reward from real-estate construction. The net effect should be more usage of real estate whose value declines in aggregate with a fall in land value and a rise in that of buildings.

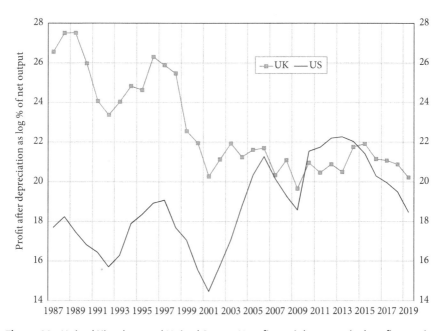

Figure 66. United Kingdom and United States: Non-financial companies' profit margins
Data sources: ONS (FARR, FACQ, JKJW, and FDBA) and NIPA Table 1.14.

In a simple example in which companies rent all their real estate their costs will fall, raising the return on their produced capital and thus the level of investment in it and the growth of the economy. Corporate savings should rise to meet the additional investment in both forms of produced capital. The argument for taxing land is widely accepted but the practical problem appears to be the difficulty in distinguishing its value from the value of the buildings on it.

Taxes on shareholders, either those on dividend income or capital gains, could lower savings if households seek to maintain consumption. The effect is, however, mitigated where savings have tax benefits. They could also affect the economy through their impact on savings or on portfolio preferences, but seem unlikely to be a significant factor, as the relative returns from risk-free bonds and equities are not obviously changed by them and retirement savings are often exempt from these taxes. Companies and households will adjust their behaviour to minimize their tax, but this seems unlikely to have much impact on investment, portfolio preferences, or pay-out ratios. The distribution of pay-out ratios between dividends and buy-backs is, however, likely to change if shareholders' effective exposure to taxes on income tax relative to capital gains alters, while leaving the broad dividend pay-out ratios unchanged.

27

Portfolio Preference and Retirement Savings

Many economic models assume that the overall return on capital is set, in the steady state, by the rate of discount, which is psychologically determined and constant. The evidence is against this. The stationarity of the equity return and its absence from returns on total capital require a wide variation in either interest rates or leverage. As real interest rates fluctuate over time within a narrow range, the cause of major divergence between the returns on equity and total capital seems bound to lie in variations in leverage. As demonstrated, the data show that this expectation is realized.

In a closed economy with a stable level of national debt, fluctuations in leverage must be matched by those in household portfolio preference. This only becomes important if leverage varies and the fluctuations are not offset by changes in interest rates. Far from the return on bonds being positively correlated with those on equity, as those who place importance on the equity risk premium seem unavailingly to expect, it would need to be negatively correlated. In practice, as I show, the returns on bonds and equities move independently, they are neither positively nor negatively correlated. The important impact of leverage on the cost of capital means that we need to understand how companies decide on it and how their decisions are matched by changes in household portfolio preference. Probably because the need for such a model is only obvious if the return on capital is not stationary, there appear to be no papers on the subject. As explained, I attribute both the management decisions on leverage and those of investors on portfolio preference to risk aversion, which in a steady state is stable in both cases, but which varies in the case of leverage with long bond yields and in the case of households on ageing and the structure of pension funds. Because the return on equity is inelastic to changes in bond yields and leverage is not, the process of adjustment only involves small changes in long bond yields and none in the return on equity.

The instability of the return on capital could have many causes. One possibility is the introduction of risk which is central to any model and which

The Economics of the Stock Market. Andrew Smithers, Oxford University Press. © Andrew Smithers 2022.
Foreword © Andy Haldane 2022. DOI: 10.1093/oso/9780192847096.003.0027

Mehra and Prescott suggested as a possible reason why, in their model, the return on equity was too high relative to bonds.[1] I explain the large gap in these returns as being due to the negative serial correlation of equity returns, combined with a significant proportion of savings being made to preserve consumption in retirement rather than for enhancing it and because individuals differ in their attitudes to risk.

As I set out in Table 18, the household sector, either directly or indirectly, owns the business sector and thus everything, which is not foreign or government owned. It also owns government debt for which it has a contingent liability, largely to itself but partly to foreigners. The equity and debts of the business sector plus government debt are the assets available for households and whose relative ownership, net of foreign holdings, are determined by their portfolio preference.

The proportion of savings that is motivated by the wish to preserve consumption in retirement is not known, but the development of pooled pension funds and the use of tax incentives to encourage it provide us with evidence of their minimum level. As Figure 67 shows they currently amount to 70 per cent of total household net financial assets and 340 per cent of personal disposable income and the speed with which these ratios have risen provides an indication of their importance for household savings.

Retirement savings appear, therefore, to dominate the sector's total savings and, as net foreign ownership is below 16 per cent (Table 20), their portfolio preference is thus likely to depend on their domestic owners' risk aversion. Economists have usually assumed that a single representative household can be used to judge the impact of risk aversion, but companies cannot raise

Table 18. Household direct and indirect ownership of US fixed produced assets 2018

	$ bn.	per cent of total
Business debt	15,318	
Federal government debt	17,865	
State and local	3,075	
US equities	25,809	
Total	62,067	100.0
Less net foreign liabilities	9,554	15.4
US households	52,513	84.6

Data sources: BEA International Table 1 and Fixed Asset Table 1.1.

[1] Mehra and Prescott (1985).

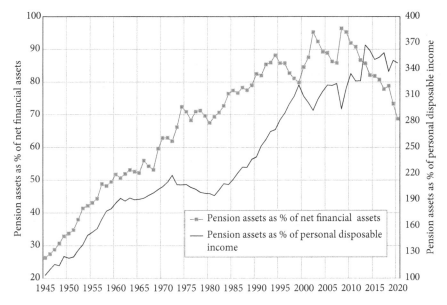

Figure 67. United States: Identifiable pensions assets as % of net financial assets and personal disposable income

Data sources: Z1 Table B. 103e and NIPA Table 5.1.

equity at different prices from different providers. As usual price is decided at the margin, so the cost of equity will be the return at which all the equity needed is provided and this will depend on the marginal supplier who will be more risk averse than average. The required return on equity is thus higher than it would be if all investors had the same level of risk aversion.

28

Life Cycle Savings Hypothesis

The model set out in this book has some similarities and many differences with the Life Cycle Savings Hypothesis (LCSH) for which Franco Modigliani was a leading exponent. Its key assumptions, are:[1]

- Young people will save so that when they are old and either cannot or do not wish to work, they will have money to spend. The young therefore save and the elderly dissave.
- As populations grow there are more savers than dissavers, so growing economies generate savings. If incomes are growing, the young will be saving on a larger scale than the old are dissaving so that economic growth, like population growth, causes positive saving, and the faster the growth, the higher the saving rate.
- The level of income itself does not matter, and poor countries save the same share of their income as rich countries. In an economy with no growth, wealth will just be passed around, no new wealth will be created.
- The total wealth in the economy depends on the length of retirement, and in simple cases, the ratio of a country's wealth to its income is a half of the average length of retirement.
- The ratio of wealth to income is lower the faster the rate of growth of the economy and is at its largest when the rate of growth is zero.

The major similarity is that both models assume that the young will save in order not to starve when elderly and that the old will often dissave either directly by spending more than their income or indirectly though annuities or final-salary pension schemes. The major difference with mine is that Modigliani implicitly assumes that the way companies behave has no bearing on savings. His model has no corporate veil, as is naturally to be expected of an approach associated with the author of the Miller-Modigliani Theorem.

The major concern of the LCSH is to explain the level of savings, while mine is to explain the stationarity of the equity return, and by examining the

---

[1] As summarized in 'Franco Modigliani and the Life-cycle Theory of Consumption' by Angus Deaton (2005) *Banca Nazionale del Lavoro (BNL) Quarterly Review* LVIII.

trade-off between the risks and returns of bonds and equities to explain how this affects the leverage of companies and the ratio of debt assets to equities in household portfolios. When the models are tested Angus Deaton remarks that 'it is consistently found that saving rates are higher where growth is higher, from the first time that Modigliani looked at the evidence until today when we have more and better data.' This expectation is common to both models, but the explanations differ. Modigliani assumes that it follows from the behaviour of individuals, which may indeed be the case, but I stress the importance of corporate savings, which he assumes must mirror the wishes of the population which is assumed not to differ from those of shareholders. Unless changes in portfolio preferences, fiscal balances, and foreign capital inflows lead to lower bond yields, companies will not increase their leverage, and net worth will have to rise at least as fast as output. I postulate that while companies will from time to time raise new equity from their shareholders, they are usually loath to do this, so that unless leverage changes corporate savings will rise and fall with the rate of growth. Figure 6 and Figure 7, which tracks changes in corporate savings required to finance the increase in corporate equity needed for economic growth, show that this hypothesis is supported by the data.

In other respects, the LCSH fails when tested. As wealth is assumed to be 'created' it must consist of produced capital, so the claim that the ratio of wealth to income rises and falls with the rate of growth of the economy is inconsistent with evidence, shown in Figure 6, that the ratio of value of produced capital to output is mean reverting. This failure cannot be avoided by defining wealth as the market price of financial assets and land. A closed economy has no net debt, so wealth can only exceed the value of produced capital if the ratio of market value of corporate equity to net worth is not mean reverting, or the value of land rises persistently faster than growth. The former is inconsistent with the mean reversion of equity q. The latter may be possible but does not seem to have occurred in the United States, since Figure 49, supported by the evidence backing Figure 61, shows that the value of land in non-financial corporate balance sheets has not risen relative to other assets since 1945 when the data series starts.

As simply stated the LCSH makes no allowance for the 'bequest motive'— the wish to leave money so that our descendants should be prosperous or even grand. Allowing for this requires assumptions about how rapidly people would be willing to spend capital to support their current consumption. It also needs to allow for the differences between income and capital, as shown in national accounts, and how they are perceived by the owners of capital. Pensions and the annual returns from annuities are represented in national accounts partly as income and partly as capital transfers, but they are seen by their recipients as coming from income rather than from capital. Allowance needs also to be made for the tax wedge between the amount left by the testator and that received by beneficiaries. The practical strength of the bequest motive does not, therefore, depend solely on the psychology of individuals but on the relative importance of directly owned assets and those intermediated by pension schemes and insurance companies and on inheritance taxes. It may therefore be possible to rescue the LCSH from its failure when tested, by introducing such modifications, but this does not yet appear to have been done. LCSH is thus not a valid hypothesis as it fails when set out in a testable form and so far appears untestable in any other.

Angus Deaton comments that: 'Many economists tend to think of the aggregate economy as if it were a single individual writ large, a "representative agent", instead of following Modigliani, and deriving a theory in which the distinction between individuals and aggregates is not only taken seriously but is used positively, to derive predictions for the economy that are quite different from the predictions for an individual, or a family.' This avoids my objection to the use by both Mehra and Prescott and Barro in their models of the 'single representative investor' but not to the failure to separate the behaviour of companies from the investors who own them. It is thus one of many macroeconomic theories which Robin Marris criticizes as fudging 'the implications of the fact that in a modern economy a large part of private investment is financed by retained profits.'[2]

I am sympathetic to the idea that people should be encouraged to save for their retirement. Effective policies to achieve this require an understanding of how savings are generated in the economy, and this is unlikely if we rely on models which ignore the crucial role of companies. I have therefore only limited sympathy with Angus Deaton when he writes that: 'Perhaps we are witnessing the movement of Modigliani's life-cycle hypothesis from a positive to a normative theory, away from description and towards prescription.' A prescriptive policy for savings is, I think, desirable, but a sound one is unlikely to follow from the LCSH with its assumption that there is no corporate veil.

[2] Marris (1991).

29

Depreciation, Capital Consumption, and Maintenance

The bundling of intellectual property (IP) expenditure with that on tangible plant and equipment raises the important question of how to estimate the rates at which they should be depreciated. It also raises the question of whether the aggregate value of intangibles is the sum of any positive values that can be ascribed to the intangible assets of individual companies or, as I suggested previously, that some companies have ill will to match the good-will of others.

The BEA assumes that 'the value of an asset changes as the result of depreciation and revaluation. Depreciation is the change in value associated with the ageing of an asset. As an asset ages, its price changes because it declines in efficiency, or yields fewer productive services, in the current period and in all future periods. Depreciation reflects the present value of all such current and future changes in productive services.'[1] In practice the BEA's data on the value and depreciation of tangible assets do not depend on this assumption, but on the results of their survey of second-hand prices.[2] This is fortunate as it does not seem to me that the BEA's definition of depreciation is a good one. It suggests that the BEA considers, mistakenly, that assets depreciate simply because they age. This is odd because it appears that the BEA appear generally to follow Robert Solow's approach to growth and he proposes an alternative model which 'assumes that capital is perfectly durable. This assumption has the advantage of simplicity, and it permits the model to bring out clearly the economics of obsolescence.'[3]

Experience points firmly to Solow's alternative view being correct. Equipment does not decay if properly maintained but it will do so if not. Houses and old cars for example last indefinitely if fully serviced and properly maintained and will continue to produce the same output as before. Maintenance is therefore the cost of sustaining the output per person from a

---

[1] 'The Measurement of Depreciation in the U.S. National Income and Product Accounts' by Barbara M. Fraumeni (1997) *BEA Survey of Current Business* 77.
[2] See Appendix 1.
[3] Solow, Tobin, von Weizsäcker, and Yaari (1971).

The Economics of the Stock Market. Andrew Smithers, Oxford University Press. © Andrew Smithers 2022.
Foreword © Andy Haldane 2022. DOI: 10.1093/oso/9780192847096.003.0029

given piece of capital equipment. This is, however, not the way in which maintenance costs are recorded. While fully maintained equipment can continue to produce the same level of output for ever, it will not be fully maintained unless it is worthwhile to do so. The value of houses and old cars lies partly in their age and perceived beauty; the value of most assets, however, falls as real wages rise and labour incomes take an increasing proportion of the value of their output, so the level of expenditure required for full maintenance becomes uneconomic over time and in the final years of the equipment's life it will often pay not to do so. This will shorten the life of the equipment but raises its profit contribution if only briefly. The recorded charge for maintenance is the amount spent, not the amount needed to keep output stable and if maintenance is defined as the cost of maintaining constant production the theoretical level of maintenance will diverge from the recorded amount. But this should not be confused, as it appears often to be, with the idea that the output of installed equipment falls over time even when it is properly maintained.

Once constructed, equipment has embedded in it the technology of its time. Its productivity depends on its vintage. Even ignoring cyclical fluctuations, equipment is not, however, always employed at its maximum potential when initially installed. Output may also be subsequently enhanced by improvements in the education of the workforce or from the experience of using the equipment. With these minor provisos the output per person employed for a given piece of equipment is stable and the value of that output will fall steadily as real wages rise.[4] The fall in value arising from rising real wages is depreciation. If the labour share of output is stable and there are no changes in the value placed on a given stream of profits, the rate of depreciation will be determined by the rise in labour productivity. In practice depreciation is calculated from changes in the value of equipment, shown by surveys, for which the rise in wages is not the only cause. The rate of depreciation as calculated by the national accountants does not fluctuate from year to year with the changes in value but is derived from the underlying trend. For the BEA: 'Revaluation is the change in value or price per unit that is associated with everything other than aging. Revaluation includes pure inflation, obsolescence, and any other impact on the price of an asset not associated with aging.'[5]

Depreciation of tangible capital assets, as measured by the BEA, is based on their value as determined by surveys. It has been argued that this

---

[4] Solow, Tobin, von Weizsäcker, and Yaari (1971).
[5] 'Depreciation of Business R&D Capital' by Wendy C. Y. Li and Bronwyn H. Hall (2016) NBER Working Paper 22473.

overstates the rate of depreciation on the grounds that these values will be determined by lemons[6] the term used when buyers are imperfectly informed about the quality of the products they are buying and assume that the quality of their individual purchases will be below average. But the BEA claims that this does not apply to their surveys as the second-hand equipment is purchased after thorough investigation and the market does not exhibit asymmetric information. In practice, therefore, the value that the BEA places on the produced tangible capital stock and the rates of depreciation they derive from it seem soundly based, and not adversely affected by their questionable definition, whose sole disadvantage is to perpetuate the myth that the output of equipment falls over time even if properly maintained.

The depreciation of intangible capital assets cannot be ascertained by surveys as the BEA acknowledges: 'The premise of my model is that business R&D capital depreciates because its contribution to a firm's profit declines over time...Although important, measuring R&D depreciation rates is extremely difficult because both the price and output of R&D capital are generally unobservable. To resolve these difficulties, economists have adopted various approaches to estimate industry-specific R&D depreciation rates, but the differences in their results cannot easily be reconciled. In addition, many of their calculations rely on unverifiable assumptions.'[7] The BEA is thus acknowledging that a valid estimate of the rate at which R&D depreciates cannot be done although it then proceeds to try. Even if the calculations of the value of IP to individual companies did not depend on 'unverifiable assumptions' the method involves the assumption that these values do not have their counterpart in the negative value that they impose on those companies which do not own them and that there is therefore no ill will to offset individual goodwill.

The lack of a suitable way to assess the value of individual items of IP means that we cannot calculate the rate at which it depreciates. Even if we could make this calculation, we should not assume that the aggregate value of IP is the sum of individual items. For example, the value of a patent is very real to the holder, but its existence will often reduce the value of the output of another company, either because the patent increases productivity or improves the quality of a new product. In the first instance, given the mean reversion of profit margins in aggregate, the additional profit to the patent holder will result in a reduction in the profit margins of everyone else,

[6] 'The Market for "Lemons": Quality Uncertainty and the Market Mechanism' by George Akerlof (1970) *Quarterly Journal of Economics* 84.
[7] 'Depreciation of Business R&D Capital' by Wendy C. Y. Li and Bronwyn H. Hall (2016) NBER Working Paper 22473.

though it will be virtually unrecognizable when spread over all other companies. In the second instance the improvement in the product will cut the profits of competitors.

I consider therefore that the decision to include expenditure on IP as a subset of the expenditure on investment was a mistake.[8] Fortunately, so long as the speed at which it is written off is as rapid as it is currently, the damage done is limited.

---

[8] A fuller discussion of the case against the decision to include IP spending as investment is set out in Smithers (2020).

30
Comparison with Other Approaches

This book seeks to explain the economics of the stock market. It differs fundamentally in its approach and conclusions to that generally taken in the past by most economists when considering equity returns and their relationship to interest rates. There have been several prominent economists who have differed strongly with the consensus that has come to dominate discussion of corporate behaviour and I have referred to the dissenting views of Robin Marris[1] and Nicholas Kaldor.[2] Nonetheless the neoclassical synthesis represents the majority and consensus approach and the differences of my views with it seem most easily explained by contrasting them with those taken by economists who adhere to it.

For the purposes of comparing the differences in my approach to that of other economists I have selected four papers:

(i)   James Tobin (1969) 'A General Equilibrium Approach to Monetary Theory' *Journal of Money, Credit and Banking* 1(1): 15–29.
(ii) Rajnish Mehra and Edward C. Prescott (1985) 'The Equity Premium: A Puzzle' *Journal of Monetary Economics* 15(2): 145–61.
(iii) Robert Barro (2006) 'Rare Disasters and Asset Markets in the Twentieth Century' *The Quarterly Journal of Economics* 121(3): 823–66.
(iv) M. Harris and A. Raviv (1991) 'Theory of Capital Structure' *The Journal of Finance* 46(1): 297–355.

Tobin's approach has many similarities with mine. His model of the economy includes money, assets, and debts, the factors that determine the demand and supply of these assets, and the markets in which prices are determined: 'As savers, people determine how much to add to their wealth; as portfolio managers, they determine how to distribute among available assets and debts the net worth they already have' (Tobin 1969). Tobin's and my model both make a distinction between the value of assets as assessed by

---

[1] Marris (1964).   [2] Kaldor (1966).

The Economics of the Stock Market. Andrew Smithers, Oxford University Press. © Andrew Smithers 2022.
Foreword © Andy Haldane 2022. DOI: 10.1093/oso/9780192847096.003.0030

the stock market or in national accounts by their second-hand value. (Second-hand value is termed replacement cost in Tobin's paper. I explain the different terms and usage of them in Appendix 1). 'Let p be the price of currently produced goods, both consumer and capital goods. I shall, how-ever, allow the value of existing capital goods, or of titles to them, to diverge from their current reproduction cost—let qp be the market price of existing capital goods' (Tobin 1969). It follows that: 'The rate of investment—the speed at which investors wish to increase the capital stock—should be related, if to anything, to q, the value of capital relative to its replacement cost' (Tobin 1969). Tobin does not assume that the rate of interest is the same as the return on capital or that there is a constant equity risk premium but points out that 'under the usual assumptions of neo-classical growth theory...investment savings equality requires a q of less than one...An alternative interpretation requires that capital is valued at its reproduction cost i.e. that $q = 1$. This may be regarded as a condition of equilibrium in the long run' (Tobin 1969).

The long-term equilibrium in which $q = 1$ is, when applied to net worth, supported by the data. Equity q is strongly mean reverting and when cor-rectly measured $= 1$ and as I have noted it follows that Tobin's Q must be also. Tobin is not precise about the mechanism that keeps q stationary, but he is usually assumed to see this as arising from the effect on investment. This interpretation is not necessarily justified as his comment on the subject is conditional: 'If the interest rate on money, as well as on all other financial assets, was flexible and endogenous...there would be no room for discrep-ancies between market value and reproduction cost. There would be no room for monetary policy to affect aggregate demand. The real economy would call the tune on the financial economy and, with no feedback in the other direction. As previously observed, something like this occurs in the long run, where the influence of monetary policy is not on aggregate demand but on the relative supply of monetary and real assets, to which all rates of return must adjust' (Tobin 1969). In my model this is exactly what does occur though the process involves the way that changes in the yield on long-dated bonds allow households and companies to make compatible adjust-ments to the former's portfolio preferences and the latter's leverage. Quoted companies are indifferent to changes in the cost of equity with the result that the net worth of the corporate sector responds only weakly to changes in the cost of capital. The main route whereby the stock market adjusts to the net worth of companies is through the mean reversion of equity returns from which it follows that q does also. Share prices are volatile and rise and fall with swings in investor confidence, but these errors in expectations cancel out over time.

Tobin does, however, also remark that 'an increase in the quantity of money is expansionary, causing a rise in the valuation of existing capital and stimulating investment' (Tobin 1969). This comment is, however, made in the context of an economy with only one private sector and two assets: money and homogeneous physical capital. Tobin may have expected the route by which the stock market value and the replacement cost of the assets they represent are brought together to be primarily through the impact on investment. It does not, however, seem to me to be a requirement of his model that this should be the case.

My model therefore follows Tobin's, though I seek to show that the route by which the real and the financial economy have a stable long-term relationship is largely through the fluctuations in the stock market rather than through the impact of monetary policy on the level of corporate investment.

The Mehra and Prescott paper is concerned with the discrepancy between the observed difference in returns on equity and the risk-free rate of return, which they term the equity premium, and their interpretation of the general equilibrium models of the neoclassical consensus: 'Intuitively, the reason why the low average real return (on cash) and the high average real return on equity cannot be rationalized in a perfect market is as follows: With real per capita consumption growing at nearly two per cent per year on average, the elasticities of substitution between the year t and year t + 1 consumption good that are sufficiently small to yield the six per cent average equity premium also yield real rates of return far in excess of those observed. In the case of a growing economy, agents with high risk aversion effectively discount the future to a greater extent than agents with low risk aversion (relative to a growing economy). Due to growth, future consumption will probably exceed present consumption and since the marginal utility of future consumption is less than that on present consumption, real interest rates will be higher on average' (Mehra and Prescott 1985).

They assume that because aggregate savings result in rising incomes the purpose of individuals when they save is to have higher incomes. This is I think fallacious. The fact that aggregate savings produce higher average incomes in the future does not mean that it is the purpose for which individuals save. Mehra and Prescott also assume that the economy has a single representative 'stand-in' household.

It is generally accepted that the utility function is such that large falls in consumption are proportionately more painful than small ones and rises are proportionately less beneficial. If the purpose of savings is to enhance future consumption, the mild benefit that it brings will need to be rewarded by a significant risk-free return and as this benefit decreases as income rises, the risks arising from the uncertain returns on equity will be moderate as will the added return needed to reward investors. If the purpose of savings is to avoid future declines in consumption the subjective discount factor will have a totally different form. Regular savings will produce a one-off decline in an individual household's annual consumption, but the assets accumulated can be used to preserve the level of future spending and if this falls through unemployment, illness, or retirement, the benefit from avoiding a large fall will have been achieved by a small sacrifice in current utility. The benefit thus heavily outweighs the sacrifice even if there is no return on the savings. Where assets are being held to prevent or at least mitigate declines in consumption after retirement, the high pain suffered by large falls relative to small ones will also render the holders of retirement savings strongly risk averse and therefore, before being willing to hold equities, they will demand a high degree of probability that they will produce a greater return than risk-free bonds.

The Mehra and Precott model thus differs from mine in that they assume the existence of a single representative investor whose motivation when saving is to enhance his future consumption, whereas I assume that different savers have different motivations and the marginal investors needed to provide the equity needed for investment are saving for retirement and are thus strongly risk averse. Equally, rainy-day savings will provide short-term funds which will also be risk averse and have a low subjective discount rate for cash assets, which rises sharply with the maturity date for debt assets which cannot be immediately realized at par.

The Mehra and Prescott paper allows for the impact of expectations and the Barro paper alters this to include greater fears of disaster 'by including the potential for rare economic disasters explains a lot of asset-pricing puzzles. I calibrate disaster probabilities from the twentieth-century global history, especially the sharp contractions associated with World War I, the Great Depression and World War II. The puzzles that can be explained include the high equity premium, low risk-free rate, and volatile stock returns' (Barro 2006).

Barro's attempt to adjust the Mehra and Prescott model to the observed level of investor risk aversion is unnecessary unless savers can be adequately represented by a single saver who wishes to enhance his future consumption which, as set out above seems unlikely. It is also incompatible with the evidence about long-term equity returns. Barro assumes that these are hit by reductions in growth arising from either capital destruction in war or through depression. However, as I have shown, the impact of these two on long-term equity returns is totally different. Losses resulting from capital destruction are permanent; those from depression are short term and non-existent over the longer term. Equity returns are stationary and unaffected by growth: the process of catching up after the loss of capital, such as that seen in Germany and Japan after World War II, is achieved by heavy investment leading to faster growth in the capital stock not by an increase in RoE.

Papers on leverage seem, invariably as far as I can find, to approach the subject from the viewpoint of individual firms rather than from a macroeconomic viewpoint. For example in their survey Harris and Ravi[3] consider two possible approaches: 'One ... is to construct or identify a very general model.' This, however, they dismiss on the grounds that 'the set of features one must include in such a general model is so large and complicated that the resulting structure would not yield clear insights.' The other 'is to ask what issues might be resolved by theories of capital structure. This "wish list" would include questions such as what the effect is on capital structure of changes in the volatility of cash flows, firm size, elasticity of demand for the product, the extent of insider private information, etc.'

The objection to the general model is surely invalid. As I wrote in the introduction 'To understand a complicated system, it is not sufficient to describe it, we also need to discard its inessential features and show that the resulting simplified model accurately simulates the system's behaviour.' The questions asked in the alternative approach involve 'volatility of cash flows, firm size, elasticity of demand for the product, the extent of insider private information, etc.' are all those which differentiate the leverage of one company with that of another. They are therefore irrelevant to the issue of how the aggregate leverage of the corporate sector is derived.

I seek to show that the leverage of the corporate sector, which must in a two-sector closed economy match household portfolio preference, is determined over time by the level of the government long bond yield. This is to discard as inessential all other variables and its validity depends on it accurately simulating the system's behaviour, which I show that it does, with the aggregate leverage of companies being strongly correlated with the yield on government long-dated bonds. I also show that this follows from the risk aversion of borrowers, rather than from that of lenders. The utility function of corporate managers is largely determined by the desire to preserve their jobs and this is threatened both by insufficient and excessive leverage. They are concerned with the specific risk of having to raise additional equity, and thereby damaging the share price of their companies. The risks to lenders lie in the specific risk of individual companies, for which the lending margin

---

[3] Harris and Ravi (1991).

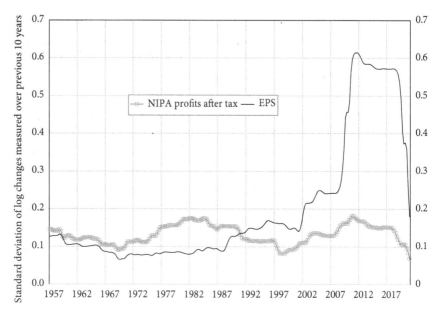

Figure 68. United States: Volatility of S&P 500 EPS and NIPA profits after tax
Data sources: NIPA Table 1.14, S&P, and BLS.

should compensate when spread over a loan portfolio and in changes to the level of bankruptcy. This systemic risk could increase with the aggregate level of leverage but does not appear to have done so in the past despite the major post-war rise in corporate debt levels. As the severity of recessions as well as aggregate leverage is likely to affect the systemic risk of bankruptcy and the former have fallen since the slump, lenders' apparent indifference to aggregate leverage is eminently reasonable.

Lending margins may well rise in the future, but this will be offset by a fall in the risk-free rate. The cost of the rise in the lending margin consequent on a rise in systemic bankruptcy risk will thus be borne by bond holders. As the long-term returns on equities are stationary the equity risk premium cannot be unless yields on risk-free long-dated bonds move with them, which they don't and can't as changes in bond yields are needed to allow the necessary *ex post* identity between leverage and portfolio preference. Leverage needs to adjust, inter alia, for changes in the systemic risk of bankruptcy, and as this is likely to vary over time it is among the reasons why bond and equity returns cannot be co-determined.

The ratio of debt to equity in corporate accounts must relate to the proportions in household investment portfolios. In a two-sector model they must be identical but as the government sector issues debt and the foreign sector buys and sells both debt and equity, the relationship is more complex in the real world. But as the actions of neither the government nor foreigners are designed to produce the necessary balance between leverage and portfolio preference, a market mechanism is required to produce the equilibrium endogenously. The assumption that corporate leverage is exogenous, as seems generally assumed in the literature is thus totally unsatisfactory.[4]

The general model for corporate leverage also has the advantage over approaches based on individual company data, in that it uses national data which are inherently less unreliable. The national data take the form of accounts in which, for example, the data on output must equal that on income, and with minor discrepancies they do. There is no similar control over the profits published by companies and these can differ substantially from those in the national accounts. I illustrate this in Figure 68 by comparing the volatility of the two sources of profits. One result of the incentives of the bonus culture has been to encourage managements to overstate the decline in profits in bad years in order to overstate the subsequent recovery. This was a marked feature of profit announcements in 2008 when profits were heavily understated with consequent overstatements in subsequent years.

---

[4] Harris and Raviv (1991).

31

The Efficient Market Hypothesis

Prior to the financial crisis most economists, though happily not all, believed in a version of the Efficient Market Hypothesis (EMH), which held that financial markets were always efficiently and thus correctly priced. The fluctuations in the equity market thus appeared to be easily explained and depended on changes in prospective returns. It followed that equity prices and value must be the same and financial bubbles could not occur. The financial crisis resulted in the EMH being discredited as, despite many warnings, it led central bankers to ignore the threat posed by excess debt and overpriced assets, which believers in this version of the EMH held to be impossible.

Stock market returns are not distributed in a random manner; they rotate around a stable long-term average. Markets which have subsequently given high returns were therefore cheap and those which gave poor returns were expensive. Although these characteristics were well known for many years before the financial crisis it was accepted with great reluctance by many economists: 'when we first presented our rejection of the Random Walk Hypothesis at an academic conference in 1986, our discussant—a distinguished economist and senior member of the profession—asserted with great confidence that we had made a programming error.'[1] Even after the invalidity of the Random Walk Hypothesis had been demonstrated many economists continued to adhere to some version of the EMH. The difficulty in persuading them to discard it was due to a significant degree to the fact that it was seldom enunciated as a well-defined and refutable hypothesis. Value, as generally understood, depends on relative returns. On this basis the EMH, when defined as holding that price and value are the same, is demonstrably wrong. But while the EMH was generally understood to be making this claim the imprecision with which it was defined meant that other interpretations were possible.

---

[1] *A Non-random Walk down Wall Street* by Andrew W. Lo and Craig MacKinley (1999) Princeton University Press.

The Economics of the Stock Market. Andrew Smithers, Oxford University Press. © Andrew Smithers 2022.
Foreword © Andy Haldane 2022. DOI: 10.1093/oso/9780192847096.003.0031

Some economists remain reluctant to drop the idea of efficiency. The intuitive basis for this lies in the apparent inability of investors to make arbitrage profits from buying low and selling high. It is not unreasonable to claim that it is therefore efficient, but it has nonetheless been a bad mistake to do so, because this has given credence to the interpretation of the EMH which holds that value and price are the same, that bubbles are therefore impossible and high asset prices therefore pose no threat to economic stability. As far as I can find, the continued claims that the market is efficient produced no hypotheses which were sufficiently well defined to be refutable. They therefore fall on the wrong side of Karl Popper's famous demarcation between science and nonscience.

I hope that I have produced a valid and thus testable hypothesis which allows prices to be rationally determined. I do not assume that all the participants always act rationally, but many do, and the actions of the irrational appear random and thus have no distorting impact on price determination. It is therefore sensible to avoid calling the price determination as being efficient as this leads to confusion by appearing to support the discredited model.

32
Summary

The model of the economy which I present has many aspects which depend on other ones and the individual points can therefore be presented in a different order to the one set out in this book. I have sought to show the robustness of each claim when tested. As each one relies on the soundness of others this makes the model as a whole open to testing. It also means that it excludes many paths that the economy might otherwise follow. It is therefore more informative and, because it makes predictions, it is more easily refutable.[1]

i) *Ex post* corporate leverage must match *ex post* household portfolio preference. Changes in demography will change *ex ante* household portfolio preference, but not *ex ante* corporate leverage, so the latter cannot be, as it is often assumed to be, exogenous. The endogenous adjustment must come from changes in the returns of either bonds or equities.

ii) The utility preferences of managers determine the investment, leverage, and pay-out policies of quoted companies, which dominate the economy. Managements avoid strategies which threaten their jobs, so (a) they seek to maximize the present value of their companies as measured by the stock market not net worth; (b) they avoid being over or underleveraged and the ratio of interest payments to pre-tax profits is therefore mean reverting; (c) they invest when expected real returns on equity (the hurdle rate) equals 6.7 per cent p.a. and refrain from those that don't; and (d) they prefer profit retentions to issuing new equity so that corporate savings rise with growth.

iii) The stationarity of equity returns is shown by historic returns and their negative serial correlation. The risks of poor returns fall sharply at longer time horizons. It is risky for companies to borrow short debt and pointless to pay more to borrow for longer than the average life of their fixed produced assets, so the yield curve is flat after twenty years.

---

[1] 'progress was towards a more informative and therefore logically less probable theory; towards a theory which was more severely testable because it makes predictions which in a purely logical sense, were more easily refutable' Popper (1963).

The Economics of the Stock Market. Andrew Smithers, Oxford University Press. © Andrew Smithers 2022.
Foreword © Andy Haldane 2022. DOI: 10.1093/oso/9780192847096.003.0032

iv) The risk aversion of managers is stable, as are those of demographically stable households, who dislike falls in income more than they like rises, and for whom the pain of decline increases more than proportionately. Most households save to avoid poverty in retirement, and their utility function leads to a low risk-free rate of interest even for twenty-year bonds and a high return on equity.

v) As the utility functions of savers and corporate managers differ, companies do not behave as if they were run by owners. The high elasticity of corporate leverage to changes in bond yields and the low elasticity of household portfolio preference results in their *ex post* identity being achieved solely through changes in bond yields. The real return on equity is thus stationary despite changes in demography.

vi) From point (ii) (a) it follows that companies do not seek to maximize the present value of their net worth. Leverage increases the present value of both stock market value and net worth. The Miller-Modigliani Theorem is invalid when applied to the corporate sector as increased leverage lowers the discount with which an unchanged flow of profits is valued.

The evidence necessary for the above claims to be valid is provided, inter alia, by (a) the mean reversion and negative serial correlation of equity returns; (b) the relative elasticities of leverage and portfolio preferences to long-dated bond yields; (c) the indifference of companies to the level of the stock market with regard to both raising equity and their level of investment; (d) the cheapness of debt relative to equity, even without any tax benefit; (e) the correlation between profit retentions and growth when leverage is stable; and (f) the lack of any long- or short-term relationship between equity returns and long-dated bond yields.

The model makes forecasts, which apply so long as the economy continues to be reasonably competitive, dominated by quoted companies, and that the definitions used in the national accounts are not changed again, for example by categorizing advertising as a form of investment. Four constants will remain:

A. The mean reversion of the real return on equity at circa 6.7 per cent.
B. The mean reversion of the profit (after depreciation) and labour shares of output.
C. The mean reversion of the ratio of interest payments to profits.
D. The mean reversion of the ratio of the value of fixed produced capital to output.

33

Comments in Conclusion

This book claims that the neoclassical synthesis has so many faults that it needs to be replaced. To do this I show that it makes numerous a priori assumptions which are shown to be false when tested. In its place I propose a model which combines theories of the firm, such as those set out by Robin Marris, with Tobin's general model of the interaction between the real and the financial economy. The former seems to have been almost completely ignored and the latter has, in recent years, tended to be unjustly overlooked despite its many virtues. I follow George Akerlof in his criticism that the neoclassical consensus has oversimplified Keynes's work by restricting the equilibria needed for a stable economy to one, namely the balance between *ex ante* savings and investment: 'Neo-classical supply had resolved that the determination of the price level and assets prices (as the inverse of the interest rate).'[1] This is not a criticism that can be levied at Tobin who specifically allows for multiple rates of return for different assets. He assumes that the ratio of stock market value to the second-hand value of the corporate assets must be stationary. This hypothesis is testable, and I show that it is robust when tested. It requires, however, that both the market value of the equity component of corporations to net worth is stationary as well as the ratio of their total market value, including both equity and debt, with the total value of their assets.

That Tobin's model has been largely neglected seems to have arisen from the possibly correct belief that he assumed that the market forces which produce the long-term stability of this ratio work through the capital stock rising to meet stock market value through stimulating investment. This has proved to be a mistake as high values of q do not stimulate investment. His model does not, however, necessarily assume this and is not therefore invalidated because the stock market adjusts to the capital stock rather than vice versa.

---

[1] Akerlof (2019).

The Economics of the Stock Market. Andrew Smithers, Oxford University Press. © Andrew Smithers 2022.
Foreword © Andy Haldane 2022. DOI: 10.1093/oso/9780192847096.003.0033

Another reason for the relative neglect of Tobin's model is that it is only compatible with the neoclassical synthesis if the mean reversion of q is driven by investment and the capital stock responds to changes in the cost of capital, and this does not occur in either case. The stationarity of q follows from the mean reversion of the stock market around fair value being driven by changes in share prices.

I am conscious that I am making very bold claims and thus laying down a challenge which I hope will be met in debate. I may then of course be shown to be wrong. My model is certainly not a complete account of the economy but if it is an improvement on the current consensus it will provide the basis for further improvement in our understanding of the economy, which recent events have shown to be badly needed, and which small adjustments to the neoclassical synthesis seem unlikely to provide.

The Duration of Bonds and Equities

The duration of a bond is conceptually different from its maturity. A bond with a coupon of 5 per cent and a maturity of twenty years, will respond to changes in interest rates differently from a twenty-year bond with a different coupon. The higher the coupon the less volatile will be the change in price for any given change in the yield. The duration is the weighted average term to maturity of the bond's cash flow.

The return and volatility of equities is, however, unchanged despite changes in their pay-out ratio. Over time periods in which leverage does not change so that net worth rises in line with growth, the pay-out ratio will vary inversely with growth but the return and volatility are the same as over periods in which trend growth is significantly different. The Gordon Growth Model assumes that returns on equities are not affected by changes in the contribution from the dividend or its growth rate. This would not, however, necessarily apply to a bond of infinite maturity whose coupon rose at a constant rate, as its duration would vary with the coupon. If two such bonds were available giving the same long-term return, the short-term price volatility of the one with the higher coupon would be lower. Unless the time horizon of all investors was certain rather than just expected and highly probable, they would prefer the bond with the lower volatility, and this would be reflected by a difference in their returns.

The Valuation of Unquoted Companies in The Financial Accounts of the United States—Z1

The Federal Reserve sets out its method of valuing quoted companies (S) and unquoted (C) as follows (FL103164123.Q). Beginning in 1996 the market value of S-corporations is estimated by multiplying the net worth data of S-corporations in non-financial industries (identified by 2-digit NAICS codes) from the IRS, SOI Table S-Corporation Returns: Balance Sheet and Income Statement Items, by major industry, by the average ratio of market value to net worth from Standard & Poor's Compustat for public companies in the same non-financial industries. The market value of C-corporations is estimated by multiplying the revenue data of companies that appear on Forbes' annual list of America's Largest Private Companies by the ratio of total market value to total revenue of public companies from Standard & Poor's Compustat with similar industry, employment, and revenue profiles. The total market value of C-corporations is split between financial and non-financial corporations using the same splits available from the S-corporations calculations. The total market value of C-corporations and S-corporations is adjusted downward by 25 per cent to reflect the lack of liquidity of closely held shares. Prior to 1996, non-financial business' closely held equity is included with non-financial business' public corporate equities (FOF series FL103164113). Series has no transactions component. Data for the most recent ten years show no significant seasonality.

Measurement of the Net Capital Stock and Depreciation in the United States

The US Bureau of Economic Analysis (BEA) estimates the value of the produced capital stock and depreciation from data on historic investment and from surveys. The latter provide evidence for the value of second-hand equipment and thereby for the value of installed capital stock and of the rate at which capital depreciates. As these values will fall in line with the return that can be achieved by the purchaser they will reflect, inter alia, the expected profitability of the equipment and this will in turn reflect the rate of growth of real wages since the capital was installed. The use of survey data thus allows for the rate of growth of productivity when valuing the net capital stock and rates of capital consumption: 'There are two basic methods for measuring net stocks. The physical inventory method applies independently estimated prices to a direct count of the number of physical units of each type of asset. The perpetual inventory method cumulates past investment flows to indirectly estimate the value of the stock.'[1] The BEA bases its estimates of depreciation on survey data: 'BEA's estimates of depreciation are based on geometric depreciation patterns, which are supported by empirical studies of the prices of used equipment and structures in resale markets.'[2]

The value of the capital stock that results from surveys of second-hand prices is often, and in my view confusingly, referred to as 'replacement' cost. In this respect the term is used differently in the United Kingdom and the United States. The Office for National Statistics (ONS) describes its approach as follows: 'Gross capital stock tells us how much the economy's assets would cost to buy again as new, or their replacement cost. All of the fixed assets in the economy, that are still productive and in use, are added up to calculate this…This measure shows the value at the end of the year. This is mainly calculated as an intermediate step towards net capital stock…Net capital stock shows the market value of fixed assets. The market value is the amount that the assets could be sold for, which will be lower than the value of gross capital stocks.'[3]

The balance sheet data for the United States (Financial Statistics of the United States Z1 Table B. 103) published by the Federal Reserve refers to replacement cost for the value of equipment and inventories (lines 3 and 6) when the UK term would be net capital value. BEA uses both survey and historic data to measure the capital stock. Tobin follows US practice when referring to replacement cost.

---

[1] 'Fixed Assets and Consumer Durable Goods 1925 to 1997' BEA (2015).
[2] 'Fixed Assets and Consumer Durable Goods 1925 to 1997' BEA (2015).
[3] 'Capital Stocks, Consumption of Fixed Capital' ONS *Statistical Bulletin* (2014).

Data Sources, Use, and Methods of Calculation

Averages are usually calculated from the geometric mean (arithmetic mean of log percentages) and the trend is then calculated from the least squares regression of the log values.

I seek to avoid data mining (aka data dredging) 'the systematic bias inherent from...only reporting what looks most interesting'[1] (or supports the author's argument) by using all the available data that I have been able to obtain.

The BEA in NIPA 1.14 calculate net output as gross value added minus depreciation, I follow most economists in also deducting 'taxes on production and imports less subsidies'.

The data in NIPA 1.14 cover all corporate domestic output and profits, whether US-owned or the subsidiaries of foreign-owned companies, though retained profits are net of dividends paid out to shareholders, net of dividends received from US foreign direct investment. The profits and output ratios for non-financial companies must therefore include foreign-owned as well as US-owned companies and pay-out ratios for US-owned companies using NIPA 1.14 data need to be adjusted as these transfers are internal when considering consolidated accounts and can differ greatly, for example, with the pay-out ratios for S&P 500 companies.

Angus Maddison

The Angus Maddison project provides long-term data for GDP and GDP per head measured at constant prices for the world and its constituent countries. I use the data for seventeen countries, updated from 2008 by national GDP data.

www.rug.nl/ggdc/historicaldevelopment/maddison

Bank of England: 'A Millennium of Macroeconomic Data for the UK'

The database provides a wide variety of long-term economic statistics for the United Kingdom. I use those for short-term interest rates, long-dated bond yields and the consumer price index.

www.kaggle.com/bank-of-england/a-millennium-of-macroeconomic-data

Bureau of Economic Analysis (BEA)

Among their published data compilations, I use the following:

The National Income and Product Accounts (NIPA). The Tables to which I refer are 1.1.5 (GDP at current prices), 1.1.6 (GDP at constant prices), 1.14.(corporate data), 3.6.5 (government data), 5.1 (data on savings and investment).

[1] *The Art of Statistics* by David Spiegelhalter (2020) Pelican.

The data on investment in 1.1.5 and 1.1.6 is solely that made in the private sector, it does not include government investment, which is included in government spending. In other countries the data are often, in this regard, presently differently. The output and profits data in 1.14 are shown in aggregate and separately for financial and non-financial companies. Profits are shown in 1.14 both with and without the adjustments for the impact of inflation on inventories (IV) and capital consumption (CC). I use those with the adjustments as they are those which are compatible with other national income data, though I refer to those without when this is relevant as these approximate more closely to the data published by companies in their accounts. The gross output of companies is shown in 1.14 by deducting from line 1 (gross value added) line 7 (taxes on production and imports less subsidies). For net output line 2 (consumption of capital) needs to be deducted and net output can then be divided into the labor share (line 4) and the profit share (net output minus line 4 = line 8). Similar calculations can be used for financial and non-financial companies.

The Fixed Asset Tables to which I refer are 1.1 (current value of fixed assets at replacement cost), 1.3 (current cost depreciation of fixed assets and consumer durable goods), and 1.9 (current cost average age of fixed assets and consumer durable goods).

NB. The BEA refer to capital consumption in the NIPA Tables and to depreciation in the Fixed Asset Tables, they have the same definition and meaning.

International Tables. I use the data in Table 1 on the net foreign ownership of US assets.
www.bea.gov

Bureau of Labour Statistics (BLS)

Among their published data compilations, I use the Consumer Price Index (CPI), Employment and Unemployment.
www.data.bls.gov

Bureau of the Census

Among their published statistics, I use their US population data, including historic and forecast numbers by age groups.
www.usa.gov/federal-agencies/u-s-census-bureau

Carola Frydman and Dirk Jenter NBER Working Paper 16585

In this paper they set out data on the salaries and bonus payments of US CEOs from 1992 to 2008.
www.nber.org/system/files/working_papers/w16585/w16585.pdf

Elroy Dimson, Paul Marsh, and Mike Staunton

Total real returns for cash, long-dated bonds, and equities since 1899 for eighteen countries. I have their data up to 2013 which I have updated for recent years by linking with national indices for equity returns and CPI.

The data up to 2001 were published in their book *The Triumph of the Optimists* (2002) Princeton University Press. I purchased the data from them up to 2013.

Robert Shiller's data on equity returns overlaps with that of Jeremy Siegel's from 1871 to 1899 and with those that I have from Elroy Dimson, Paul Marsh, and Mike Staunton, for 1899 to 2013. There are differences in data from different sources, but the long-term returns do not depend to any significant extent on the source used.

Federal Reserve

Among their published data compilations, I use The Financial Accounts of the United States— Z1. The Tables to which I refer are B. 101e (the balance sheet of the household sector including indirect ownership of equities and debt assets held via insurance companies and pension funds), B. 103 (the balance sheet of non-financial corporations), B. 104 (the balance sheet of non-incorporated non-financial businesses), F. 103 (flow data of non-financial corporations, i.e. profits, dividends, capital consumption, and investment), F. 104 (flow data of non-incorporated non-financial businesses), F.223 (purchases, sales, and issues of corporate equities), L. 101 (the balance sheet of the household sector, showing value of insurance policies and pension funds), L. 105 (the balance sheet of the government sector, i.e. includes the federal, state and local government), L. 133 (balance sheet data for the rest of the world), and L.223 (ownership and market value of corporate equities).

Different editions of the Federal Reserve's Financial Accounts of the United States—Z1 can have different line numbers in the Tables for a given data series compared with earlier editions. Unless otherwise stated the line numbers below are those of the Q1 2021 edition, published on 10 June. I have taken the annual data from B. 103 from the quarterly series as the Federal Reserve has warned that there has been an error in the annual data which will presumably be corrected when the new data are published in September.

I also use their selected interest rates H 15. These give the data on interest rates paid by the federal government on debt of different maturities and their Money Stock Measures H 6.

www.federalreserve.gov

Jeremy J. Siegel

US total real returns for cash, long-dated bonds and equities since 1801.

The broad conclusions from his data are available in his book *Stocks for the Long Run* (1994) Richard D. Irwin. The detailed data that I use were kindly provided to me by the author.

Office for National Statistics (ONS)

The official source for UK data includes detailed economic data which can be accessed from the website by inserting the relevant 'signifier'. The ones that I use are (a) for private non-financial companies NG2S (produced non-financial assets), E43J (land), FBDA (labour incomes), FARR (gross value added), FACQ (taxes on production), JQJW (subsidies on production), NSRK (consumption of fixed capital), FACU (operating surplus), NG27 (intangible produced assets), and (b) for national data NG22 (produced non-financial assets), CGRD (inventories), YBHA (GDP at current prices), and NQAE (capital consumption).

www.ons.gov.uk

Òscar Jordà, Moritz Schularick, and Alan Taylor

They have compiled US data from 1870 of which I use short-term interest rates, long bond yields, and CPI.

Data on bond yields and CPI from Òscar Jordà, Moritz Schularick, and Alan Taylor (2016b) and Robert Shiller are virtually identical. I have used both without preference.

I update these from 2016 with data from the Federal Reserve and the BLS.

https://www.nber.org/system/files/working_papers/w22743/w22743.pdf

Robert Shiller

Data on US equity market prices, EPS, dividends per share, CPI, and long bond yields from 1871 to 2021.

www.econ.yale.edu/-shiller/data

Stephen Wright

US net worth and equity market value from 1900, which I link with Z1 B. 103 data from 1952.

Stephen Wright (2004) 'Measures of Stock Market Value and Returns for the US Non-financial Corporate Sector 1900–2002' *The Review of Income and Wealth* 50(4): 561–84.

Glossary

Arbitrage Selling one asset and buying another with equal amounts of money thus exploiting market prices to profit from price anomalies.

Asset class Financial assets divided into three groups cash, bonds, and equities.

Bequest motive The wish to save or preserve capital for the benefit of future generations.

Bonus culture The attitudes and behaviour that results from the dramatic change in the amounts and bonus element of management remuneration that took place in the decade from 1990 to 2000.

Bonus element The proportion of total remuneration which does not depend on a fixed salary.

Broad dividend The amount of cash distributed to its shareholders by the corporate sector. It comprises the dividend, as normally defined, plus the amount of new equity raised minus the amount reduced either through buy-backs or takeovers.

Business sector The sector of the economy which includes incorporated companies, whether or not quoted, and unincorporated firms.

Buy-backs The reduction of the equity capital of companies through share purchases.

Capital consumption The loss in the value of plant and equipment that arises from depreciation (see below).

Capital consumption adjustment (CC) Company profits habitually use historic cost for calculating depreciation. But in real terms depreciation will be affected by inflation and this adjustment seeks to remove the resulting distortion from the national accounts.

Capital destruction The physical destruction, usually in wartime, of capital before it is due to be scrapped.

Capital stock value (capital value) The second-hand value of plant and equipment as shown by surveys by the ONS for the United Kingdom and the BEA for the United States.

Capital/output ratio The ratio of the capital stock to output both measured at current prices.

Cash The asset class which can be immediately used to pay debts or acquire goods and services at their nominal value.

Cobb-Douglas production function Shows that, with constant returns to scale, the labour and profit share of output is stable when profits are measured net of capital consumption.

Coefficient of determination R^2 A measure used to assess the strength of any underlying relationship between two variables. It is the square of the correlation coefficient (see below).

Corporate veil The barrier which allows and causes companies to behave other than if they were directly operated by their shareholders.

Correlation coefficient A measure used to assess the strength of any underlying relationship between two variables. It is the square root of the R^2 (the coefficient of determination, see above).

Cost of capital The combined cost of equity and debt.

Cost of equity The return needed on new investment to match the cost of adding to a company's equity. In the United States it appears to have been mean reverting in the long run, around 6.7 per cent p.a. in real terms.

Cyclically adjusted PE (CAPE) One of two valid measures of the value of the US equity market (q is the other). Measured at constant prices it is the ratio of the mean EPS of the S&P 500 over the past ten years EPS to the Index, divided by the long-term mean of the ratio. Its validity depends on the mean reversion of the real return on equities and the assumption that the overstatement of US profits in published accounts is stable over time.

Demographic deficit (−)/surplus (+) The annual growth rate of the numbers of working age, usually defined as between 15 and 65, minus the annual growth rate of the total population.

Depreciation The loss in the value of plant and equipment that arises mainly through the rise in real wages and the consequent fall in profit margins; often misrepresented as the cost of maintenance. The value of the resulting fall in the flow of profits is also affected by changes in the cost of capital. In US national data the term is used interchangeably with capital consumption.

Discount rate The rate at which future receipts must be discounted to give their value.

Dividend yield The dividend per share × 100 divided by the price.

Duration The equivalent of the maturity of a debt when allowance is made for the amount and timing of interest or dividend payments as well as the date at which the principal of the debt is due to be repaid. It is the weighted average term to maturity of a bond's cash flows.

Earnings per share (EPS) Net profit after tax divided by the number of shares outstanding.

Earnings yield The EPS × 100 divided by the share price. It is therefore equivalent to 100/PE (see below); for example a PE of 20 is the same as an earnings yield of 5 per cent.

Efficient Markets Hypothesis (EMH) States that every security's price equals its investment value at all times.

Elasticity The degree to which a change in price or return alters the object's desirability.

Endogenous Having an internal cause or origin.

Equity q The market capitalization of the corporate sector divided by its net worth.

Equity Risk Premium (ERP) The difference in returns, either historic or prospective, in equities compared to debt instruments, usually represented by long-dated bonds.

ex ante **and** *ex post* There are identities, such as leverage and portfolio preference and savings and investment which must exist after the event (*ex post*) but for which prior intentions (*ex ante*) can differ.

Exogenous Having an external cause or origin.

Fair value The price that a security, or the stock market in aggregate, would have if it were correctly valued. It follows that price and fair value would always be the same if the EMH held.

Fallacy of composition This occurs when the validity, or near validity, of a relationship which holds for an individual constituent of a set, taken in isolation, is assumed wrongly to hold for the set in total.

Final output The value of the output of the economy or a company after deducting intermediate output (see below) to avoid double counting. It differs from sales which include intermediate output.

Fiscal deficit (–)/surplus (+) Government income minus government spending.

Full employment The level of unemployment consistent with a stable level of inflation.

Hard-baked clay Investment in which the technology is embedded in the equipment. One of the two divisions into which Robert Solow classed new investment—(see putty-putty).

Hindsight value The value of the stock market at any given time measured by the return it would subsequently have given relative to average returns.

Household sector Satisfactory models of the economy require its division into sectors. This one includes non-profit making institutions serving the household sector (NPISH).

Hurdle rate The minimum return on equity required to justify new investment.

Incorporated Businesses which operate under the protection of limited liability.

Incremental capital/output ratio (ICOR) The rise in output resulting from additional new investment.

Intangible assets (intangibles) These are the assets of companies which are neither financial, such as cash on deposit, or physical, such as plant and equipment. They are typically represented by brand names and patents but can cover many other things.

Intellectual property (IP) The assumed value of intangibles.

Intermediate output The value of goods and services which are used to produce final output and whose value must be deducted to avoid double counting of output.

Investors (i) those who spend money on plant and equipment or **(ii)** those who acquire financial assets.

Investors' time horizon The length of time over which investors expect to hold a portfolio of securities invested in one asset class.

Inventory adjustment (IVA) A rise in the current prices of inventories will affect profits based on the historic cost convention; no profit in real terms has been made and this adjustment is used in the national accounts to try to allow for this difference.

Labour productivity (productivity) Output, measured either before or after capital consumption, divided by numbers employed or hours worked.

Labour share of output Employee remuneration as percentage of output net of capital consumption.

Lending margin The difference between the risk-free rate, applicable to the maturity of the debt, and that charged by the lender. It is needed to cover the reduction in liquidity, the risk specific to the borrower, and the systemic risk of corporate bankruptcies.

Leverage (aka gearing) The proportion of capital employed which is provided by debt rather than equity. Alternative measures are the ratio of debt, gross or net, to output.

Life Cycle Savings Hypothesis (LCSH) A model expounded by Franco Modigliani which assumes, inter alia, that people save when young and spend in retirement.

Log normal distribution A regular pattern of distribution of events, such as returns, with standard probabilities using log values.

Maintenance The cost of maintaining equipment so that its productive capacity is undamaged.

Maturity The date at which a debt is due to be repaid—see also duration.

Mean Either the arithmetic mean which is the sum of the values of n numbers in a series divided by n, or the geometric mean which is the nth root of their product.

Mean reversion Some series, of which examples are the ratio of capital value to net domestic product, q, and CAPE, have a tendency to rotate around their average. It is statistically measured by the Augmented Dickie-Fuller Test. If sufficient data are available when measured in logs the arithmetic mean will be the same as the linear trend and I illustrate this in some of the figures. Also known as stationarity.

Miller-Modigliani Theorem This holds, wrongly, in my view, that the value of corporate assets is not altered by changes in leverage.

Median The number at which the sum of those of higher value equal those of lower.

Model A simplification of a complex system made to understand it and test its properties.

Money-weighted return The return given by cash received from an asset and its current value. This is the rate of interest which equals the present value of all past cash distributions to shareholders plus the change in the capital value of the stock market at the end of the period— see time-weighted return.

National accounts The data for the combined income, output, and expenditure of a nation, together with the more detailed data used in their compilation and associated series.

National savings The total amount of GDP that is not spent on consumption, either by the household or public sectors. It is equal to the total amount of investment plus or minus the current account's surplus or deficit.

Negative serial correlation The behaviour of a series, such as the real return on equities, in which above-average past returns indicate the probability of below-average future returns and vice versa.

Neoclassical synthesis (aka Keynesian-neoclassical synthesis) The generally agreed body of theories. George Akerlof suggests that this was first comprehensively set out by Gardner Ackley in *Macroeconomic Theory* (1961) New York: Macmillan but it has since been subject to subsequent modifications, for example over inflation.

Net debt Interest-bearing liabilities minus interest-bearing assets.

Net worth The net value of companies' assets after deducting their financial liabilities. It is therefore the same as corporate equity. In national data the produced assets are usually valued at their second-hand values shown by surveys.

Nominal returns Those measured and defined in terms of current prices.

Non-accelerating inflationary rate of unemployment (NAIRU) The minimum level of unemployment consistent with a stable rate of unemployment in conditions of stable inflationary expectations.

Non-financial companies and non-financial corporate sector The corporate sector is divided into non-financial and financial companies. The dividing line is obvious with banking, insurance, and financial advice being distinguished from manufacturing and non-financial services. Where manufacturing companies have financial subsidiaries, their activities are split in the national accounts between the two sectors.

Non-technology variables (NTV) In my Total Factor Productivity (TFP) model the amount of current technology in which it is worth investing, is determined by leverage, interest rates, corporation tax, profit margins, and the equity hurdle rate, which constitute NTV in aggregate.

Normal distribution A regular pattern of distribution of events, such as returns, with standard probabilities using natural numbers.

Obsolescence The consequence of rising real wages on the value of the output of plant and equipment.

Participation rate The rate of those employed plus those seeking work as a percentage of those of working age.

Pay-out ratio The proportion of profits after tax that is paid out in dividends

either as normally defined or as broad dividends.

PE (aka PE multiple and P/E) The price per share divided by the EPS, therefore also the market value of the company, or of the stock market in aggregate, divided by profits after tax.

Polymorphic The ability to take multiple forms. Individual risk aversion is polymorphic, it varies between individuals and these variations remain stable proportions of the population over time.

Portfolio preference The desired balance in an asset portfolio between equities and debt assets.

Present value The value of a stream of income discounted at the appropriate rate.

Private sector The economy is divided into four main sectors: households, business, government, and foreigners. The first two together comprise the private sector.

Produced capital The result of investment, it thus excludes land.

Profit margins The ratio of profit, measured in various ways, to output or sales.

Profit maximization Action to maximize the present value of a firm.

Public sector The government sector of the economy.

Putty-putty Conditions where the labour to capital ratio is as flexible on new investment as it is for the existing capital stock. One of the two divisions into which Robert Solow classed new investment—see hard-baked clay.

Quoted/unquoted companies (aka listed and unlisted companies) Companies quoted or not quoted on stock markets.

Rainy-day savings Amounts saved for short-term and uncertain events, including holidays, unemployment, and illness.

Random Walk Hypothesis This is the restricted versions of the EMH which assumes that the variations in future returns from their long-term averages are independent of past returns. Shown to be false by, inter alia, the variance compression (see below) of equity returns.

Real returns Those that are measured and defined in constant prices, thereby allowing for inflation.

Refinancing risk The possibility that leverage is so high that it will need to be reduced, for example, by an infusion of new equity capital.

Required return on equity The expected return on the amount of equity sufficient to justify new investment—see hurdle rate.

Replacement cost The value of second-hand equipment, not the current cost of producing such equipment.

Research and development (R&D) Costs incurred in finding new or improved products or more efficient ways to produce existing ones.

Return on equity (RoE) Profits after tax as a percentage of new worth.

Risk aversion The extent to which individuals prefer the probability of a benefit relative to its size.

Risk-free The return over different maturities available on lending to governments in countries with their own monetary systems ('fiat money') borrowing in that currency.

R^2 **(R squared)**— see correlation coefficient.

Savings propensity The proportion of income saved by different individuals or sectors.

Scrapping Ceasing to employ equipment.

Scrap value The price at which equipment can be sold when its output has ceased to have value due to obsolescence.

Second-hand market The market for old equipment ascertained by surveys.

Sectors Different parts of the economy respond in different ways to changes in incentives and threats. To allow for this, satisfactory models must divide the economy into different sectors. These are the public sector, the household sector, the foreign sector (rest of the world), and the business sector, which is itself divided into incorporated firms, both quoted and unquoted, and those which are unincorporated.

Serial correlation The relationship of two datasets over time. With negative serial correlation a rise in the ratio over one time period is likely to be reversed over the next one and with positive serial correlation it is likely to become more pronounced.

Single representative investor The fictional person used in economic models in which all investors are assumed to behave as if there is only one.

Specific risk The risk of a specific event such as the bankruptcy of an individual firm or destruction of a property by fire—see systemic risk.

Standard deviation This measures the variability of distributions, for example of returns. It is the square root of the squared difference between observed returns and their average. It is the square root of the variance (see below).

Stationarity See mean reversion.

Systemic risk The general but often fluctuating risk applying to events, such as the incidence of bankruptcy among companies or fire loss for a country's housing stock—see specific risk.

Tangible assets In contrast to intangibles these are the physical assets of companies, such as plant and equipment.

Testable The ability of a proposition to be shown to be false by reference to data, an essential condition for a valid hypothesis.

Time horizon The number of years ahead when an owner of a financial asset class expects to sell it, or the owner of a productive asset expects it to be scrapped.

Time-weighted return The return given by the rise in the value of an asset assuming that all income is reinvested in the same asset at the price applicable at that time.

Tobin's Q The market value of the corporate sector, including both debt and equity, divided by the value of corporate assets.

Total factor productivity (TFP) The rise in output resulting from improvements in technology, thus excluding those that arise from increases in the volumes of labour and capital.

Total shareholder return (TSR) The percentage increase per annum in shareholders' wealth arising from dividends and capital gains combined.

Treasury Inflation-Protected Securities (TIPS) Bonds issued by the government in which the coupon and the principal are adjusted for changes in the CPI.

Unincorporated Businesses which operate without the protection of limited liability.

Utility function The change in satisfaction, or misery, that comes from changes in circumstances such as wealth, income, or consumption.

Valid Model One that satisfies the two conditions set out by Karl Popper, which are that it must be testable and robust when tested.

Value Stock market's value is its current level relative to the level at which it is neither over nor underpriced. It is therefore the level at which equity market capitalization/net worth = 1—see fair value.

Variance Like the standard deviation this is a measure of the variability of distributions and is its squared value.

Variance compression This occurs when variance falls over time by more than it would if returns were random.

Volatility Is measured by the standard deviation or the variance.

Wealth The current market value of individuals' assets.

Working-age population The internationally agreed definition, which I use, is the number of people aged 15 to 65. The BLS define it as those over 16 not in jail or mental homes.

Write-offs Reductions in the book values of assets.

Yield curve The relationship between the risk-free interests rates of debt instruments of differing maturities.

Bibliography

Akerlof, George (1970) 'The Market for "Lemons": Quality Uncertainty and the Market Mechanism' *The Quarterly Journal of Economics* 84(3): 488–500.

Akerlof, George (2019) 'What They Were Thinking Then: The Consequences for Macroeconomics during the Past 60 Years' *Journal of Economic Perspectives* 34(4): 171–86.

Asker, John, Joan Farre-Mensa, and Alexander Ljungqvist (2013) 'Corporate Investment and Stock Market Listing: A Puzzle?' *Review of Financial Studies* 28(2): 342–90.

Bank of England (2016) 'A Millennium of Macroeconomic Data' dataset, https://www.bankofengland.co.uk/statistics/research-datasets.

Barro, Robert (2006) 'Rare Disasters and Asset Markets in the Twentieth Century' *The Quarterly Journal of Economics* 121(3): 823–66.

BEA (2015) 'Fixed Assets and Consumer Durable Goods 1925 to 1997' US Department of Commerce, Bureau of Economic Analysis. Washington, DC: US Government Printing.

Bernanke, Ben (2004). 'The Great Moderation' remarks at meeting of the Eastern Economic Association, Washington, D.C. February.

Bullard, James (2020) Interview by Christopher Jeffery. Central Banking August. www.centralbanking.com/central-banks/financial-stability/7668906/james-bullard-on-the-feds-policy-review-fsoc-and-forecasting-jobs-data.

Burnham, James (1941) *The Managerial Revolution*. New York: The John Day Company.

Chan-Lee, James (1986) 'Pure Profits and Tobin's q in Nine OECD Countries' OECD Working Paper. Paris: OECD.

Corrado, Carol, Charles Hulten, and Daniel Sichel (2006) 'Intangible Capital and Economic Growth' *Federal Reserve Board, Finance and Economics Discussion Series* 24.

Deaton, Angus (2005) 'Franco Modigliani and the Life-cycle Theory of Consumption' *Banca Nationale del Lavoro (BNL) Quarterly Review* LV111: 233–4.

Dimson, Elroy, Paul Marsh, and Mike Staunton (2002). *The Triumph of the Optimists*. Princeton, NJ: Princeton University Press.

Dornbusch, Rüdiger (1976) 'Exchange Rate Expectations and Monetary Policy' *Journal of International Economics* 6(3): 231–44.

Fair, Ray C. (2015) 'Reflections on Macroeconometric Modelling' *B. E. Journal of Macroeconomics* 15(1): 445–66.

Fleming, J. Marcus (1962) 'Domestic Financial Policies under Fixed and Floating Exchange Rates' *IMF Staff Papers* 9: 369–79.

Frydman, Carola and Dick Jenter (2010) 'CEO Compensation' NBER Working Paper 16585. Cambridge, MA: NBER.

Fraumeni, Barbara M. (1977) 'The Measurement of Depreciation in the U.S. National Income and Product Accounts' *BEA Survey of Current Business* 77: 7–23.

Gutiérrez, Germán and Thomas Philippon (2016) 'Investment-less Growth: An Empirical Investigation' NBER Working Paper 22897. Cambridge, MA: NBER.

Harris, M. and A. Raviv (1991) 'Theory of Capital Structure' *The Journal of Finance* 46(1): 297–355.

Hayashi, Fumio (1982) 'Tobin's Marginal q and Average q: A Neoclassical Interpretation' *Econometrica* 50(1): 213–24.

Hicks, J. R. (1939) *Value and Capital: An Enquiry into Some Fundamental Principles of Economic Theory*. Oxford: Oxford University Press.

Hulten, Charles R. (2000) 'Total Factor Productivity: A Short Biography' NBER Working Paper 7471. Cambridge, MA: NBER.

Jensen, Michael C. and William H. Meckling (1976) 'Agency Costs and Ownership Structure' *Journal of Financial Economics* 3(4).

Jordà, Oscar, Moritz Schularick, and Alan Taylor (2017) 'Macrofinancial History and the New Business Cycle Facts' NBER Working Paper 22743. Cambridge, MA: NBER.

Kaldor, Nicholas (1966) 'Marginal Productivity and the Macroeconomic Theories of Distribution: Comment on Samuelson and Modigliani' *Review of Economic Studies* 33 (4): 309–19.

Li, Wendy C. Y. and Bronwyn H. Hall (2016) 'Depreciation of Business R&D Capital' NBER Working Paper 22473. Cambridge, MA: NBER.

Lo, Andrew W. and Craig MacKinley (1999) *A Non-random Walk down Wall Street*. Princeton, NJ: Princeton University Press.

Malkiel, Burton G. (1953) *A Random Walk down Wall Street*. New York: W. W. Norton & Co.

Marris, Robin (1964) *The Economic Theory of 'Managerial Capitalism'*. London: Macmillan.

Marris, Robin (1991) *Reconstructing Keynesian Economics with Imperfect Competition*. Cheltenham: Edward Elgar.

Medawar, Peter (1990) *The Threat and the Glory*. Oxford: Oxford University Press.

Mehra, Rajnish and Edward C. Prescott (1985) 'The Equity Premium: A Puzzle' *Journal of Monetary Economics* 15(2): 145–61.

Meyer J. R. and E. Kuh (1957) *The Investment Decision: An Empirical Study*. Cambridge, MA: Harvard University Press.

Minsky, Hyman P. (2008) *Stabilizing an Unstable Economy*. New York: McGraw-Hill.

Mitchell, James (2009) 'Appendix 3: Interest Rates, Profits and Share Prices' in Andrew Smithers, *Wall Street Revalued: Imperfect Markets and Inept Central Bankers*. Chichester: John Wiley & Sons.

Modigliani, Franco and Merton H. Miller (1958) 'The Cost of Capital, Corporation Finance and the Theory of Investment' *The American Economic Review* 48(3): 261–97.

Modigliani, Franco and Merton H. Miller (1963) 'Corporate Income Taxes and the Cost of Capital: A Correction' *The American Economic Review* 53(3): 433–43.

Mundell, Robert A. (1963) 'Capital Mobility and Stabilization Policy under Fixed and Flexible Exchange Rates' *Canadian Journal of Economics and Political Science* 29(4): 475–85.

ONS (2014) 'Capital Stocks, Consumption of Fixed Capital' *ONS Statistical Bulletin* https://www.ons.gov.uk.

Peters, Ryan H. and Lucian A. Taylor (2017) 'Intangible Capital and the Investment-q Relation' *Journal of Financial Economics* 123: 251–72.

Philippon, Thomas (2019) *The Great Reversal: How America Gave Up on Free Markets*. Cambridge, MA: Harvard University Press.

Popper, Karl (1963) *Conjectures and Refutations*. London: Routledge & Kegan Paul.

Reinhart, Carmen M. and Kenneth S. Rogoff (2009) *This Time is Different: Eight Centuries of Financial Folly*. Princeton, NJ: Princeton University Press.

Robertson, Donald and Stephen Wright (2009) 'Testing for Redundant Predictable Variables' Working paper downloadable from http://www/econ.bbk.uk/faculty.wright.

Ross, Stephen (1977) 'The Determination of Financial Structure: The Incentive Signalling Approach' *Bell Journal of Economics* 8(1): 23–40.

Samuelson, Paul (1965) 'Proof that Properly Anticipated Prices Fluctuate Randomly' first published in the *Industrial Management Review* and subsequently reprinted as Chapter 2 in The World Scientific Handbook of Futures Markets (2015) pp 25–38 from World Scientific Publishing Co. Pte. Ltd. pp 3–25.

Shiller, Robert (2000) *Irrational Exuberance*. Princeton, NJ: Princeton University Press.

Siegel, Jeremy (1994) *Stocks for the Long Run*. Homewood, IL: Richard D. Irwin.

Smith, Adam (1776) *An Inquiry into the Nature and Causes of the Wealth of Nations*. London.

Smithers, Andrew (2018) 'A Critical Review of Thomas Piketty's *Capitalism in the Twenty-first Century*' *World Economics* 19(3): 13–25.

Smithers, Andrew (2019a) 'The NTV Model for Total Factor Productivity' *World Economics* 20(2): 1–26.

Smithers, Andrew (2019b) *Productivity and the Bonus Culture*. Oxford: Oxford University Press.

Smithers, Andrew (2020) 'The Debate over the Depreciation of Intangible Capital' *World Economics* 21(1): 11–38.

Smithers, Andrew and Stephen Wright (2000) *Valuing Wall Street: Protecting Wealth in Turbulent Markets*. New York: McGraw-Hill.

Smithers, Andrew and Stephen Wright (2002) 'Stock Markets and Central Bankers: The Economic Consequences of Alan Greenspan' *World Economics* 3(1): 101–121.

Solow, Robert M. (1962) 'Substitution and Fixed Proportions in the Theory of Capital' *Review of Economic Studies* 29(3): 207–18.

Solow, Robert M., J. Tobin, C. C. von Weizsäcker, and M. Yaari (1971) 'Neoclassical Growth with Fixed Factor Proportions' *The Review of Economic Studies* 33(2): 79–115.

Summers, L. H. (1981) 'Taxation and Corporate Investment: A q Theory Approach' *Brookings Papers on Economic Activity* 11.

Taylor, Lance (2020) ''Savings' Glut Fables and International Trade Theory: An Autopsy' Institute for New Economic Thinking, https://www.ineteconomics.org.

Tobin, James (1969) 'A General Equilibrium Approach to Monetary Theory' *Journal of Money, Credit and Banking* 1(1): 15–29.

Tolkien J.R.R. (1954) 'Prologue' in *The Lord of the Rings—Part 1: The Fellowship of the Ring*. London: George Allen & Unwin.

Wiles, P. J. (1956 and 1961) *Price, Cost and Output*. Oxford: Basil Blackwell.

Wright, Stephen (2004) 'Measures of Stock Market Value and Returns for the US Non-financial Corporate Sector 1900–2002' *The Review of Income and Wealth* 50(4): 561–84.

Index

Note: Tables and figures are indicated by an italic '*t*' and '*f*' following the page number.

Akerlof, George 12, 15, 62, 65 n1, 145 n6,
     158, 174
Andy Haldane xiii
Angus Maddison project 28*t*, 77*t*, 78*t*, 79*t*,
     82*t*, 167
arbitrage *ix*, *x*, 2–3, 15, 32, 51, 75, 155
     definition 171
Asker, John 92 n10, 113 n2
asset class 12, 14–16, 20 n9
     cash and 171
     definition 171
     time horizon and 173, 177
asset prices *ix*, *x*,14, 107, 130, 155
     short and long-term fluctuations 14–15
assets
     debt *see* debt assets
     equity assets, household ownership of 66*f*
     financial 6, 14–16, 19, 30, 65–6, 97, 138–9,
          139*f*, 141, 148
     fixed produced 26*f*, 138*t*
     household ownership of 138*t*
     intangible *see* intangible assets
     investors and 173
     land and 108*f*
     overpriced *see* overpriced assets
     pensions 139*f*
     tangible *see* tangible assets
     time horizon and 177
     see also asset class; asset prices
Australia 76
     equity returns 82*f*
     GDP and equity returns, growth of 77*t*,
          78*t*, 79*t*

balance, fiscal *see* fiscal balance
Bank of England 44, 167
     Millennium of Macroeconomic Data for
          the UK 167
banking/banks *x*, 175
     central 9, 14–15, 65–6, 97, 130
     deposits 41
     investment *xiii*
     see also Bank of England

Barro, Robert 13 n6, 19 n8, 142, 147, 150
behaviour
     borrowers *see* borrower behaviour
     corporate 87–94
     investor *see* investor behaviour
     management *see* management
          behaviour
Belgium 76
     equity returns 82*f*
     GDP and equity returns, growth of 77*t*,
          78*t*, 79*t*
     real return index values 80*f*
bequest motive 141–2
     definition 171
Bernanke, Ben 98
bond yields 26*f*, 32*t*, 38*f*, 43*f*, 44*f*, 47*f*
     changes in 20, 23, 25, 31, 137, 152, 157
     equity returns, independence from 6,
          19, 47–9
     government 32
     long/long-dated 4, 6, 8, 11–13, 16, 24–7,
          42–4, 47, 62, 65, 75, 99, 114, 132, 137,
          141, 151, 157, 167, 170
     nominal 5, 75
     risk-free 11
bonds
     bond returns 47*t*
     duration of 161
     equities and 59–60
     foreign demand 32*t*
     long dated 12
     return on *see* return on bonds
     risk-free 19–20
     United States 46*f*, 60*f*
     yields *see* bond yields
     see also return on bonds
bonus culture 22, 91, 113–14, 153
     definition 171
bonus element
     definition 171
borrower behaviour
     corporate borrowers 37
     financial stability 127

borrower behaviour (*cont.*)
  preferences 37
  risk for borrowers 8, 99, 130, 151, 173
  see also lending margin
broad dividend 9, 18, 27–9, 32–3, 35–6, 85,
    89, 103, 107, 122, 136
  definition 171
  pay-out ratio and 175
Bullard, James 97
Bureau of Economic Analysis
    (BEA) 143, 165
  data and sources 167–8
Bureau of Labour Statistics (BLS) 168, 170
  data sources 38*f*, 42*f*, 44*f*, 46*f*, 47*f*, 52*f*, 53*f*,
    54*f*, 56*f*, 152*f*
  working-age population, definition of 177
Bureau of the Census 29*t*, 168
Burnham, James 87
business(es) *see* companies
business investment
  corporation tax rates 114, 132
  cost of capital and 100
  cost of equity and 101*f*
  depreciation and 121–2
  housing and 118 n5
  intangible spending 119*f*, 122*t*
  quoted companies 92
  time horizon 11
  types of 87
business sector 14–15, 35, 74, 92, 138, 176
  definition 171
buy-backs 18, 27–8, 36, 97, 102, 129
  definition 171

Canada 76, 81
  equity returns 82*f*
  GDP and equity returns, growth of 77*t*,
    78*t*, 79*t*
CAPE *see* cyclically adjusted PE (CAPE)
capital
  consumption *see* capital consumption
  consumption adjustment *see* capital
    consumption adjustment (CC)
  cost of *see* cost of capital
  destruction *see* capital destruction
  investment *see* capital investment
  produced *see* produced capital
  ratio *see* capital ratio
  return on *see* return on capital
  stock value *see* capital stock value
  value *see* capital stock value

capital consumption 84, 115, 123, 132,
    143–6, 165, 168–9
  definition 171
  depreciation and 172
  labour productivity and 173
  labour share of output and 173
capital consumption adjustment (CC)
  definition 171
capital destruction 5–6, 76, 79–80, 150
  definition 171
  global comparisons 77*t*, 78*t*, 79*t*
capital investment 112
capital ratio 118
  definition 171
capital stock value
  definition 171
  increases 122*t*
  net additions 110*f*
  net, measurement of 165
  tangible, value of 27*f*
capitalization *see* market capitalization
cash
  cash relative returns 45–50
  definition 171
  United States 46*f*
central banks *see* banking/banks
Chan-Lee, James 95 n3, 100 n8, 109 nn1–2
Cobb-Douglas production function 123 n4
  definition 171
coefficient of determination R^2
  definition 171–2
companies
  behaviour of 87–94
  non-financial *see* non-financial companies
  quoted *see* quoted companies
  unquoted *see* unquoted companies
  value of *see* company value
  see also businesses
company value *see* value
comparative approaches 147–53
compression, variance *see* variance
    compression
consensus theory 1–2, 6, 15, 18, 31, 91–2,
    94, 97, 102, 118, 147, 149, 158–9
consumption of capital *see* capital
    consumption; capital consumption
    adjustment (CC)
corporate debt 97–9, 128*f*, 152
corporate earnings 48, 70
  see also earnings per share (EPS);
    earnings yield

corporate equity 3, 17, 22, 27–9, 65, 68–9, 74, 84, 108–9, 141, 175
  growth of 34–6
corporate leverage 3, 32*t*, 36
  aggregate leverage 104
  changes in 4, 20, 23, 27, 35, 62
  corporate capital and 6
  elasticity of 11, 16–17, 20, 25–7, 59, 75, 157
  ex ante 16, 156
  ex post 15, 17, 156
  exogenous approach 153
  financial stability, role in 127
  managers and 8
  non-financial 128*f*
  portfolio preference, household 20, 31–3, 49–50, 65–6
  sensitivity of 9, 65
  tax rates and 131
  see also leverage
corporate pay-out ratios 28*f*, 30
corporate savings 9, 17–18, 33, 136, 141, 156
  corporate investment and 28 n3
  definition 33 n4
  growth and variation 18
corporate sector
  assets, value of 97
  behaviour of firms 87
  broad dividend 171
  corporate investment 95–6, 102
  debt levels of 21, 34
  equity of 35
  equity *q* 172
  independence of 7–9
  leverage of 65, 151
  market value of 177
  net worth of 148
  non-financial 175
  portfolio balances 63
  total output share (US) 88*f*
  see also Miller-Modigliani Theorem
corporate veil 2, 7, 92, 140
  definition 171
corporation tax 8, 23, 96, 99–100, 102, 104, 111–14, 130, 132–3, 175
  effective rate (US) 133*f*
  see also tax
Corrado, Carol 116 n2, 120 n8, 121 n1
correlation coefficient 176
  business investment 101*t*
  definition 171–2

cost of capital 6, 14, 17–18, 32, 66, 91–2, 95, 97, 100–4, 111, 129, 137, 148, 159
  business investment 101*t*
  definition 172
  investment and 100*f*
cost of equity 5, 8, 14, 90–2, 96, 99–104, 139, 148
  business investment and 101*f*
  definition 172
cyclically adjusted PE (CAPE) 68–72, 86, 174
  definition 172
  hindsight value 72*f*

data sources 167–70
Deaton, Angus 140–2
debt 21–30
  assets 127, 141, 150, 169, 175
  corporate *see* corporate debt
  excess *see* excess debt
  net *see* net debt
deficit
  demographic *see* demographic deficit
  fiscal *see* fiscal deficit
demographic deficit
  definition 172
demographic surplus
  definition 172
demographics 5–6
  US population statistics 29*t*
  see also demographic deficit; demographic surplus
Denmark 76
  equity returns 82*f*
  GDP and equity returns, growth of 77*t*, 78*t*, 79*t*
depreciation 143–6
  definition 172
  intangible investment 122*t*
  investment and cost of capital 100*f*
  net, measurement of 165
  profits before 24*f*
destruction of capital *see* capital destruction
deviation, standard *see* standard deviation
Dimson, Elroy 46–7, 52–4, 56, 71–3, 76–8, 80–3, 168–9
discount rate 8, 95, 97, 110, 150
  definition 172
disposable income 66*f*, 138, 139*f*
dividend yield 34–6
  definition 172

dividends 18, 27–8, 70, 84–5, 89–90, 107, 117, 122, 136, 167, 169–70, 175, 177
    quoted companies (US) 70*t*
    see also broad dividend; dividend yield
Dornbusch, Rüdiger 32
duration
    definition 172

earnings per share (EPS) 28, 29*f*, 68, 70*t*, 111, 113, 170, 175
    definition 172
    S&P 500 152
earnings yield 70
    definition 172
earnings, corporate *see* corporate earnings
economic data 167, 169
economic growth 108, 118, 140–1, 140–1
economic history 22, 51, 150
economic policy 1, 98
economics
    financial *see* financial economics
    structure of the economy 14
Efficient Market Hypothesis (EMH) 154–5, 173, 176
    definition 172
elasticity 6, 11, 16, 20, 26–7, 31, 75, 99, 151, 157
    definition 172
employment *see* full employment; non-accelerating inflationary rate of unemployment (NAIRU)
endogenous 15–16, 31, 49, 148, 153, 156
    definition 172
equities/equity
    bonds and 59–60
    corporate *see* corporate equity
    cost of *see* cost of equity
    duration of 161
    equilibria for 12
    real returns on 60*f*
    required return on *see* required return on equity
    return on *see* return on equity (RoE)
    risk premium (US) 46*f*
    risks of 55–8
    United States 46*f*, 52*f*, 53*f*, 56*f*, 60*f*
    value 47*f*
equity *q* 14, 103–4, 109, 141, 148
    definition 172
equity returns 3–6, 10, 12–20, 23, 27, 30, 31, 45–6, 49, 51, 53, 55, 62, 68–9, 75–8, 81–3, 99, 150–2, 157

consumption, desire to maintain 12–13
global comparisons 77*t*, 82*f*, 83*f*
international growth and 82*f*
stationarity of 6, 156
United States 57*f*
equity risk premium (ERP) 4, 6, 12, 19–20, 45–6, 48, 63, 137, 148, 152
    definition 172
    United States 46*f*
ex ante 3, 9, 12, 16, 49–50, 62–3, 65–7, 156, 158
    definition 172
ex post 15–18, 49, 62, 152, 156–7
    definition 172
excess debt 154
exogenous 9–10, 12, 14, 16, 20, 23, 31–2, 41, 49, 75, 119, 153, 156
    definition 172

fair value 68, 73, 109–10, 159
    definition 172–3
    value and 177
Fair, Ray C. 9 n3
fallacy of composition 8, 96
    definition 173
Farre-Mensa, Joan 92 n10, 113 n3
Federal Reserve 41, 89, 91, 97, 129, 163, 165, 169–70
final output
    definition 173
financial crisis *see* Global Financial Crisis
financial economics 55
financial stability 127–31
fiscal balance 11, 14–15, 31, 141
fiscal deficit 11, 31–2, 49
    definition 173
fiscal policy 4, 9, 16, 31–2, 49, 66–7, 104, 110, 131
fiscal surplus
    definition 173
Fleming, J. Marcus 32 n2
foreign direct investment (FDI)
    United States 113*f*, 167
France 76
    equity returns 82*f*
    GDP and equity returns, growth of 77*t*, 78*t*, 79*t*
    real return index values 80*f*
Fraumeni, Barbara M. 143 n1
Frydman, Carola 112, 168
full employment 4, 15–17, 33, 49, 67
    definition 173
    see also employment

GDP (Gross Domestic Product)
  business investment and 101*t*
  corporate pay-out ratios 28*f*
  corporate profit retentions 29*f*
  growth, global comparisons 77*t*
  monetary base as % of 67*f*, 129*f*
gearing *see* leverage
Germany 75–6, 113, 151
  GDP and equity returns, growth of 77*t*,
    78*t*, 79*t*
  equity returns 83*f*
  real return index values 80*f*
Global Financial Crisis *ix, x, xi*
  see also recessions
Gordon Growth Model 34, 161
Gutiérrez, Germán 121 n1

Hall, Bronwyn H. 144 n5, 145 n7
'hard-baked clay' 105, 117
  definition 173
Harris, M. 147, 151, 153 n4
Hayashi, Fumio 87 n3, 95 n3, 109 n4
Hicks, J. R. 122
hindsight value
  definition 173
  United States 71*f*, 72*f*, 73*f*
household sector 2, 18, 22, 34–5, 65, 73, 138,
    169, 176
  definition 173
households
  equity assets, ownership of 66*f*, 138*t*
  portfolio preference and 31–3
  sector *see* household sector
Hulten, Charles R. 116 n2, 119 n7,
    120 n8, 121 n1
hurdle rate 3, 17, 20, 22, 27, 61, 90–1, 96,
    103–4, 108, 132–4, 156, 175, 176
  definition 173
  fluctuations 111–14

incorporated businesses
  business sector 171
  definition 173
  sectors 176
  types of 87
  (un)incorporated companies 87, 89, 94,
    103, 169, 177
incremental capital/output ratio (ICOR)
    124–5
  definition 173
  gross 125*f*
  net 125*f*

inflation 127–31
  global 81*f*
  see also non-accelerating inflationary
    rate of unemployment (NAIRU);
    Treasury Inflation-Protected
    Securities (TIPS)
intangible assets 101*t*, 115–20, 127, 143
  definition 173
  see also tangible assets
intellectual property (IP) 115, 121, 143
  definition 173
  expenditure, mislabelling of 121–6
interest rates
  non-financial companies 96*f*
  real short-term 42*f*
  return on equity (RoE) 130*t*
  risk-free 39*f*, 41–4
  short-term equilibria 12
intermediate output
  definition 173
inventories 35, 105–8, 133, 165, 168, 169
  non-financial companies 106*f*
inventory adjustment (IVA)
  definition 173
investment 21–30
  business 100*f*, 101*f*, 101*t*, 119*f*, 122*t*
  capital *see* capital investment
  corporate 95–104, 112*f*
  cost of capital and 100*f*
  fixed non-residential 89*t*
  intangible 119*f*, 122*t*
  non-financial corporate 88*f*
  return on *see* return on investment
  tangible 100*f*, 101*f*
investors
  definition 173
  portfolio preferences 32*t*
  see also single representative investor
investors' time horizon 59–60
  definition 173
Italy 76
  equity returns 83*f*
  GDP and equity returns, growth of 77*t*,
    78*t*, 79*t*
  real return index values 80*f*

Japan 76, 81, 113, 151
  equity returns 83*f*
  GDP and equity returns, growth of 77*t*,
    78*t*, 79*t*
  real return index values 80*f*
Jensen, Michael C. 93–4

Jenter, Dick 112, 168
Jordà, Òscar 38, 42, 44, 170

Kaldor, Nicholas 1, 5 n5, 22 n1, 28 n3, 90, 147
Keynesian-neoclassical synthesis
  see neoclassical synthesis
Kuh, E. 28 n3

labour productivity 17, 21, 105, 108, 116–17,
  121, 132, 144
  definition 173
labour share of output 2, 84, 124, 126,
  132–3, 144
  definition 173
land 105–8
  non-financial companies 106*f*
  price changes 107*f*
  tangible assets, as % of 108*f*
  see also property
lending margin 8, 98–9, 151–2
  definition 173
leverage 127–31
  corporate *see* corporate leverage
  definition 174
  monetary policy 65–7
  non-financial companies' 25*f*, 128*f*
  portfolio preferences 65–7
Li, Wendy C. Y. 144 n5, 145 n7
Life Cycle Savings Hypothesis (LCSH) 140–2
  definition 174
Ljungqvist, Alexander 92 n10, 113 n3
Lo, Andrew W. 154 n1
log normal distribution
  definition 174

MacKinley, Craig 154 n1
maintenance 143–6
  definition 174
Malkiel, Burton G. 51 n1
management behaviour 21–30
  incentives 112*f*
market capitalization 14, 172, 177
market returns 51–3, 76, 154
  see also fair value
market share 3, 17–18, 21–2, 90, 116
market value 14, 47–8*f*, 65–6, 68–9, 86, 89, 95,
  102–4, 109, 113*f*, 120, 122, 141, 148–9,
  157–8, 163, 165, 169–70, 175, 177
Marris, Robin 8 n1, 14 n1, 87 n4, 92–3, 142,
  147 n1, 158
Marsh, Paul 46–7, 52–4, 56, 71–3, 76–8,
  80–3, 168–9

maturity 19, 37, 39*f*, 39*t*, 41, 43*t*, 55, 60*f*, 63,
  150, 161, 173
  definition 174
  duration and 172
mean reversion 2, 48, 68–9, 109, 132, 141,
  145, 148, 157–9, 172
  definition 174
  tangible capital stock (US) 27*f*
Meckling, William H. 93–4
Medawar, Peter 16 n4
median
  definition 174
Mehra, Rajnish 12 n5, 19 n8, 63, 138, 142,
  147, 149–50
Meyer, J. R. 28 n3
Miller, Merton H. 95–6, 102 n10, 122, 157
Miller-Modigliani Theorem 95–104, 122,
  140, 157
  definition 174
Minsky, Hyman P. 1
Mitchell, James 48 n1, 105 n3, 126 n8
model(s)
  definition 174
  see also Gordon Growth Model; Mundell-
    Fleming Model; Tobin's Q model;
    valid model
Modigliani, Franco 95 n1, 140–2, 174
monetary policy 16, 49, 62, 98,
  109–10, 148–9
  leverage 65–7, 130
  portfolio preferences 65–7
money-weighted returns 84–6
  definition 174
motive *see* bequest motive
Mundell, Robert A. 32 n2
MundellFleming Model 32

NAIRU *see* non-accelerating inflationary rate
  of unemployment (NAIRU)
national accounts
  definition 174
The national income and product accounts
  of the United States (NIPA) 167–8
national savings 18 n6, 33 n4, 107, 115,
  118, 122, 141, 148, 153, 157, 171,
  173, 175
  definition 174
NBER Working Paper (16585) 168
NDP (net domestic product) 27*f*, 88*f*, 121,
  122*t*, 124, 125*f*, 134*f*
negative serial correlation 2 n4, 3, 5, 15, 19,
  52–5, 81, 138, 156–7, 176

definition 174
see also serial correlation
neoclassical synthesis 1, 4–5, 7, 12, 62, 65,
    104, 109, 147, 158–9
definition 174
net debt 14, 34, 73–4, 96, 104,
    127–8, 141
definition 174
net worth 17, 22, 24, 28, 31, 33–5, 47*f*, 61,
    65–6, 68–70, 75, 84, 86*f*, 89, 94, 96,
    102–4, 109, 115, 122, 127–9, 133,
    141, 147–8, 156–8, 161, 163, 170,
    172, 177
definition 6, 14, 174–5
non-financial companies 86*f*
New Zealand 76
equity returns 83*f*
GDP and equity returns, growth of 77*t*,
    78*t*, 79*t*
nominal returns
definition 175
non-accelerating inflationary rate of
    unemployment (NAIRU) 65, 126
definition 175
non-financial companies 87, 123, 167–9
debt 128*f*
definition 175
importance of 89*t*
interest rate of net debt 96*f*
inventories 106*f*
land and 106*f*, 108*f*
leverage 128*f*
net profit margins 123*f*
net worth 86*f*
profits/profit margins 107*f*, 135*f*
tangible assets 106*f*
tax and interest rates 130*t*
trade credit 106*f*
non-financial corporate
    sector 101 n9
definition 175
non-technology variables (NTV)
definition 175
normal distribution 58*f*, 59
definition 175
see also log normal distribution

obsolescence 143–4, 176
definition 175
Office for National Statistics (ONS) 108,
    134–5, 165, 169, 171
output growth 32, 35, 119–20

output ratio 2, 24, 35 n2, 73, 80, 124, 127,
    134–5, 167, 173
definition 171
overpriced assets 154

participation rate 126
definition 175
pay-out ratios 21–30
corporate (US) 28*f*
definition 175
PE multiple
definition 175
pensions
annuities 141–2
assets 139*f*
funds and schemes 10–11, 17, 19–20, 37,
    64, 137–8, 140–2, 169
savings 11, 19, 75, 102
see also retirement savings
Peters, Ryan H. 121 n1
Philippon, Thomas 121 n1, 124
policy
economic *see* economic policy
fiscal *see* fiscal policy
monetary *see* monetary policy
polymorphic 11, 16
definition 175
Popper, Karl 13 n7, 155, 156 n1, 177
portfolio preference 4–6, 97–9, 114, 136,
    141, 148, 172
changes in 20
corporate leverage and 31–3
definition 175
household 15–17, 23, 25, 27, 31–3, 49–50,
    59, 62, 65–7, 75, 129, 151–3, 156–7
investors' 32*t*, 94, 104
monetary policy and 65–7
retirement savings 137–9
savings levels, independence
    from 9
wealth ownership 9–11
positive serial correlation 52
definition 176
see also serial correlation
Prescott, Edward C. 12 n5, 19 n8, 63, 138,
    142, 147, 149–50
present value 5–6, 84–5, 93–4, 102, 143,
    156–7, 174
definition 175
private sector 2, 7, 14–15, 62, 67, 92, 118,
    149, 168
definition 175

produced capital 11, 17–18, 20, 25, 34–5, 37,
  65, 105–6, 109, 133–6, 141, 157, 165, 175
  definition 175
production function *see* Cobb-Douglas
  production function
productivity, labour *see* labour productivity
profit margins 21, 84, 105, 116, 123–4,
  126 n8, 134–5, 145
  corporate 85*f*
  definition 175
  depreciation and 172
profit maximization 6, 93
  definition 175
profit(s)
  corporate margins 85*f*
  corporate retentions 29*f*
  depreciation, before 24*f*
  NIPA 152*f*
  non-financial companies 107*f*, 123*f*,
    124*f*, 135*f*
  tax, before 24*f*
  see also profit margins; profit
    maximisation
property
  destruction by fire 176
  enemy, appropriation of 75–6
  intellectual *see* intellectual property (IP)
  ownership 90
  see also land
public sector 7, 31, 174, 176
  definition 175
'putty-putty' 105, 117–18, 173
  definition 175

quoted companies 1–3, 8, 22, 87, 89–94, 103,
  113–14, 148, 156–7, 163
  definition 175
  dividends, growth of 70*t*
  importance of 89*t*
  valuation, method of 163

R^2 (R squared) *see* coefficient of
  determination R^2; correlation
  coefficient
rainy-day savings 9–10, 19, 64, 150
  definition 176
Random Walk Hypothesis 154
  definition 176
  stock markets 51–4
rate of return 34, 41, 61, 84–5, 95, 149
Raviv, A. 147, 153 n4

real returns 3, 5, 15, 41, 46*f*, 47–9, 52, 56*f*, 58*f*,
  59–60*f*, 69, 70*t*, 75, 156, 168–9
  definition 176
recessions
  financial stability and 127–30
  severity of 1, 98–9, 152
  see also Global Financial Crisis
refinancing risk 37
  definition 176
Reinhart, Carmen M. 43 n1
replacement cost 69, 95–7, 104, 109, 128*f*,
  148–9, 165, 168
  definition 176
required return on equity 18, 61, 95–6, 139
  definition 176
Research and Development (R&D) 115
  definition 176
retirement savings 6, 19, 64, 136, 150
  portfolio preference and 137–9
  see also pensions
return on bonds 45–50, 59, 99, 137
  risk-free 43*t*
return on capital 73–4, 102, 116,
  137, 148
return on equity (RoE) 2–3, 5–6, 9, 11–12,
  21–2, 29, 34–5, 45–50, 55, 59, 61, 63,
  68, 70, 74, 84, 90, 94–6, 100, 103, 108,
  111, 116–17, 122, 127, 130, 132–3,
  137–9, 149, 157, 173
  definition 176
  differences 19–20
  global comparisons 75–83
  interest rates 130*t*
  stability of 'real' 17–18
return on investment 96
returns
  long-term 15–16
  money-weighted 84–6
  owners and managers 16–17
  time-weighted 84–6
  see also risk
reversion *see* mean reversion
risk aversion 3, 5–6, 8–18, 20, 23, 27, 35, 49,
  55, 59, 75–6, 97, 111, 137–9, 149–51,
  157, 175
  aggregate, changes in 61–4
  definition 176
  owners and managers 15–16
risk
  aversion *see* risk aversion
  equities, at different time horizons 55–8

equity premium *see* equity risk
        premium (ERP)
    investment *see* investment risk
    owners and managers 16–17
    refinancing *see* refinancing risk
    'risk-free', definition of 176
    risk-free bonds 19–20
    risk-free interest rates 39*f*
    risk-free return on bonds 43*t*
    specific *see* specific risk
    systemic *see* systemic risk
Robertson, Donald 85
robustness 156
Rogoff, Kenneth S. 43 n1
Ross, Stephen 8 n1, 95 n1

S&P 500 46*f*, 47*t*, 52–4*t*, 56*f*, 71–3*f*, 85
    CEO total pay 113
    companies 167
    EPS of 152*f*, 172
Samuelson, Paul 1 n1, 51 n1
savings
    portfolio preferences and 9
    propensity, definition 176
    retirement 137–9
    see also Life Cycle Savings Hypothesis
        (LCSH); pensions
Schularick, Moritz 38, 42, 44, 170
science, non-science *vs.* 155
scrap value 105
    definition 176
scrapping 133, 135
    definition 176
second-hand market 95
    definition 176
sector(s)
    business *see* business sector
    corporate *see* corporate sector
    definition 176
    household *see* household sector
    private *see* private sector
serial correlation 48
    definition 176
    equity returns, global comparison of 82–3*f*
    negative *see* negative serial correlation
    positive *see* positive serial correlation
shareholders 7, 17–18, 22, 27–8, 75, 84, 90,
        92–3, 102–4, 109, 114, 132, 136, 141,
        167, 171, 174, 177
Shiller, Robert 26, 28–9, 43, 47, 57–8,
        68–70, 170

Sichel, Daniel 116 n2, 120 n8, 121 n1
Siegel, Jeremy 46–7, 52–6, 71–3, 169
single representative investor ix, 10, 12–13,
        63, 142, 150
    definition 176
Smith, Adam 87
Smithers, Andrew 35 n2, 48 n1, 92 n12,
        105 n1, 105 n3, 113 n2, 115 n1, 118 n4,
        122 n2, 124 n5, 124 n7, 126 n8,
        130 n2, 146 n8
Solow, Robert M. 105 n2, 117 n3, 143, 144 n4,
        173, 175
South Africa 76
    equity returns 83*f*
    GDP and equity returns, growth of 77*t*,
        78*t*, 79*t*
Spain 76
    equity returns 83*f*
    GDP and equity returns, growth of 77*t*,
        78*t*, 79*t*
specific risk 98–9, 151
    definition 176
    systemic risk and 177
standard deviation 52, 152*f*
    definition 176
    equity returns 57*f*, 59
    negative serial correlation 54*t*
    variance and 177
    volatility and 177
stationarity *see* mean reversion
Staunton, Mike 46–7, 52–4, 56, 71–3, 76–8,
        80–3, 168–9
stock market
    random walk hypothesis 51–4
    US stock market, valuation of 68–74
    value, data insights 69*f*, 73*f*
stock value *see* capital stock value
Summers, L. H. 109
Switzerland 76
    equity returns 83*f*
    GDP and equity returns, growth of 77*t*,
        78*t*, 79*t*
systemic risk
    bankruptcy, of 98–9, 152, 173
    definition 177
    specific risk and 176

tangible assets 106–8, 115–20, 118, 121,
        127–9, 143
    definition 177
    see also intangible assets

tax 132–6
  profits before 24*f*
  rates 112*f*
  revenue 130–1
  see also corporation tax
Taylor, Alan M. 38, 42, 44, 121 n1, 124 n6, 170
Taylor, Lance 124
Taylor, Lucian A. 121 n1
testability 13 n7
  'testable,' definition of 177
  profits after tax 152*f*
The Netherlands 76
  equity returns 83*f*
  GDP and equity returns, growth of 77*t*,
    78*t*, 79*t*
time horizon
  business investment 11
  definition 177
  equities, risks of 55–8
  investors 59–60
  investors' *see* investors' time horizon
  US investors, equities and bonds 60*f*
time-weighted returns 55, 84–6
  definition 177
TIPS *see* Treasury Inflation-Protected
    Securities (TIPS)
Tobin, James 14, 69, 95, 105 n2, 143–4,
    147–9, 158, 165
Tobin's Q model 14, 69–70, 87 n3, 92, 95 n3,
    104, 147–9, 158–9, 177
  definition 177
Tolkien, J. R. R. 1 n3
total factor productivity (TFP) 118, 120, 175
  definition 177
total shareholder return (TSR) 111, 113
  definition 177
trade credit 35, 105–8, 133
  non-financial companies 106*f*
Treasury Inflation-Protected Securities
    (TIPS) 41, 47–8
  definition 177
  yields 48*f*

unemployment *see* non-accelerating
    inflationary rate of unemployment
    (NAIRU)
unincorporated companies 89
  definition 177
  importance of 89*t*
United Kingdom (UK)
  equity returns 83*f*

GDP and equity returns, growth of 77*t*,
    78*t*, 79*t*
  long bond yields 44*f*
  non-financial companies:
    land and assets 108*f*
    profit margins 135*f*
  tangible produced assets 134*f*
  US bond yields, compared 44*f*
United States (US)
  annual volatility and returns 52*f*
  assets, household ownership of 138*t*
  bond yields 38*f*, 43*f*, 44*f*, 47*f*
  bonds 46*f*
  business investment 88*f*, 100*f*, 101*f*,
    101*t*, 119*f*
  capital stock, net additions to 110*f*
  cash 46*f*
  corporate investment 112*f*
  corporate pay-out ratios 28*f*
  corporate profit margins 85*f*
  corporate profit retentions and GDP 29*f*
  corporate sector, output share 88*f*
  corporation tax rates 133*f*
  cost of capital 100*f*, 101*f*, 101*t*
  equities 52*f*, 53*f*
    real returns 46*f*, 56*f*
  equity assets, household ownership of 66*f*
  equity log returns, distribution of 58*f*
  equity risk premium 46*f*
  equity value 47*f*
  fixed produced assets, average life of 26*f*
  foreign direct investment (FDI) 113*f*
  GDP and equity returns, growth of 77*t*,
    78*t*, 79*t*
  Gross ICOR 125*f*
  hindsight value 71*f*, 72*f*, 73*f*
  intangible investment 119*f*, 122*t*
  management incentives, change in 112*f*
  monetary base as % of GDP 67*f*
  negative serial correlation 53*f*, 54*t*
  net ICOR 125*f*
  non-financial companies:
    assets of 106*f*
    net worth of 86*f*
    debt 128*f*
    interest cover 24*f*
    interest rate of net debt 96*f*
    investment 88*f*
    leverage 25*f*
    profit/profit margins 107*f*, 123*f*, 124*f*, 135*f*
  pensions assets 139*f*

population statistics 29*t*
profits:
    depreciation, before 24*f*
    tax, before 24*f*
real bond yields, rolling averages of 26*f*
real equity returns, stability of 57*f*
real log % equity 47*t*
real long-term bond yields 43*f*
real return:
    on equities 60*f*
    to equity investors 56*f*
real short-term interest rates 42*f*
S&P 500 EPS 152*f*
stock market, valuation of 68–74
    q and CAPE 69*f*
tangible capital stock, value of 27*f*
tangible produced assets 134*f*
tax rate 112*f*
types of businesses, importance of 89*t*
UK bond yields, compared 44*f*
yield curve 38*f*, 39*f*
yields on TIPS and *q* 48*f*
unquoted companies 22, 90–3, 163
    definition 175
    importance of 89*t*
    valuation, method of 163
utility function 6–8, 10, 14, 16, 19, 149,
        151, 157
    definition 177

valid model 2
    definition 177
value
    definition 177
    fair *see* fair value
    hindsight *see* hindsight value
    market *see* market value
    present *see* present value
    scrap *see* scrap value

variance 52–4, 82–3*f*
    definition 177
variance compression 176
    definition 177
veil, corporate *see* corporate veil
volatility 19, 37, 51–2, 55, 57*f*, 98, 106,
        151–3, 161
    definition 177
von Weizsäcker, C. C. 105 n2, 143 n3,
        144 n4

wealth
    definition 177
    ownership of 9–12, 16, 99
Wiles, P. J. 93
working-age population
    definition 177
worth, net *see* net worth
Wright, Stephen 68–9, 85–6, 101, 110, 115,
        130 n2, 170
write-offs
    definition 177

Yaari, M. 105 n2, 143 n3, 144 n4
yield(s)
    bond *see* bond yields
    curve *see* yield curve
    dividend *see* dividend yield
    earnings *see* earnings yield
    investment *see* investment yields
    spread 38*f*, 67*f*, 129*f*
yield curve 37–40
    business investment, time horizon
        of 11
    definition 177
    long-term 39*t*
    risk-free interest rates 39*f*
    shape of 18–19
    United States 38*f*, 39*f*